The Government and Politics of France

Dr Wright was reader in French politics at the London School of Economics before taking up his present post as official Fellow of Nuffield College, Oxford. He has also taught at the Universities of Bordeaux, Newcastle and Paris. He has written extensively on modern French history and French politics in British, American and French journals. He is currently joint editor, with Gordon Smith, of *West European Politics*, and a member of the editorial board of *Political Studies*. He is the author of a book on the French Council of State, and joint author of one on the French Prefects.

The Government and Politics of France

Vincent Wright

Hutchinson of London

Hutchinson & Co (Publishers) Ltd
3 Fitzroy Square, London WIP 6JD

London Melbourne Sydney Auckland
Wellington Johannesburg and agencies
throughout the world

First published 1978

Set in Monotype Times New Roman

Printed in Great Britain by The Anchor Press Ltd
and bound by Wm Brendon & Son Ltd
both of Tiptree, Essex

British Library CIP data

Wright, Vincent
    The government and politics of France.
    1.   France – Politics and government
    – 1945-
    I.   Title
    320.9′44′082   JN2594

ISBN 0 09 133310 5 cased
         0 09 133311 3 paper

Contents

to Dorothy and William Pickles

Preface

All books which claim to describe 'The Government and Politics' of a country are presumptuous, and short books are doubly so. All suffer, too, from being out of date the moment they are written (and even more so by the time they are published), but those on France are in a particularly hazardous position, for every national election – and they are frequent – may produce a political and constitutional crisis which damages or even destroys the assumptions and arguments of the book. Nor can any book pretend to capture in any real detail the immensely rich and complex interplay of social, economic, political and psychological forces which comprise the political process. The author of a book on politics is like the practitioner of the art: he is constantly squeezed into unpleasant choices, and in ordering his priorities he betrays his idiosyncrasies and prejudices, and reveals his indolence and ignorance.

The priorities of this book centre upon an examination of the stages of, and the reasons for, the growth of presidential government in France. It also analyses the obstacles to, and the limits of presidentialism. Its general theme is that, compared with the previous régime, there is now a closer focus of authority on the office of the Presidency, but that political power continues to be highly fragmented and subtly suffused amongst a vast number of public, semipublic and private bodies whose relationships – when they exist – range from contented co-operation to bilious antagonism.

I am aware that the organization of the book leaves something to be desired: the need to be brief frequently competes with the desire to be coherent, and clarity of presentation often does disservice to highly complex truths. But, on the whole, I hope that I have not over-sacrificed either coherence or truth in seeking a framework which allows a logical development of the main theme of the book.

Needless to say, this book owes a great deal to my present and former research students and to my colleagues and friends on both sides of the Channel and of the Atlantic. They will find their ideas pilaged and perverted in this short book, so may I take this opportunity of thanking and apologizing to them in advance.

Finally, I should like to thank Eileen Gregory, my secretary, whose patience, good humour and efficiency greatly facilitated the writing of the book.

April 1978

Introduction: the Fourth Republic and the Gaullist critique

It is easy to sneer at the Fourth Republic; most Frenchmen did and continue to do so. Yet its defects should not be exaggerated nor its achievements belittled. During the period 1945 to 1958 France was geared to meet international economic competition and was firmly linked to Europe through the Coal and Steel Community, Euratom and, finally, by the Treaty of Rome, the European Common Market. The country was also firmly integrated into the NATO alliance, and relations with Germany, the traditional enemy, were improved (the settlement of the Sarre problem in October 1955 greatly helped). Diplomatically, France of the Fourth Republic may have been weak, but it was not isolated. Even in the colonial field, progress, although slow, begrudged and often achieved at a terrible price, was made with the granting of independence to Indo-China (1954), Morocco (1956) and Tunisia (1956). In black African states, measures taken by Gaston Defferre in 1956 were to help smooth the path to the independence achieved during the Fifth Republic. And if the Algerian problem proved intractable, it should be remembered that it was to take all the ruthlessness, the courage and the guile of General de Gaulle to impose a solution upon an army, part of which did not hesitate to resort to rebellion and assassination. Moreover, the first President of the Fifth Republic was able to count upon the massive support of a war-weary public, a support which had been denied his predecessors.

On the domestic level, too, the record of the régime is far from dishonourable. It was during the Fourth Republic that the social gains of the Popular Front Government of 1936 and the family welfare schemes of the Vichy régime were consolidated and extended. The foundations of the much vaunted French 'economic miracle' were also laid during this period. The achievement was all the more remarkable in view of the economic situation of the country in 1945 after four years of war, invasion and enemy occupation. Large areas of France, it must be recalled, were a battlefield not only in 1939–40 but also in 1944–5, and by the time of the Liberation, about a fifth of all French real estate was destroyed or seriously damaged. So, too, were more than half a million houses and three-quarters of a million farms, half the country's railway engines, a third of its merchant navy, and three-quarters of its harbour installations and freight yards. Key mines had been put out of action and innumerable bridges blown up, and those factories which had survived the holocaust were geared to the war effort. An acute food and fuel shortage was not helped by a widespread and highly lucrative black market. By 1958, the situation had been transformed by what was arguably the most revolutionary period in French economic history. It is true that economic progress was accompanied by financial instability and fragility (with occasional bouts of excessive inflation and a humiliatingly weak franc), thus giving substance to the Gaullists' oft-repeated accusation that the politicians of the Fourth Republic had left the country bankrupt. It is equally true, however, that French financial policy was, in some measure, deliberate, and that a large part of the problem lay in the financial strain of the colonial wars and heavy defence commitments, both of which were applauded and encouraged by the same Gaullists.

Even on the purely political level, it is to the credit of the régime that it repulsed determined and often violent onslaughts from the extreme Right and the extreme Left, and that by 1958 France was still a parliamentary and pluralistic democracy and not a dictatorship. Furthermore, like so many of its predecessors it was defeated by forces outside France: if Wellington destroyed the First Empire and Bismarck the Second Empire and if Hitler smashed the Third Republic, it was left to the French army in Algeria to overthrow the Fourth. For twelve years the régime took France through a period of unprecedented social and political tension and disruption, which was due to the consequences of the Second World War and military occupation and of the Cold War, to momentous economic changes and to the colonial wars. It should also be added that amongst the régime's most virulent critics were those who were partly responsible for its defects: the extreme Right demanded 'order', yet flirted with disruptive and disorderly minorities; the moderate Right clamoured for greater political stability, yet by its undisciplined and irresponsible behaviour in Parliament ensured instability; the Communists appealed for greater social justice, but by their intransigence and short-sightedness helped to sabotage any effective means of achieving it. The Gaullists were no less culpable of this fatal ambivalence:

they agitated for stronger authority, yet many of them made it difficult to impose such authority by encouraging dissidence in Metropolitan France and by fanning rebellion in Algeria.

In spite of its real achievements, the Fourth Republic remained unloved – *la mal aimée*. The régime, like the present Italian régime, could probably have survived, lurching from one ministerial crisis to the next, but it was clear by 1958 that the very legitimacy of the régime – that intangible yet essential ingredient of any political system based on consent – was seriously undermined. As Dorothy Pickles has pointed out, already by 1951 nearly half the electorate was voting for parties that rejected the parliamentary system as it prevailed. Faced with the challenge of May 1958 the régime simply could not call upon the loyalties of its citizens. Even those politicians who defended the régime regarded the system with a mixture of resignation, lassitude and even despair. In January 1958, barely four months before the *coup* which resulted in the downfall of the régime, the President of the Republic solemnly reiterated his warning that 'our basic institutions are no longer in tune with the rhythm of modern times'. It was a view shared by many but especially by General de Gaulle, the régime's most persistent and bilious critic, and by Michel Debré, his faithful lieutenant whose vehemence outstripped that even of his master.

Shortly after his return to power, General de Gaulle, in a radio broadcast of 27 June 1958, told the nation that the country was facing three pressing problems: Algeria, the financial and economic situation, and the 'reform of the State'. In fact, he was faced with five distinct, yet related problems: he had to

put an end to the war in Algeria;
challenge the political power of the army which had become a 'State within a State';
remedy a disastrous financial situation and strengthen a promising yet precarious economic position;
re-establish French power and prestige abroad; and
forge new political institutions which were effective, 'Republican', democratic and respected.

For de Gaulle and his political and constitutional advisers, those problems were inseparable one from the other, and all sprang from a common source. That source was the chronic weakness of French political institutions, which paralysed State authority, which, in turn, led 'infallibly' (to use de Gaulle's own word) to trouble in the colonies and the army, to social disruption and to the loss of national in-dependence. General de Gaulle's main constitutional ideas had been outlined in his celebrated speeches at Bayeux and Épinal in June and September 1946. He attributed much of the weakness of the Fourth Republic to the lack of executive authority which was prey to a divided Parliament. During the Fourth Republic there were no fewer than twenty-five Governments and fifteen Prime Ministers (during the same period in Britain there were only four): only two Prime Ministers, Henri Queuille and Guy Mollet, lasted for more than a year. Associated with ministerial instability were ministerial crises – those periods between the fall of one Government and the successful investiture of another. Such crises were not only frequent (an average of two a year) but they were also increasingly difficult to resolve: in the year before the collapse of the Fourth Republic France was ruled by a caretaker Government for one day in every four. Whilst the extent and impact of instability and crises should not be exaggerated (there was a surprising degree of continuity in personnel and policies throughout the period) both undoubtedly brought the régime into disrepute and occasionally paralysed badly needed action.

De Gaulle saw the fault of the régime in its defective Constitution, which gave too much power to Parliament, which was itself at the mercy of the many and divided parties. For the Gaullists, political parties were, by their very nature, the spokesmen and defenders of sectional interests, and they reflected, articulated and perpetuated the basic divisions of French society. Since France was so bitterly divided over many issues there could only be many bitterly divided parties, and with many bitterly divided parties government could only be unstable. Parties had, therefore, to be kept firmly in their subordinate place. The logic was implacable, yet faulty: the problem of the Fourth Republic was not that it was dominated by the parties but rather that those parties which formed successive coalition Governments were so internally divided and so undisciplined in their voting behaviour.

Two other important premises underpinned Gaullist constitutional ideas. The first related to the precariousness of the French national fabric: for many Gaullists the unity of the nation itself was under constant threat. This was scarcely surprising, given the diversity of the country: the cultural and historical links between the inhabitants of Picardy, Provence and Normandy, of Lorraine, Roussillon and Savoy, of Brittany, the Basque Country and the Auvergne, to men-tion but a few of the many provinces which compose France, were seen to be very tenuous. It was, therefore, scarcely surprising that the concern for national unity was an obsession of the chauvinistic Gaullists. Certainly, the past activities of separatist movements were never forgotten and rarely forgiven. The second basic premise of Gaullist constitutional thinking related to the view of the French as being not only diverse and divided but also as being somehow 'ungovernable'. It was claimed that, compared with the regimented Germans or the socially virtuous British, the French, that 'effervescent' and individualistic people, were socially undisciplined, and only too ready to defy established authority. The claim was made with a mixture of despair and pride: de Gaulle was both fascinated and appalled by the fissiparous nature of his compatriots. The Gaullist response to the divisions, the diversity and the 'perpetual effervescence' of the French was the need to construct a strong, centralized and respected State based on an Executive authority capable of governing and of eliciting obedience. And that was what the Fourth Republic had failed to do; for Michel Debré, it was 'a régime of chaos and confusion'. The terms *crise de l'État, crise de l'autorité, carence de pouvoir* (power vacuum) figure prominently in the Gaullist critique of the Fourth Republic. With sufficiently strong institutions such problems could have been avoided. In other words, the Gaullists proposed a series of constitutional and political reforms which would serve to compensate for certain defects or inadequacies of political behaviour, themselves rooted in the nature of French history and society. But constitutional reforms designed to strengthen the authority of the State (by reinforcing the Executive against a Parliament dominated by the despised parties) were insufficient. They had to be accompanied by resolute action against those groups whose actions were undermining the State. Those groups included not only the political parties and the pressure groups whose intrinsic role was to further sectional interests, but also comprised the administration (especially that in the colonies) and the army which were supposed to be obedient custodians of the national interest but whose autonomy threatened the very integrity of the State.

The most striking exercise of autonomous and uncontrolled authority took place in the French colonies, where initiatives were often taken by local civil servants, themselves prisoners of other local forces whose sole concern was the maintenance of the colonies in French hands. Representatives of the French government in the colonies such as General Leclerc and Admiral Thierry-d'Argenlieu in Indo-China, General de Hautecloque in Tunisia and General Juin in Morocco played crucial parts in shaping French policy, often in defiance of instructions emanating from Paris. Successive prime ministers and foreign ministers complained that they were unable to get any orders obeyed or that they were constantly faced with embarrassing *faits accomplis*. Thus, in March 1952, it was the French Resident-General, General de Hautecloque, who took the initiative in having the Tunisian Prime Minister arrested. Similarly, in August 1953, the deposition of the Sultan of Morocco was much more the inspiration of colonial officials than French politicians. Indeed, in both cases, the Government was unhappy and embarrassed about the decisions but did nothing to prevent them.

The Algerian 'cancer' which was to undermine and eventually to destroy the Fourth Republic was contracted in Indo-China and spread unchecked in Morocco and Tunisia. The dreadful tissue of lies, evasion and irresponsibility which characterized the Algerian war had already been evident in the six and a half years war in Indo-China, which had ended in the military humiliation of Dien-Bien-Phu and which cost the French 92 000 dead and 114 000 wounded. The cost of the Algerian war, which began in November 1954, was even more appalling, and may, in some respects, be likened to that of the Vietnam war for the United States: it sacrificed many men; it was a cause of governmental and financial instability; it weakened the country's already feeble diplomatic position; it sapped the moral probity of the régime; it eroded some of the very bases of the State – the loyalty of its army, of its administration and of its citizens. In short, it slowly undermined the legitimacy of the régime. It was in Algeria that the authority of French Governments was most acutely contested. Residents-General who were sent from Paris to Algiers with the task of introducing liberal measures were quickly seduced or intimidated either by the French settlers or by the army. Soustelle, a Left-wing Gaullist, Lacoste, a Socialist, and Salan a 'Republican' general, were amongst those Residents-General whose liberal intentions were quickly transformed into illiberal practices. More dangerously, civil authority gradually relinquished power to the army, often (as was the case with Lacoste in 1957) only too willingly. In the development of the relationship between Paris and Algiers there were thus two distinct yet related stages: first, decisions were increasingly taken in Algeria, and secondly, power within Algeria was gradually transferred from civilian to military hands. A multitude of incidents served to illustrate the inability and unwillingness of Paris to impose its will on a suspicious, obdurate and rebellious local administration and army. In October 1956, for example, Ben Bella, one of the leaders of the Algerian independence movement, who was flying from Morocco to Tunisia was forced by the French airforce to land in Algeria where he was immediately arrested. The Government in Paris, which was in highly secret and sensitive negotiations with the Algerian 'rebels', was horrified: Savary, the Minister for North African Affairs, resigned in protest (a singularly effective gesture). But Prime Minister Mollet, although stupefied by the action, accepted and then justified it. Another example of governmental impotence and cowardice, no less revealing and certainly more tragic, was the Sakhiet incident of February 1958. Prime Minister Gaillard had no foreknowledge of the French bombing of the Tunisian village of Sakhiet, which was suspected by the French army of harbouring Algerian independence fighters. Sixty-nine Tunisians (including twenty-one children) lost their lives, the Tunisian Government was outraged, the French Government astonished and angry, international opinion indignant. But the Prime Minister, fearful of army reactions, was forced to condone the bombing. Such acts of defiance by the army were clearly intolerable to General de Gaulle – once in power.

The creation of a strong, centralized, democratic and respected State, based on a powerful Executive headed by the President and protected against a previously omniscient and omnipotent Parliament, served by an obedient and efficient administration and army, and willing and able to resist the particularist demands of the groups and of the parties – such were the aims of the Gaullist reformers. They were a response to a pressing situation but they also corresponded to a deeper political philosophy. For the first President of the Republic, those aims had to be carried out 'within the context of Republican legality': there could be no recourse to vulgar dictatorship, which de Gaulle abhorred for reasons based on historical experience and on a tactical reading of contemporary French politics. How the Gaullists attempted to fulfil their aims and how successful the régime they founded has been in achieving them serve as two of the underlying themes of this book.

1 The emergence of presidential government: constitutional powers and presidential practice

In his *Conduire le changement*, published in 1975, Michel Poniatowski, Minister of the Interior, intimate friend and political advisor of President Giscard d'Estaing, advocated 'a further push towards presidentialism'. The reaction of some observers was to ask whether such a push was possible, since the régime had already become so ostentatiously presidential. Those observers could be excused their reaction, for the emergence of the presidential office as the major centre of political decision-making has been perhaps the most important single institutional change since the collapse of the Fourth Republic in 1958. This chapter will briefly examine the Presidency under the Third and Fourth Republics and then consider how far the present superiority of the Presidency may be attributed to the 1958 Constitution. It will then examine the major functions of the Presidency and show that successive presidents have exploited political circumstances in order to extend the number and scope of presidential functions.

The Presidency of the Republic before 1958

When de Gaulle decided to stand for election to the Presidency of the Republic he was making clear that the office was destined to become the real power-house of French politics. It was, in many senses, a surprising choice, for its image had been somewhat politically tarnished during the Third and Fourth Republics. Occupants of the Presidency before 1958 were depicted, at best, as distinguished yet colourless figures or, at worst, as harmless nonentities. They were seen as the creatures and prisoners of the Members of Parliament who had elected them and who, when choosing the President, had sought to avoid the election of a strong personality – a man who might prove a danger both to the privileges and prerogatives of Parliament and to the Republic itself. The successful *coup d'état* of 2 December 1851 which ended the Second Republic and the abortive one of 16 May 1877 which threatened the Third Republic were both carried out by incumbent Presidents of the Republic. Those two dates (*le deux décembre* and *le seize mai*) remained anchored in the parliamentary consciousness: a strong-minded and popular choice, such as Clemenceau, for the Presidency was to be avoided. In order to be elected President of the Republic by a highly divided Parliament a candidate had to project himself as a man of no decided views. Occasionally, Parliament was so divided that it took many ballots before a compromise candidate could emerge. René Coty, the second and last President of the Fourth Republic, was elected in December 1953 after thirteen time-consuming and somewhat humiliating ballots: it was a system which seemed designed to ensure the survival of the weakest. The nondescript were preferred to the brilliant, the safe to the adventurous, the cautious to the ambitious, and of the long list of Presidents of the Republic only Thiers, Grévy, Poincaré, Millerand and possibly Auriol emerged from the ranks of obscure worthies. Amongst de Gaulle's predecessors at the Élysée were Sadi Carnot, who secured his place in French history by his assassination (an unkindly contemporary remarked that Carnot's life had been unworthy of his death), Félix Faure, who was remembered for his romantic yet compromising death in the arms of his mistress, Paul Deschanel, whose nocturnal and half-naked perambulations and other bizarre activities finally led to his forced resignation, Gaston Doumergue, who is remembered for his bitter complaints about his own powerlessness, and Albert Lebrun, whose reputation was sullied by his procrastination during the terrible events of 1939–40. It was small wonder that the office was the object of a derision and contempt which was summed up by Clemenceau's famous jibe that the Presidency was as superfluous as the prostate gland. Yet to depict the presidential office during the Third and Fourth Republics as a constitutional superfluity is seriously to mistake the nature of the post, since its power depended to some extent on the personality of the incumbent. And however discreet, that power could be considerable. This was true during the Fourth Republic even though the framers of the Constitution of 1946 had deliberately created a weak Presidency.

During the Fourth Republic there were two Presidents: Vincent Auriol (1947–54) and René Coty (1954–8). Neither may be described as entirely impotent. It is a point worth emphasizing, since the powerful Presidents of the Fifth Republic are all too frequently contrasted with their apparently powerless predecessors of the

Fourth. The two Presidents of the Fourth Republic exercised their power in several ways. First, both were always intimately involved in the delicate negotiations which preceded the formation of any new Government and also in marshalling parliamentary support for that Government once it presented itself to the Assembly for investiture. Both Auriol and Coty took their duties seriously in that area, and both made controversial interventions: the appointment of the very conservative Pinay as Prime Minister in 1952 owed much to the wily manoeuvring of President Auriol, whilst the choice of Socialist Guy Mollet after the elections of January 1956 was engineered in part by President Coty, who disliked Mendès-France, the man many assumed the obvious candidate for the post. Secondly, both Auriol and Coty gave constant advice and warnings to successive Governments and they represented continuity during periods of great ministerial instability. They were constantly informed of all major decisions, especially in the area of foreign, colonial and defence policy, and they had highly developed political antennae sensitive to the ever-changing moods of Parliament. Thirdly, Auriol and, to a lesser extent, Coty directly intervened in the formulation of policy. The former's antipathy towards German rearmament was public knowledge (his public utterances frequently made clear his disagreement with governmental policy), whilst the latter's support for the cause of *Algérie française* was certainly no secret, especially to the army. The importance of the role played by Auriol in foreign affairs and in certain controversial domestic issues (the breaking of the Communist-inspired political strikes of the winter of 1947–8, and the problem of Church–State relations) should not be underestimated, and it is only now beginning clearly to emerge. President Coty was more discreet, but it should not be forgotten that his attitude and activity in the troubled days of May 1958 were to be a vital factor in easing de Gaulle's path back to power. Naturally, in the face of a resolute and hostile Prime Minister the President could not insist on having his way. On the other hand, a determined President could try to block proposals and wait for the ineluctable collapse of the ministry: the succeeding Prime Minister might prove more sympathetic or more pliable.

Whilst the power of the Presidency during the Fourth Republic should not be underestimated, it should be emphasized that presidential power was exercised only so long as it was tolerated by Parliament and the Government. It was not rooted in constitutional texts, in time-honoured conventions or in strong party backing. It was

highly personalized and its exercise hinged upon the tenacity, discretion and patience of the President and good-will (or tolerance) of
the Government and Parliament. Moreover, as an ex-Member of
Parliament of long-standing, the President of the Republic was all
too aware of the limits of his own power. To that extent, the office
was clearly an unsatisfactory power base for General de Gaulle, a
man who had no parliamentary experience, who disliked being
ignored and who hated being over-ruled. Why, then, choose the
Presidency, an ultimately weak office, as his power base? Several
factors seem to have influenced him. First, it was an office which
would enable him more easily to take his distance from the despised
politicians. In his conception of his role, de Gaulle wished to be
'above politics and politicians', and as Prime Minister running a
Government he would inevitably be dragged into the tawdry business
of day-to-day bartering and bargaining. The Presidency was an
office which better ensured a certain aloofness which suited both his
temperament and his view of his role. Moreover, the office may have
had a politically tarnished image, but it was not morally compromised.
Previous incumbents may have been grey mediocrities, but no neurotic
liar had ever disgraced the office as was shortly to be the case in the
United States. But the French Presidency, although strategically
well-placed, had to be reshaped and strengthened. The fulfilment of
that task was commenced by de Gaulle in the Constitution of 1958
and pursued by him for the following ten years. His successors were
no less assiduous in pursuing the same aim, and there is no doubt
that less than twenty years after the collapse of the Fourth Republic
the Presidency had been radically reinforced in a way that even
General de Gaulle could not have envisaged.

The constitutional arrangements of 1958

The text of the present Constitution was adopted by the Government
on 3 September 1958 and presented to the nation on the following
day. It was the first Republican Constitution not to have been drawn
up and debated in Parliament. The Constitution was accepted by the
nation on 28 September 1958 in a referendum in which only 15 per
cent of the electorate abstained. Four out of five voters accepted the
proposed Constitution, and there was a majority for acceptance in
every one of the then ninety *départements* of metropolitan France.
The electorate appears to have been moved by mixed motives. Some
electors were voting against the Left, some for a solution to the

Algerian problem, some for de Gaulle: the Constitution itself was regarded with supreme indifference. This did not prevent the Government from claiming that the new constitutional arrangements were firmly rooted in public assent: this contrasted sharply with the two previous Republican constitutions, since that of the Fourth Republic was accepted by a small margin in a low poll and that of the Third was never put to the nation. If the decision of the electors in September 1958 seemed clear it was more than could be said for the text they had accepted, for it was the result of unhappy compromises between men who held basically conflicting views on the future distribution of political power.

Directly involved in the drafting of the Constitution were a small group of Members of Parliament (who participated in a consultative role and who wished, not unnaturally, to preserve the prerogatives of Parliament), Michel Debré (the recently appointed Minister of Justice who was clearly determined to strengthen the Executive branch of government in its relations with Parliament), and General de Gaulle (who was intent on reinforcing the Presidency to which he was shortly to accede). Since General de Gaulle was at that time still currying parliamentary favour and since Parliament was keen not to displease the General, both sides were prepared to make concessions, yet the result of those concessions was not a happy compromise but a constitutional mess. The unfortunate constitutional experts of the Council of State were called upon to juxtapose and superimpose conflicting ideals, and in the resulting lengthy text confusion competed with contradiction and ambiguity with obscurity. In essence, the lawyers were trying to fuse two ultimately incompatible notions: on the one hand, the separation of powers with a strong Head of State (which smacked of presidentialism), and on the other, the principle of governmental responsibility to Parliament (which implied a parliamentary régime).

The central question of any constitution – who rules? – is fudged. Is it the President of the Republic who is given certain potentially important powers, including that of appointing the Prime Minister? Or is it the Prime Minister who is put 'in general charge of the work of government' which 'decides and directs the policy of the nation' (Articles 20 and 21 of the Constitution) and which is responsible to Parliament? Certain articles of the Constitution clearly suggest that the Prime Minister governs, whilst successive Prime Ministers and Presidents of the Republic have so far claimed that the President rules: with the French Constitution of 1958 we enter the world not

of Descartes but of Lewis Carroll. In spite of presidential claims to
the contrary, the Constitution clearly establishes a dyarchy at the
top, a twin-headed or bicephalous Executive. In practice, the problem has been solved by prime ministerial acceptance of presidential supremacy, but such a happy situation may not last, and the
prospect of a major constitutional crisis has haunted the minds of
politicians throughout the Fifth Republic.

Two major facts emerge from the constitutional morass of 1958:
first, the Presidency was undoubtedly strengthened, and secondly,
the Executive was strengthened *vis-à-vis* of Parliament. The second
fact will be considered at some length in Chapter 5 (pages 107–23),
and it is the first fact that must be now examined. If the Constitution
of the Fifth Republic does not create a presidential régime, it does,
undeniably, confer new powers and an enhanced prestige upon the
presidential office. In the first place, the Constitution changes the
electoral source of presidential power. Presidents of the Third and
Fourth Republics were elected in a joint session of the two Houses of
Parliament, a system which was clearly intolerable to General de
Gaulle, whose opinion of Parliament was not always very flattering.
Initially, both he and Debré, his constitutional *alter ego*, also rejected
the idea of electing the President of the Republic by universal
suffrage. The result was that in the 1958 text of the Constitution the
President was to be elected by an electoral college, comprising about
80 000 political *notables*. But this method of electing the President
was changed by the referendum of October 1962: henceforth, the
President of the Republic was to be elected by universal suffrage.

The change accepted in October 1962 conferred no new functions,
privileges or prerogatives upon the Presidency. But Professor
Duverger has rightly argued that if it granted no new *powers* it did
afford him an important new *power*. From 1965, the date of the first
presidential election, successive Presidents could claim (and have
claimed) that their mandate came directly from the people, that the
source of their authority was impeccable, that their democratic
legitimacy was at least equal to that of the National Assembly, which
was also elected by universal suffrage. The President was, in the full
sense of the term, the *élu de la nation*, and exercised his functions as
the result of the sovereign decision of the electors. The political
significance of the October 1962 reform cannot be over-estimated,
for it completely upset, in favour of the President, the uneasy and
ambiguous balance established in the 1958 Constitution. As President
de Gaulle claimed in his January 1964 press conference, 'we behave

in such a way that power . . . emanates directly from the people, which implies that the Head of State, elected by the nation, must be the source and holder of power . . . that is what was made clear by the last referendum'.

Apart from strengthening the source of his authority, the Constitution confers upon the President all the powers traditional to the office. The traditional rights he inherited as Head of State and Commander-in-Chief of the Armed Forces include those relating to the presiding of the Council of Ministers and important committees, the negotiating and ratifying of international treaties, the appointing of the Prime Minister and important officials, the signing of decrees in the Council of Ministers, the promulgating of laws and the granting of pardons. In the exercise of these powers, many of which are purely formal, the President of the Republic, according to the Constitution, must act with the agreement, and on the initiative of the Prime Minister together with that of any other appropriate minister. This stipulation was included to underline the constitutional myth of the political irresponsibility of the President. And it led to the claim of Michel Debré that the President was essentially a *solliciteur*, a word with unfortunate connotations in English but which implied that the President had to 'solicit' the intervention of the Prime Minister or the appropriate minister before he could act. In practice, this has not proved the case: ministerial countersignatures have become a mere formality.

A number of new powers are also given to the President in the 1958 Constitution, and in order to exercise them he does not need to solicit ministerial intervention. These powers were included to enable him to fulfil the presidential role, as defined in Article 5 of the Constitution. That article is one of the most important and most controversial of the Constitution, and it is worth quoting in full:

The President of the Republic sees that the Constitution is respected, ensures by his arbitration the regular functioning of the organs of government and the continuity of the State. He is the protector of national independence, of territorial integrity, and of respect for agreements with the [French] Community and for treaties.

The concept of *arbitrage* contained in Article 5 has excited the minds of some constitutional experts and stimulated the imagination of others: the most awful twaddle has been employed to rationalize the prejudices (often political) of the lawyers in the interpretation of the notion. Incorrigible supporters of parliamentary supremacy insist that the notion requires the President to be an objective referee, an impartial observer, an olympian arbitrator, whilst Gaullist lawyers (and notably Marcel Prélot) have unearthed the ancient Latin sense of *arbitrium* which involves the right of the President to make decisions on the basis of his own judgement. This Gaullist interpretation naturally attributes a much more dynamic and interventionist role to the President of the Republic. In truth, Article 5 is sufficiently vague to enable successive Presidents to interpret it as they wished.

In order to carry out his role as arbiter, the President receives certain powers not accorded to Presidents of the Fourth Republic:

He has the right to submit a Bill or a treaty to the Constitutional Council for judgement on its constitutionality. He also has the right to appoint three of the nine appointed members of the Council.

He may have a message read out for him in either or both Houses of Parliament.

He is empowered to grant or refuse a request of either the Government or the two Houses of Parliament jointly for a referendum.

He has the right to dissolve the National Assembly before the official end of its term of office, although he is prevented from dissolving the Chamber again in the following twelve months.

Article 16 of the Constitution enables the President, after consultation with the Prime Minister, the Presidents of the National Assembly, the Senate and the Constitutional Council, to take whatever measures he sees fit, 'when there exists a serious and immediate threat to the institutions of the Republic, the independence of the nation, the integrity of its territory or the fulfilment of international obligations, and the regular functioning of the Constitutional public authorities has been interrupted'. This so-called emergency-powers provision gives the President total and unchecked power in circumstances defined by himself. In the early years of the Fifth Republic it caused a storm of controversy, for many observers were rightly concerned about its possible abuse. It was included on the insistence of General de Gaulle, who had in mind the traumatic events of May 1940 when, in the face of an advancing German army, political authority was completely paralysed. Since 1958, the Article has been used only once, by General de Gaulle, between 23 April and 30 September 1961, following a military *putsch* in Algeria.

The President of the Republic is given, therefore, three fairly distinct sets of powers: one to carry out his normal duties as Head of State, one to act in a politically charged situation, and one to take complete control in very exceptional circumstances (Article 16). But these fairly wide-ranging powers were clearly insufficient to meet the demands of the first President of the Fifth Republic, who not only fully exploited the constitutional powers given him but did not hesitate to violate the Constitution and even, in October 1962, to change it (by unconstitutional means). It has been said that the 1958 Constitution was 'tailor-made' for General de Gaulle, but since it was so frequently abused by the General one might conclude either that the tailor was totally incompetent or that the statement is untrue.

Presidential practice – the functions of the Presidency

Whatever the intentions of the framers of the Constitution, presidential supremacy has clearly been established by the practice of successive Presidents. Since 1958 that practice has transformed the nature and scope of the office. The President of the Republic has now five basic functions: he is the ceremonial Head of State, the guardian of the national interest, the fountain-head of patronage, the country's most prominent politician and, finally, the head of the Executive. The priority given to each of these functions, their interpretation and their execution have depended on the taste, the temperament and the ability of the incumbent, but under successive Presidents of the Republic the office has been much more powerful, more interventionist and more political than the constitutional texts appear to imply.

The first function of the President of the Republic concerns his role as Head of State, which involves him in a great deal of time-consuming ceremony. Like Presidents of the Fourth Republic, he receives foreign Heads of State, makes courtesy visits abroad and accredits ambassadors. The President is also expected to make frequent visits to the French provinces. These visits, which are a veritable ordeal for local officials (particularly the local prefects who are responsible for the smooth running of the visit), are seen as a useful means of keeping the President in touch with the people. In the performance of these ceremonial duties there have been marked contrasts in the style of the three Presidents of the Fifth Republic. As the Head of State, the President of the Republic has some unpleasant duties to perform. It is he, for example, who exercises the right of pardon, and since France and Spain share the dubious privilege of being the only countries in Western Europe to retain capital punishment this duty can be, in the words of President

Pompidou, 'very painful'. All three Presidents have taken the duty seriously: President de Gaulle would often meet the defence lawyers to hear their final plea, whilst his successor, Pompidou, openly admitted his revulsion for the guillotine, and only after prolonged agonizing did he not exercise his right to pardon. The present President of the Republic, although equally revolted by the practice, has so far allowed the execution of four men, presumably on the grounds that chopping human beings in two is an integral part of that 'advanced liberal society' so close to his heart.

The second main presidential function relates to his role as the guardian of the national interest, the leader of the nation, the physical embodiment of its traditions and its continuity and the guide to its future actions. The President has become the nation's principal pedagogue, using this role to emphasize the essential unity of the nation, constantly calling for effort and sacrifice. The presidential New Year message always stresses these themes. In moments of crisis, the President attempts, not always successfully, to rise above the political fray and to perform the role attributed to him by the Constitution – that of the ultimate arbiter of the national interest. The role was assumed with superb aplomb by the first President of the Fifth Republic: at his best, de Gaulle was unsurpassable: his television appeal to the nation after the army revolt in Algeria in April 1961 was as moving and as resolute as it was effective, a rare combination of high drama and deep sincerity. The role of national leader was assumed less convincingly but no less readily by de Gaulle's successors. Thus, during the economic and financial crisis of the summer of 1976, Giscard d'Estaing appeared on television and in sombre tones exhorted his countrymen to greater efforts, criticized the selfish attitude of certain sectional interests and appealed for national consensus in dealing with the country's problems. Unfortunately, such appeals have often a hollow ring: patriotism, the last resort of the scoundrel, is often the first device of the desperate politician.

The President's third main function relates to his constitutional power of appointment to key posts in politics, in the armed forces, in the top ranks of the civil service and in the judiciary. His most important appointments concern the choice of Prime Minister and his Government. According to the Constitution (Article 8),

The President of the Republic appoints the Prime Minister. He terminates his period of office on the presentation by the Prime Minister of the resignation of the Government. He appoints and dismisses the other members of the Government on the proposal of the Prime Minister.

There is no doubt that presidential interpretation of this article has been exceedingly elastic. Prime Ministers have not only been appointed but also dismissed (although the dismissal often took the form of a forced resignation) – often in summary fashion and to the astonishment of at least one Prime Minister (Chaban-Delmas in 1972). Moreover, Presidents have not been reluctant to meddle in the choice and removal of ministers and have also protected ministers who did not enjoy the confidence of the Prime Minister. Until 1974 the choice of ministers was generally the result of agreement between the President and the Prime Minister. Since that date there is evidence to suggest that for many appointments the President has merely consulted or informed the Prime Minister. He has also ignored prime ministerial advice and overruled his objections. By his liberal interpretation of the Constitution, the President has increasingly turned the Government into an instrument of his own ascendancy. He has become the principal dispenser of political rewards and revenge, able to make or break the career of the aspiring and the ambitious. This distribution of patronage is an important component in the President's political armoury, since by his choices he determines the political complexion of the Government.

In other spheres, too, the President has an important source of patronage. He appoints in the Council of Ministers to key posts in the judiciary. He nominates all members of the Higher Council of the Judiciary (a body which makes recommendations to the Government on appointments to top judicial posts, advises the President on the exercise of his right to pardon, and acts as a disciplinary court for judges) and also appoints three of the nine members of the increasingly influential Constitutional Council (the body which is called to give judgement in constitutional disputes). The President of the Republic also appoints, in the Council of Ministers, Ambassadors, Councillors of State, Prefects, Rectors of Academies, senior members of the Court of Accounts and the civil service heads of the divisions in the ministries. Unofficially, he may, of course, propose candidates for other posts, and few people are likely to refuse presidential requests. The extent of presidential patronage in the administration should not be exaggerated: there is no highly developed spoils system in France, and senior appointments are most often dictated by considerations of ability and well-rooted conventions (such as the seniority rule). Furthermore, politically inspired appointments are certainly not peculiar to the Fifth Republic. Nevertheless, posts at the discretion of the President can be, and have been, used to reward the faithful, to tempt the waverers, to punish the recalcitrant and the hostile, and to get rid of the embarrassing. The presidential right of appointment was skilfully exploited by de Gaulle when he was cleansing the army of its dissident elements and purging the French Foreign Office of diplomats suspected of being too pro-American or too pro-European. President Pompidou displayed no reticence in rewarding loyal political and personal friends: several young members of his private staff enjoyed meteoric promotion. President Giscard d'Estaing has not been over-scrupulous in the exercise of his power of patronage and several top civil servants with a history of *anti-Giscardisme* have fallen victim to his rancour.

The fourth function of the President is purely political. The Constitution of 1958 proclaimed the principle of the political irresponsibility of the President of the Republic, and it may well be that the first President of the Fifth Republic had no intention of sullying his hands by playing politics: he wished to be, as he so frequently declared, 'above politics'. But whatever the pious implications of the Constitution or the intentions of General de Gaulle, each President of the Republic has been obliged to descend into the political arena. Indeed, in January 1976, President Giscard d'Estaing could openly admit that politics were 'part of his mission', a confession which would never have been made by General de Gaulle. Presidential intervention in political matters takes three basic forms. First, as the effective (if not the constitutional) head of the Government, the President constantly defends governmental policies and criticizes those of the Opposition. Like his two predecessors, President Giscard d'Estaing appears frequently on television to explain, comment upon and justify the Government's record. In one important respect President Giscard d'Estaing differs from his predecessors: unlike de Gaulle and Pompidou, he meets frequently, officially and openly representatives of important pressure groups. Such contacts had always been expressly refused by General de Gaulle who disliked and despised the 'intermediaries', the representatives of sectional interests.

The second area of presidential political activity concerns his relations with his own supporters, for the President increasingly intervenes to marshal party and parliamentary support for governmental policies. General de Gaulle was content to leave most of that activity to his willing Prime Minister or to Foccart, a 'Gaullist baron' who exercised great influence behind the scenes. But both Pompidou and Giscard d'Estaing were quickly drawn directly into this area, although the former was generally (though not always) more discreet in his methods. Amongst Pompidou's political acts were his interventions in the choice of the General Secretary of the Gaullist party in January 1971 and in the election of the Speaker of the National Assembly in 1973. President Giscard d'Estaing regularly meets leaders of the parties which compose the governmental coalition in order to ensure some co-ordination between them, to iron out differences, or to mobilize support behind a minister in difficulty. In November 1974, he had to back his Minister of Health in her battle over the abortion Bill, which was being given a rough passage by the Government's own supporters. He intervened again in June 1976 to support his Minister of Finance, who was struggling to push through Parliament a capital gains tax in the teeth of fierce opposition from members of the governmental coalition, and in November he tried to impose on the Government coalition his own candidate, Michel d'Ornano, for the local elections in Paris.

The third and most obvious area of presidential action is electoral. In the first place, like the British Prime Minister, he has to time the general election in a way most favourable to his supporters. The power of the President to dissolve the National Assembly is now considered to be an important political weapon at his disposal, although it was felt by most constitutional experts at the beginning of the Fifth Republic that the power of dissolution was unlikely ever to be used. The last time it had been invoked was in May 1877 when the Royalist President MacMahon dissolved a National Assembly dominated by the Republicans. The ensuing elections were won by the Republicans, and a year later the President of the Republic was forced to resign. The dissolution of 16 May 1877 was a perfectly valid constitutional act, yet for good Republicans it was considered to be a *coup d'état* against them, and for that reason no subsequent President ever used the power. It was not until October 1962 that a President of the Republic, General de Gaulle, dared dissolve a hostile National Assembly. He was to do so again in May 1968 when the Government's majority was both small and precarious. On both occasions, the desired result – an increased majority for the Government – was achieved. It is revealing that the President's right to dissolve the National Assembly is now accepted by everyone: the weapon is not only constitutionally theoretical but is now rooted in convention. Nevertheless, however effective it may be (and has proved to be), the right to dissolve is also, as Wilson and Heath in Britain were bitterly to discover, a double-edged weapon: an error of judgement may be very costly indeed.

Presidential electoral action also used to extend to the choice of governmental candidates in the general elections. Under de Gaulle and Pompidou pressure was exerted on the Government coalition parties to present only one candidate at the first ballot of the elections. This naturally gave rise to fierce disputes in the constituencies, and arbitration at national level was needed. During General de Gaulle's period of office, this duty of arbitrating between the conflicting claims was left almost exclusively to the Prime Minister who, for the general elections of 1962, 1967 and 1968, was Georges Pompidou. When Pompidou became the President of the Republic he was unable or unwilling to relinquish this task which he had performed so well. President Giscard d'Estaing's power in this domain has been drastically reduced, because the major party of his coalition, the Gaullist party, now rejects his right to arbitrate, and the task is now carried out by representatives of the various parties of the coalition.

The final area of presidential electoral intervention is in marshalling support for the Government's candidates. Both General de Gaulle and President Pompidou appeared on television openly to support their candidates and to attack the Opposition. In the June 1968 general elections, for example, de Gaulle unscrupulously exploited a non-existent Communist menace, whilst in the March 1973 elections, Pompidou denounced the opposition in terms which gave the lie to his claim to be 'the President of all the French'. His successor at the Élysée, obsessed with the prospect of a Left-wing victory at the polls in March 1978, started his election campaign as early as 1976, following severe governmental defeats in the local elections.

The President of the Republic has, therefore, three major political roles: first, he is the general spokesman of the Government and its principal pedagogue; secondly, he is the guardian of the unity of the coalition which supports him; finally, he is the coalition's principal electoral guide and agent. This politicization of the presidential function was inevitable, since the President has become the effective head of the Executive during the Fifth Republic, and that function can only be carried out if it is accepted or tolerated by Parliament. Yet presidential entanglement with domestic politics and involvement in the polemics of his supporters, whilst inevitable, are dangerous, for the President is bound to become a main target for Opposition attacks and his supporters' disgruntlement. In such circumstances he is led inevitably to defend himself, thus inviting further political attacks, and tarnishing his image as 'the President of all Frenchmen'. The vicious circle is established and closed. There was once a fiction of the President being 'above politics', of his being the statesman who stands aloof from party polemics, parliamentary strife and electoral warfare. That fiction was quickly eroded under de Gaulle and Pompidou and has been shattered under Giscard d'Estaing.

The fifth and final function of the President of the Republic is policy-making, for, whatever the constitutional texts may declare, the President of the Republic has emerged as the effective head of the Executive. He does not 'solicit'; he commands: the Prime Minister and the Government are not his equals but his servants. The President's role as chief policy-maker in France is examined in detail in the following chapter.

In extending the powers of the Presidency, successive Presidents have not hesitated to exploit all the powers given them by the Constitution. When the President of the Fifth Republic 'presides over the Council of Ministers' he does so in a way totally different from his predecessors of the Third and Fourth Republics, for he fixes the timetable and the agenda and even decides who may or may not speak. Similarly, the constitutional power 'to negotiate and ratify treaties' has not been viewed in any narrow or formalistic manner but has been seen as signifying presidential primacy in the field of foreign affairs: the French President is fully in charge of the conduct of foreign policy and, in that field, enjoys an independence far greater than the American President, who is constantly having to keep a wary eye on the reactions of Congress.

Successive Presidents of the Fifth Republic have also shown a remarkable facility for interpreting loosely (and advantageously) certain ambiguous articles of the Constitution. If French constitutional lawyers discuss with theological intensity the exact meaning of the term 'arbitration' contained in Article 5, Giscard d'Estaing, like his two predecessors, has always acted as though it involved much more than a purely representative, consultative and advisory role for the Presidency. General de Gaulle argued that it gave him 'supremely important responsibility for the destiny of France and of the Republic', which meant, in effect, that it empowered him to govern the country. Neither Pompidou nor Giscard d'Estaing demurred at that interpretation. Finally, the first President of the Fifth Republic did not hesitate to act unconstitutionally to strengthen his position. There were a number of celebrated examples: his refusal to convoke a special session of Parliament in March 1960 even though a majority of the National Assembly had requested it; his abuse of Article 16 in April 1961 (its use was extended well beyond the time required to crush the army *putsch* which had provoked its use in the first place); his method of amending the Constitution in October 1962 and his attempt to amend it in April 1969 by use of referenda, instead of by the means outlined in the Constitution.

The steady violation of the spirit and the occasional infringement of the letter of the Constitution in order to strengthen the presidential office caused little stir amongst the French. They belong to a country which has never displayed undue respect for the prevailing Constitution. And whereas in the USA the Constitution is regarded as a quasi-sacred text and as binding upon the President as upon the most humble citizen, in France the Constitution has always been regarded, to use Professor Goguel's phrase, as 'a mechanism, a rule in the game'. It is not the foundation of the political and social system but an elaborate device for trying to make the system work. If it does not appear to work it may be discarded. The first President of the Republic exploited, sometimes in spectacular fashion, this public indifference to the Constitution. Like his two successors, he was also able to exploit political circumstances to assert presidential pre-eminence. President Pompidou carefully played upon the fears of the Right, anchored in anti-Communism and heightened by the events of May 1968, to forge a powerful electoral and political coalition under his leadership. President Giscard d'Estaing skilfully exploits the fatal ambivalence of the position of the Gaullists (who could cause him trouble), because whilst many of them have no particular affection for him they have a deep-rooted respect for his office and recognize (albeit ungraciously) his position as *de facto* leader of the anti-Left forces. But the greatest expert in seizing the chances offered by propitious political circumstances was the first President of the Fifth Republic. He brilliantly manoeuvred himself back to power during the confusion and fear of May 1958; his admirers claim that he came to power perfectly legally, but the fact remains that he did so by exploiting an illegal situation – an armed rebellion against the authority of the French State. He later used the attempt against his life at Petit-Clamart in August 1962 to propose the introduction of universal suffrage for the election of the President. In September 1962, when the National Assembly passed a motion of censure against the Pompidou Government, he immediately dissolved the Chamber, and the ensuing election gave him a comfortable majority. Similarly, in May 1968, he employed the existing chaos to dissolve a troublesome National Assembly where his majority was only wafer-thin: the Chamber which had been elected only a year previously, had, in de Gaulle's memorably arrogant phrase, 'the vocation to be dissolved'.

It was in Algeria that de Gaulle was fully to exploit political circumstances in order to strengthen his office. Indeed, it is probably the case that without Algeria de Gaulle would never have come to power at all and may not have survived the first four years of his office. General de Gaulle once noted that '*l'Algérie bloque tout*'. By 'everything' he really meant the pursuit of a more active and independent French foreign policy. But the Algerian war also blocked something else very important: the political opposition to himself. That opposition was hostile to many of his other policies, but it recognized that only de Gaulle could 'solve' the Algerian problem. Lack of space precludes a detailed account of the war which broke out in November 1954 and which dominated the life of the last three years of the Fourth Republic and the first four years of the Fifth. It was no manichean affair although it was viewed as such by extremists on both sides. All the major groups involved in the war – the Government, Parliament, the political parties, the white settlers, the army, the Algerian population and the independence fighters – were divided both between and within themselves over ends and means, over motives, strategy and tactics. It was an immensely complex war rendered poisonous by all the instruments of modern war: military might and urban guerilla warfare, political persuasion and moral blackmail. The war consumed French manpower, money and diplomatic energy and was punctuated by bloody and dramatic incidents (notably in January 1960 and April 1961), some of which appeared to threaten the very existence of the Fifth Republic. De Gaulle had neither sentimental attachment for, nor aversion towards, *Algérie française*. Nor had he any pronounced doctrinal penchant for Algerian independence, but he saw it as the only means of ridding France (and himself) of a huge economic, political and diplomatic millstone. By a mixture of brutal cynicism, prudent opportunism, calculated idealism and characteristic audacity, he imposed not a solution (there was no solution, since the participants were so irreconcilably opposed) but an end to the war. In order to do so he exploited the divisions of his opponents, the loyalty of his own supporters (Michel Debré, the Prime Minister, was notably lukewarm about Algerian independence) and the war-weariness of a frustrated

French population. Nowhere was the skill of the General more evident and nowhere was his achievement more resounding: by mid 1962, the war was over, the political power of the army was destroyed, the extremists were crushed, and his popular support was high. The Opposition parties had been reduced to silent disapprobation of many of his acts, but their silence was more significant than their disapprobation. For the four formative years of the Fifth Republic they had been content to stand back and allow the General to violate the Constitution, to consolidate his personal position and to strengthen his office. They could do little else, since to bring down de Gaulle involved their being once again saddled with the Algerian problem – a problem which had caused their own demise and provoked their ultimate downfall. Thus, for those four key years Algeria prevented the Opposition from acting against the President of the Republic: the Algerian war, noted Raymond Aron, was an effective substitute for a parliamentary majority. And it is revealing that less than six months after peace was restored in Algeria, the Opposition parties passed their only successful motion of censure against the Government.

Successive Presidents have exploited not only specific and short-lived political circumstances, they have also been able to take advantage of the continuing unpopularity of the previous régime. That unpopularity emerges from all the opinion polls. A constant theme of Gaullist propaganda since 1958 (and, indeed, long before that date) has been that the Fourth Republic was a chaotic and unstable régime, and the very considerable success of such propaganda must be explained by the fact that it coincided with a widely held perception: when General de Gaulle intoned his dark and frequent warnings about the dire consequences of returning to the disorder of the Fourth Republic he touched a responsive chord in the electorate. The French yearned not for dictatorship but for Governments which at least gave the appearance of governing. They not unnaturally resented the reputation of their country as the sick man of Europe (the Americans and the British were prolific in wounding and condescending sneers), and whilst they may not have liked some of de Gaulle's acts they appreciated his efforts in restoring their sense of national pride. Even eighteen years after the fall of the Fourth Republic, President Giscard d'Estaing could still exploit an imaginary threat of a return to the 'disastrous régime of parties'.

Finally, the President of the Republic has been able to exploit the increasing acceptance of presidential government. The Prime Minister, the Government, Parliament, most of the parties and the pressure groups now fully recognize the dominance of the Presidency, and focus their attention and energies in that direction. So, too, does the electorate. The exceptionally high turn-out at the last presidential elections (85 per cent at the first and second ballots) was an eloquent affirmation of the importance that the voters attached to the office. Moreover, opinion polls clearly reveal that a great majority of people, when casting their votes, considered that they were voting for the man who was going to govern the country (Table 1).

Table 1 *Results of the Publimétrie poll May 1976: 'When you voted in the presidential elections of May 1974 for Giscard d'Estaing or François Mitterrand, did you think that you were voting for the man who was going to govern the country?'*

	Yes	No	Don't know
		(percentage)	
Electorate, total	78	10	12
Electorate, men	80	9	11
Electorate, women	77	10	13
Giscard voters	89	4	7
Socialist voters	75	15	10
Communist voters	82	9	9

That people now see the Presidency as the real power-house of French politics is confirmed in small but revealing ways, such as the number of letters received at the Élysée: de Gaulle received an average of 50 000 letters a year, Pompidou 180 000, whilst Giscard now receives over 220 000 letters, and the number is increasing.

The present power of the Presidency may be traced to the 1958 Constitution and the October 1962 constitutional reform. But it has undoubtedly been reinforced by the activities of successive occupants of the office, who have not hesitated to exploit propitious political circumstances in order to increase the scope of each of their functions. The most remarkable extension of presidential power has undoubtedly been in their function as effective head of the Executive, which is the subject of the next two chapters.

2 The extension of the presidential sector: the personal factor

If the old adage that office maketh man is arguable, the Fifth Republic provides irrefutable proof that man also maketh office. The French Presidency, its powers, power and its functioning owe a great deal to the will, the style and the personality of the incumbent President. For that reason it is worth briefly looking at the three men who have so far occupied the office under the Fifth Republic.

The importance of General de Gaulle, the first President of the Fifth Republic, in shaping the presidential office cannot be overestimated. Elected President, 21 December 1958, by 78 per cent of the 80 000 electors who comprised the presidential electoral college, he was re-elected for a further seven years in December 1965. But on the latter occasion he was elected by direct suffrage, beating François Mitterrand, the Left-wing candidate, at the second ballot. He occupied the Presidency until April 1969, when he resigned after the defeat of his proposals in a referendum. He was thus President of the Republic for ten years. General de Gaulle intervened both directly and indirectly in the framing of the Constitution, and later, by his actions, he secured the supremacy of the office he occupied. He came to the Presidency with clear ideas about the need for strengthening the State and reinforcing Executive authority. Those ideas emerged from a long and bitter historical experience, for de Gaulle had witnessed the steady decline of his beloved country and had participated in some of its greatest tragedies. His long life was marked by bitter personal and political memories: the impotence of squabbling politicians in the 1930s; the gutlessness of the political elite in the black days of May 1940; the humiliation of his country's occupation and his self-imposed exile; his acrimonious relations in the provisional government after the Liberation of France; his withdrawal from government in 1946 and his long and lonely 'crossing of the desert' until 1958. He had witnessed the total collapse of his country once and had experienced the progressive degradation of the State, and he was determined to prevent the former and reverse the latter. For de Gaulle, strong governmental authority was required and he was determined to provide it. Yet such authority would have to be legitimate, Republican and democratic: General de Gaulle may have had dictatorial tendencies but he was no vulgar dictator, and some of his finest lines dissect the moral and political bankruptcy of dictatorship. There were thus limits which de Gaulle refused to transgress in the means he employed to extend presidential power. But within those limits, he felt free to act. Authoritarian pronouncements, impassioned and emotional outbursts, extremely moving exhortations, paternal jocularity and a natural charm were all weapons in his considerable personal armoury.

In this extraordinarily rich and complex character, in this monarch who destroyed one Republic and founded another, certitude competed with paradox, faith with scepticism, high principles with brutal cynicism. He was at once a Jesuit and a Jansenist, a Florentine and a Venetian, a man of world vision and a carping chauvinist. This mountain of insensitivity (who could crush his close associates with his ingratitude) could also display a profound, touching and tragic concern for his mentally handicapped daughter. He disdained politicians and despised 'politics' yet he proved himself a consummate practitioner of the art. He was a profound realist who nevertheless took up his sword against diplomatic windmills: Cervantes would have done him proud. This intense nationalist accelerated the process of decolonization, and this army officer broke the army as a powerful political force – perhaps his greatest political achievement. There were, in truth, the elements of several folk-heroes in de Gaulle: like Don Quixote he defied the inevitable, like Till Eulenspiegel he cocked a snook at traditional authorities, like William Tell he frequently displayed great physical and intellectual courage.

A man of action, de Gaulle was also a philosopher and writer with a highly developed (if tendentious) view of history. He was a born pedagogue who used the public platform and the television screen to great effect, and his elegant writings all profess those eternal truths he so cherished. His mastery of the French language was proverbial ('*il gouverna par le verbe*', noted one critic) and he could use words, often simple in appearance, to disguise obscurity: verbal decisiveness often masked profound equivocation. De Gaulle also had a finely attuned sense of theatrical moment. His sense of theatre and the dramatic found expression on several occasions: on 18 June 1940 when he flew to England to lead the Free French in a continued struggle against Germany; on 29 May 1968 when he suddenly disappeared from a Paris which was in political turmoil to visit high-ranking army officers in Germany. Yet allied with the taste for striking gestures were an empiricism, a prudence, a capacity for improvisation and an occasional calculated prevarication, all of which he displayed during his accession to power in May 1958 and in his conduct of the Algerian war between 1958 and 1962. Furthermore, if circumstances demanded, he would resort to silence, secrecy and even deceit.

General de Gaulle lived at several different levels: as the personification of the values and virtues of French civilization; as the living embodiment of the State; as the man of Providence defying the elements; as the author conscious of writing his own place into world history; as the Cassandra who foresaw the collapse of his own country in May 1940 and as the prophet who forecast the inevitable defeat of Germany; as President of the Republic resolutely constructing a strong Executive authority; as a bilious politician constantly marshalling support for his dreams and schemes; as an anguished and perceptive spectator of his times. This extraordinary man, who could refer to himself in the third person, was partial prisoner of his own myth. As a national leader, General de Gaulle elicited both deep-seated hatred and also an admiration which bordered occasionally on adulation: the political magic of the man was sufficient to create a fervent and sometimes fanatical following. And if that support declined during his long period of office, it must be remembered that in the referendum which led to his resignation he was still backed by a percentage of the voters greater than that enjoyed by any British Prime Minister since the war. Intelligent and powerful men accepted without question his moral authority – however illegal or unconstitutional his activity. In his genius for communication he displayed an uncanny ability to touch a responsive chord in the national consciousness. When he resigned in 1969, after ten years in office, he handed over to his successor a Presidency which enjoyed both power and prestige.

The successor of General de Gaulle was Georges Pompidou, who was elected to the Presidency in June 1969. His rise to the Presidency was, in many senses, spectacular. When de Gaulle appointed him Prime Minister in April 1962 he was totally unknown to the general public, and his appointment was interpreted by many as an act of defiance by de Gaulle towards the Gaullist party and towards Parliament, since he had never been a member of either. That he was to become undisputed master of both was a measure of the man's uncanny ability. Pompidou had not rallied to the call of 10 May 1940, he had fought no battles for the Resistance, he had taken no part in the heroic episode of the RPF (the first Gaullist party) from 1947 to 1951, he had played no part in the Gaullist conspiracy in Algiers and Paris which helped to pave the way to de Gaulle's return to power in May 1958, he had suffered none of the many setbacks of Gaullist diehards such as Michel Debré and had taken no active part in Gaullist party propaganda. During the Fourth Republic he enjoyed a short yet distinguished career in the Council of State and a longer and infinitely more lucrative one in Rothschild's bank in Paris. It was during that period that Pompidou acquired his business contacts, a certain financial security and a taste for modern art (with which he was to desecrate certain rooms of the Élysée after his election to the Presidency). He made money, read poetry and lived the good life. His background seemed less suited for the battlefront of politics than the salons of the well-heeled, the well-bred and the well-read. But Pompidou was an able and trusted confidant of General de Gaulle who appreciated his discretion, his fidelity, his literary ability and his managerial efficacy. And whilst he had played no active role in politics, his Gaullist credentials were well established: he had been a member of de Gaulle's private office in 1945 and was recognized as one of the Gaullist 'barons' (together with men such as Chaban-Delmas, Foccart and Frey) who met weekly to discuss political tactics. He was known to be in frequent contact with de Gaulle from 1946 to 1958 (and gave the General financial advice), and from 1958 to 1962 carried out several confidential missions for the President.

Pompidou remained Prime Minister for six years – for the longest period in French Republican history – and by 1968, when he 'resigned', he had created for himself a very powerful political base. He had nursed his parliamentary constituency with the assiduity of an old-style politician, he had emerged as a skilful parliamentary debater and a powerful public speaker, he had established himself as the undisputed leader of the Gaullist party, he had been successful in forging unity of action (if not of attitude) between the parties which composed the governmental coalition (which he led to electoral victory in 1962, 1967 and 1968) and he proved himself a remarkably effective Prime Minister, especially during the disorders of May 1968. More dangerously, he had emerged as the *dauphin*, the legitimate and apparently inevitable successor of de Gaulle. For the latter it was an intolerable situation. In June 1968, Pompidou was gracelessly replaced as Prime Minister by the lack-lustre Couve de Murville. Then began his personal *traversée du désert*, a short but painful period marked by a total breach with de Gaulle and by ugly rumours, as scurrilous as they were unfounded, of his being involved in an underworld scandal. With de Gaulle's resignation in 1969 Pompidou immediately declared himself a candidate for the Presidency, and, after an unexciting campaign, was elected at the second ballot against Poher, an avuncular mediocrity whose political opinions were as colourless as his personality.

De Gaulle's apocalyptic prophecy of the political deluge which would engulf France after his departure was to be disproved by Pompidou's Presidency. Until he was undermined by his appalling illness he was a strong and effective President who considerably extended the presidential sphere of government. Rumours of Pompidou's illness were circulating long before his death: this was scarcely surprising, since he was literally dying a public death. In his last two years, in spite of terrible suffering, he clung tenaciously to office and continued to make and shape the major policies of the régime. He made frequent visits abroad and to the French provinces and continued to preside over the weekly Council of Ministers. But he had neither the will nor the strength closely to control the activities of his ministers or even his own personal staff. Increasingly, both his personality and style of government changed. His well-known ability to take quick and decisive decisions was replaced by a disquieting procrastination, his personal joviality by lassitude, his enthusiasm by indifference, his opportunism based on acute political sensitivity by an over-prudent conservatism, his good-living by an introspective piety, his worldly scepticism by a deepening religiosity which bordered on mysticism: Pompidou, a prize product of the secular Republic, ended his days firmly in the embrace of the Church.

Pompidou, as President, was a firm political and social conservative. His profound scepticism about men and the world was expressed in his highly personal *Noeud gordien*, published in June 1974 but written when he was out of office in 1968–9. This son of a Socialist primary school teacher from one of the poorest parts of France (the Cantal in the Massif Central) reached the top through his local *lycée* and the École Normale Supérieure. Talented, intelligent and ambitious, Pompidou made good, and like many of his kind, had little understanding of those unable or unwilling to do the same. In one important respect, however, he was a radical: he was obsessed by the need economically to transform France, by the need to make his country a great industrial power. And to that end a great deal was sacrificed: the environment and greater social justice were amongst the victims. When Pompidou died, 2 April 1974, he must have been satisfied by his work, for France had become one of the greatest economic powers in the world.

The third, and present, President of the Fifth Republic, Valéry Giscard d'Estaing, comes from the same region – the Auvergne – as his predecessor. But there ends all similarities in origins. Giscard d'Estaing hails from an old and distinguished family of political and industrial *notables*: indeed, ingenious genealogists, encouraged by the President, trace part of his ancestry to the French royal family. He is the great-grandson of a minister of Marshal MacMahon and a Vice-President of the Senate, the grandson of an influential Deputy and the son of an *inspecteur des finances* who became a director of several banks and a member of the French *Institut*. Many of his relatives are prominent in banking, industry and the higher reaches of the civil service. His wife is the grand-daughter of Eugène Schneider, the immensely wealthy industrialist and ex-Speaker of the National Assembly

Giscard d'Estaing inherited from his family great wealth, many political contacts and a ferocious intelligence. This latter quality was admirably displayed in the highly competitive examinations to and within the École Polytechnique and the École Nationale d'Administration (ENA) – the two schools which together form so much of the present French elite. His performance at the ENA enabled him to follow his father in choosing a career in the highly prestigious financial inspectorate. In 1953 he had his first taste of politics when he entered the private office of Edgar Faure, then Minister of Finance. Thereafter, his political ascension was meteoric: Deputy of the Puy-de-Dôme in 1956 at the age of thirty (his grandfather was unceremoniously bundled out of the seat to make way for his ambitious grandson); Junior Minister in the Ministry of Finance in the Debré Government from January 1959 to January 1962; Minister of Finance from January 1962 to January 1966. In the meantime he was building a secure political base for himself – both locally as Deputy and as Mayor of Chamalières (a wealthy suburb of Clermont-Ferrand) and nationally as leader, from 1962, of the newly formed Independent Republican Party. His dismissal as Minister of Finance in January 1966 came as a humiliating shock to him (he was dismissed like a common servant, he later bitterly claimed). De Gaulle, who had performed relatively badly in the December 1965 presidential elections, attributed part of his failure to his Finance Minister's unpopular economic policies.

Relations between Giscard d'Estaing and de Gaulle deteriorated from that moment, with the former making increasingly pointed remarks about the authoritarian aspects of the régime and the Gaullists responding by refusing to elect him to the chairmanship of the Finance Committee of the National Assembly. In the referendum which led to the resignation of General de Gaulle in April 1969, Giscard d'Estaing publicly announced that 'regretfully' he would vote against the presidential proposals. This act of *lèse-majesté* was to earn him the lasting enmity of the diehard Gaullists who nicknamed him *Judas Giscariot*. In the presidential elections of June 1969, after some hesitation, he finally declared his support for Pompidou. His reward after Pompidou's election was the Finance Ministry, and he kept this key post, without interruption, throughout Pompidou's Presidency (22 June 1969 to 2 April 1974). When Pompidou died, Giscard d'Estaing was not the inevitable successor but he was an obvious candidate. He was elected to the Presidency after one of the most exciting election campaigns in recent history, beating Mitterand, his Left-wing opponent, by a wafer-thin majority.

The present President of the Republic has many personal qualities. He is, by all accounts, an immensely nice man (in this respect, he contrasts sharply with the first President), and clearly lacks neither intelligence nor courage. He is also no less sensitive than de Gaulle to his own image, and constantly projects himself as a high-powered and technically competent leader. If de Gaulle was a slightly strict father and Pompidou a jovial uncle, Giscard d'Estaing is the clever brother. He has also cultivated another image – that of the dynamic, easy-going, youthful and accessible Kennedy figure. To that end he has been photographed behind the wheel of his car, shaking hands with the inmates of a Lyons prison, dining with a garage mechanic and receiving dustmen at the Élysée. He has even been seen in swimming-trunks (the mind rebels at the very idea of de Gaulle in such apparel). Furthermore, for personal and political reasons, this scion of the upper classes has to demonstrate his sensitivity to the needs of the ordinary Frenchman. But there is something rather sad and pathetic about this impeccably well-bred man displaying his aristocratic knees on the sportsfield of his home town of Chamalières or his musical talents on the accordion to his local electors, or dining with garage mechanics and firemen. But for the President these latter antics were part of his campaign to change the style of the Presidency: a more relaxed atmosphere has replaced the previous stifling formality of the office.

In his *Démocratie française*, published in October 1976, Giscard d'Estaing declared his ambition to create 'a peaceful and thoughtful democracy' untainted by 'the timidity of conservatism and by revolutionary confrontations'. He is especially disturbed by the 'gratuitously dramatic' nature of French political controversy, and argues that the source of that controversy is no longer sociological but ideological: he rejects the idea of his country being divided into two warring classes – the bourgeoisie and the proletariat – but rather discerns the emergence of 'an immense central group' capable, eventually, of integrating the whole of French society. The President's ideas are not free from contradiction, since he praises the principle of pluralism yet rejects its most eloquent expression, which is class conflict. Giscard d'Estaing's second ambition, as expressed in *Démocratie française*, is to modernize and to liberalize French society without anguish or torment, and in certain important respects (the lowering of the voting age to eighteen, penal reform, the introduction of divorce by mutual consent, the easing of legislation on abortion and contraception) he has already had an important impact on French society. The present President of the Republic oscillates between a certain audacity and a prudent realism: he wishes to reform French society but is all too aware of the political constraints imposed by his supporters and, in that respect, he sometimes gives the impression of being rather like a London street busker, with one eye on the crowd and the other anxiously peering over his shoulder for the reactions of the forces of order.

Giscard d'Estaing differs greatly from his two predecessors in social origins, in educational background and in professional training. He also differs in several other important ways. First, he differs in his working methods: both de Gaulle and Pompidou worked very much alone whereas Giscard d'Estaing works more closely with his team in his private office. Secondly, as already noted, he differs in the style he has imposed upon the presidential office. Thirdly, he differs in temperament and personality: whilst de Gaulle was imbued with a profound scepticism rooted in his reading of history, and Pompidou was pervaded by a sense of peasant caution tinged with fatalism, Giscard has a largely optimistic view of mankind. Fourthly, he has a different view of French society: de Gaulle was obsessed with its deeply divisive nature and attempted to create political institutions to soften the divisions and ensure that they did not tear apart the nation. Pompidou believed that, below the tensions, the bases of the nation were sound and healthy and should not be disturbed by political and social reforms. Giscard d'Estaing whilst sharing Pompidou's basically optimistic view on the nature of French society nevertheless sees the need for social change. Fifthly, the present President of the Republic is not a Gaullist, but belongs to a moderate conservative and parliamentary political tradition. Finally, Giscard d'Estaing differs from his two predecessors in the ends he is pursuing. If de Gaulle's peculiar and archaic obsession was France's place in the world and if Pompidou's passion was with the modernizing of the French economy, Giscard d'Estaing appears more concerned with the creation of 'an advanced liberal society' in which the problems of Frenchmen transcend those of France. In other words, Giscard d'Estaing wishes to humanize a society the political institutions of which were strengthened by de Gaulle and the economic bases of which were improved by Pompidou.

The three men also have much in common. Giscard shares his predecessors' qualities of intellectual ability, political sensitivity and personal courage. He also shares their aversion to political instability and to collectivist political ideals and practices. Like his predecessors, too, Giscard is an inveterate pedagogue and careful image builder. And part of both the pedagogy and the image-building is directed to stressing the primacy of the presidential office. Only a few days after his election in December 1958, General de Gaulle could declare that 'as the guide of France and Head of the Republican State I shall exercise the supreme power in as wide-ranging a manner as necessary'. When he resigned in 1969 it was clear that he had certainly carried out his wish. President Pompidou was no less specific about his role, and very few of his major political speeches failed to insist upon the supremacy of his office. The present President made it clear during his election campaign that he wished 'to push the régime further in a presidential direction' and all the evidence suggests that he has done so. The strengthening and consolidation of the Presidency corresponds, therefore, to the expressed wish of successive incumbents. So, too, in very large measure, does the scope of the presidential sector.

The presidential sector

In 1967, Valéry Giscard d'Estaing, then an embittered and ambitious ex-Finance Minister, made a celebrated attack on General de Gaulle's methods of government: the President of the Republic, he alleged, was concentrating too much power and too many decisions in his own hands. Ten years later, the same accusations are being made, with greater justification, by the Gaullists against Giscard d'Estaing, now President of the Republic. Such attacks are inevitable, for the steady and uninterrupted growth of the presidential domain constitutes one of the more striking characteristics of the present régime.

In November 1959, Chaban-Delmas, then President of the National Assembly, in a speech to the Gaullist party congress, defined the so-called presidential 'reserved domain' as encompassing foreign affairs, defence matters, questions relating to the French Community and Algeria. This restrictive interpretation was rejected by the President both by his practice and in his speeches. On 31 January 1964, de Gaulle insisted that it was the President himself who defined his own field of responsibility. De Gaulle, however, did not interfere in all areas of decision-making: he was content to leave a great deal of discretion to his Prime Minister and his ministers. His main interests were foreign policy, defence policy (especially after 1962), colonial and French community questions (with Algeria dominating all else until April 1962) and European questions. But as shall be made clear, de Gaulle would not hesitate to intervene in any policy area he considered of importance or interest.

When Georges Pompidou became President in June 1969 he inherited the presidential domain as defined by General de Gaulle, and added to it his own field of interests (mainly economic and political) which he had acquired during his long premiership (1962–8). The presidential domain was further extended with the election of Giscard d'Estaing in May 1974: he was unwilling to relinquish any of the established fields of presidential policy-making and was keen to add to them his own interests in financial, social and environmental questions. Thus, the steady accretion of presidential power has been rather like the accumulation of geological strata, each President bequeathing to his successor a new layer of responsibility. It was revealing that no one was at all surprised when the President invited the leaders of the parties and the major pressure groups after the March 1978 elections to the Élysée to help him to decide the future political, social and economic policies of the nation.

At the beginning of 1976, President Giscard d'Estaing claimed that there were only two areas in which he would never intervene – justice and information, so presumably any other area was vulnerable to presidential interference. However, both the areas he mentioned had already been invaded. The President makes key appointments to the judiciary and to the Council of State. General de Gaulle, during the Algerian drama, had several altercations with members of the judiciary, a celebrated clash with the Council of State in 1962, and established special courts to deal with offences arising out of the Algerian crisis. The area of public information has also received a fair share of presidential attention. Like his predecessors, President Giscard d'Estaing has shown more than a passive interest in the relationship between the State and television: certainly the 1974 Act which completely reorganized the French television network was carefully supervised from the Élysée. Moreover, the affairs of the Paris press are also closely watched by the Presidency.

The Presidency has apparently become omnipresent – a phenomenon which is all the more surprising since it has little basis in the Constitution.

There are essentially four components of the presidential domain:

Foreign and European affairs, defence matters, and colonial and French community matters. This was the area defined by Chaban-Delmas in 1959 as constituting the presidential 'reserved domain', and may be described as the traditional domain.

Economic, financial and industrial matters, which became increasingly important after the election of Georges Pompidou to the Presidency in June 1969.

Political, social and environmental, issues which have figured prominently in the presidential domain since May 1974 when Giscard d'Estaing was elected to the Presidency.

Questions which become politically delicate or explosive or which attract presidential attention for purely personal reasons. These questions involve presidential intervention of a sporadic nature.

The traditional domain

The supremacy of the Presidency was quickly established in this area since it was during the Algerian crisis that General de Gaulle took decisions with little regard to either the Government or Parliament. By a combination of tenacity, guile, mendacity and courage he imposed his policies towards Algeria on a rebellious army, a discontented Prime Minister, a divided Parliament and an unhappy Gaullist party. Time and again he stressed the personal nature of his policies. In his direction of French policy towards French colonies and ex-colonies he was equally autocratic: his decisions in the Bizerta affair of July 1961 and his sending of troops to Gabon in February 1964 were never discussed in the Council of Ministers. Presidential interest in these areas has continued: Presidents Pompidou and Giscard d'Estaing both extensively visited ex-French colonies in black Africa. The supremacy of the President in foreign affairs is unquestionable and unquestioned, and Foreign Ministers have been chosen simply as faithful executants of presidential policy. The policy of *rapprochement* with Eastern Europe, the recognition of China, the decision not to sell arms to Israel, the outrageous proclamation in Quebec were amongst the many personal acts of the first President of the Fifth Republic. The French Memorandum of 24 September 1958 which defined the bases of French policy towards the Atlantic Alliance remained a closely guarded secret for a long time, and was only revealed to ministers as the result of the indiscretion of a journalist. President de Gaulle's decisions to take France out of NATO and to order the Americans to withdraw their troops from French soil were discussed in the Council of Ministers three days after the American President had already been informed. The Presidency has clearly retained its supremacy in foreign affairs, and amongst President Giscard d'Estaing's personal initiatives have been the Rambouillet meeting of November 1975, the Paris Conference (or so-called North–South summit meeting) of December 1976, and the offer to act as mediator in the Lebanese crisis (an offer he made whilst he was in the USA and which surprised many ministers). French foreign policy has not only been highly personal. It has also been highly personalized. President Giscard d'Estaing, like his two predecessors, has travelled abroad a great deal, has had personal meetings with representatives of foreign powers at the Élysée and has represented France at major international conferences.

In European affairs the supremacy of the President has been equally manifest. De Gaulle had the disconcerting habit of making pronouncements on European affairs at press conferences where apprehensive ministers learnt, at the same time as the rest of the world, of changes in French policy. On 15 May 1962, for example, European-minded ministers sat in grim-faced disapproval as de Gaulle attacked their cherished ideas: some were to resign immediately after. President de Gaulle's two vetoes of British entry into the Common Market were also highly personal decisions, and neither enjoyed the unanimous support of his ministers, who were informed of his decisions at the same time as the rest of the French public. President Pompidou's decision to lift the French veto on British entry was equally highly personal, a fact readily admitted by Pompidou himself: it has been claimed that the Prime Minister learnt the decision at the same time as television viewers. Giscard d'Estaing has been no less determined to assert presidential supremacy in European affairs: when Britain was renegotiating the terms of its entry into the Common Market, in Dublin in March, 1975, the French President made concessions without first consulting or informing the Council of Ministers. Similarly, the decision in the early summer of 1976 to press ahead with the direct election of the European Parliament was taken at Brussels by the President and announced to the Council of Ministers on his return. Prime Minister Chirac, who was known to be less than lukewarm about the pro-European ideals of the President, was later to reveal that he was informed only at the same time as his ministerial colleagues, and that at no stage was he consulted or kept informed on the issue. As in the general field of foreign policy, European policy-making became highly personalized. De Gaulle attended the important Rome meeting of the six European members of the European Common Market in May 1967; Pompidou represented France at The Hague summit conference of 'the Six' in December 1969; Giscard d'Estaing personally conducted French negotiations at the Dublin meeting in March 1975. De Gaulle's friendly and fruitful relationship with Konrad Adenauer, the German Chancellor, was followed by a similar relationship between Pompidou and Edward Heath and then between Giscard d'Estaing and Helmut Schmidt (this was to sour after the Chancellor was reported to have made some very uncomplimentary remarks about the French President).

Defence has always fallen within the presidential domain, although when General de Gaulle was preoccupied with the Algerian problem during the first three years of his Presidency the Prime Minister, Michel Debré, took many important decisions. The President of the Republic plays three key roles in defence policy; as effective head of the Executive, as official Commander-in-Chief of the Armed Forces and as Chairman of the National Defence Committee. He may determine the main lines of French defence policy as was demonstrated by de Gaulle's decision to withdraw from NATO or by successive Presidents' pursuit of an independent nuclear deterrent. He may also shape the strategy to be employed: for instance, President Pompidou effectively opposed the military High Command's desire to reorganize French territorial forces, and defended his predecessor's ideas on the size and role of French classical forces. Or the President may recommend specific courses of action: hence President Giscard d'Estaing's insistence in December 1974 on maintaining a fleet of classical strike and reconnaissance aircraft and his arbitration on the type of aircraft to carry out that task.

The President of the Republic also defends the defence budget in the Council of Ministers (it was on President Giscard d'Estaing's insistence that the defence budget was raised in 1976 from 17 to 20 per cent of the total State budget), appoints to key military posts, arbitrates between the conflicting claims of the various branches of the military establishment and between the various sections within each branch, and arbitrates between his ministers and the military High Command. Presidential supremacy in the area of defence was highlighted in May 1976 when the President personally amended the Defence White Paper proposed by the Minister of Defence and when he presented the Government's defence proposals on television. In the following month he insisted before an assembly of high-ranking officers that defence policy should be imbued with his own conceptions and ideas, and reminded them that the President of the Republic was responsible both for the guidelines of policy and the means for implementing them. He ended his speech by quoting Louis XV before the battle of Fontenoy in 1745: 'Gentlemen, I invite you to keep quiet. The battle plan has been drawn up, the Commander has been chosen. It is up to him to take charge of the action.'

Economic, financial and industrial matters

In this area, presidential power has gradually increased. Initially, General de Gaulle intervened only occasionally in this field and generally to emphasize the main lines of policy. From the mid 1960s he showed increased interest in economic affairs, possibly as the result of the influence of Jacques Rueff, that arch-apostle of pre-Keynesian economic and financial orthodoxy. In August and September 1963 he presided over several interministerial committees devoted to the economic stabilization plan, and in June 1964 he took an active part in the discussions in the Council of Ministers on the problem of rents and prices in the public sector. Nor would President de Gaulle hesitate to intervene directly and personally if he felt a problem critical. In the autumn of 1968, on the advice of Raymond Barre, then a little-known civil servant in Brussels, he astounded the financial world, his own Prime Minister and Finance Minister, by refusing to devalue the franc (reputable newspapers had already reported the decision to devalue as certain). On the whole, however, General de Gaulle tended to leave economic and financial matters to his Prime Minister and Finance Minister.

President Pompidou was initially very interventionist in this domain; this was scarcely surprising, since this ex-banker had, as Prime Minister, exercised considerable influence in shaping French economic and financial policy. It was he who was mainly responsible for the devaluation of the franc in 1969. Furthermore, as a sensitive politician President Pompidou kept a keen eye on the State budget and would occasionally arbitrate between the conflicting claims of the spending ministries on the one hand, and, on the other, between the spending ministries and the Ministry of Finance, the protector of the public purse. And his constant defence of the agricultural budget was an open secret. Most of the time, however, President Pompidou left the role of budgetary arbiter to the Prime Minister. In his last year of office, when Pompidou was seriously ill and when the Prime Minister was the ineffectual Pierre Messmer, the Minister of Finance gained more and more power. That Finance Minister was Giscard d'Estaing who, when he became President of the Republic, was unwilling to surrender his financial prerogatives. As expected, when he became President he retained tight control over economic and financial policy. His first Finance Minister, Fourcade, was a personal and political friend who was happy to bend to presidential directives. The reintegration of the French franc into the European monetary snake in July 1975 and the decision to leave it in March 1976 were both presidential decisions. In May 1976 the President publicly committed the Government to rejecting an incomes policy, and in the summer of the same year he pushed his reluctant Finance Minister into pressing ahead with a controversial capital gains tax. He corrected the first draft of the Bill, demanded that it be introduced as quickly as possible in Parliament and defended it throughout its passage against the hostility of many of his nominal supporters. With the appointment of Raymond Barre as Prime Minister and Finance Minister in September 1976 presidential economic and financial power weakened somewhat. Nevertheless, the Prime Minister's resolution in October 1976 to reject a timid wealth tax was first motivated by presidential hostility (the resolution was later reinforced when the Paris stock exchange almost collapsed at the thought of such a revolutionary measure). In the following month, the President of the Republic announced on radio his intention of asking the Prime Minister to introduce measures to protect people with small savings by a system of indexation.

French industrial policy-making has also reflected presidential ideas. The first two Presidents of the Fifth Republic actively pursued policies for the restructuring of French industry: massive subsidies and tax incentives were given to encourage the formation of giant industrial complexes which were equipped for European and international competition. President Giscard d'Estaing, on the other hand, seems to be keener on helping small and medium-sized industries, and in March 1976 announced several measures to help them. The first two Presidents also had a penchant for projects which they assumed would add to French prestige: their support for massive and prestigious projects such as the petrochemical complex at Fos (an industrial, social and ecological disaster), their attempt through large-scale office-building in the Défense area of Paris to make the French capital the business centre of Europe, and their obstinate defence of projects such as Concorde and the Channel tunnel reflected this preoccupation. President Giscard d'Estaing has a healthy disregard for such considerations, and his decision to scrap several prestige projects (including a particularly expensive and nasty aerotrain which was axed almost immediately) was helped by the changed economic circumstances when the folly of prestige projects became more apparent. The differences in policy between General de Gaulle and President Giscard d'Estaing were most clearly marked in their approach to the computer industry. It was de Gaulle who personally decided in 1967, for political reasons, to create the Compagnie Internationale pour l'Informatique (CII), an exclusively French computer complex which he protected against its own inefficiency and savage American competition by subventions and guaranteed orders. The purpose of the move was to protect the home computer industry, since de Gaulle was rightly convinced that an independent defence policy was dependent upon the existence of a national computer industry. Eight years later, in May 1975, after months of tergiversation, President Giscard d'Estaing personally decided to authorize the dismantlement of the CII in its existing form and its merger with the American-dominated firm of Honeywell-Bull. The personal nature of the decision was underlined in the *communiqué* which accompanied the announcement of the measure.

Political, social and environmental questions

President Giscard d'Estaing was elected in May 1974 on a programme of reforms (although not *for* a programme of reforms, since the great majority of his supporters were for the *status quo* and voted for him because he was likely to do less damage than François Mitterrand, his Left-wing opponent). In three areas at least – the political, the social and the environmental – he has kept his promises, and it would be churlish to deny his achievements in that area. Amongst the political reforms which have been introduced since May 1974 have been the reduction in the voting age to eighteen, and a no-less-welcome reduction in telephone-tapping, which had become so widespread in the last years of Pompidou. Political asylum has been made easier, the police have been told to make their presence less felt in the streets of Paris, and Left-wing newspapers are now allowed into army messes (*Charlie-Hebdo*, an extreme Left-wing satirical newspaper, celebrated with a provocative and indelicate headline: *Merde à l'Armée*). Of greater significance was the presidential decision to provide access to the Constitutional Council to Members of Parliament who are concerned about the constitutionality of an Act. The President also announced that no one would be pursued in the courts for politically motivated attacks upon him. The general effect of these political reforms has been to give a decidedly more liberal hue to the régime.

The record in the social field has been somewhat less impressive. Presidential *intentions* were made clear when he appointed Ministers for Prison, Immigrant and Feminine Affairs and nominated Jean-Jacques Servan-Schreiber, a vociferous political maverick, to the post of Minister of Reforms. Although the latter was to survive less than a fortnight (he publicly denounced Government nuclear defence policy) some reforms were quickly forthcoming. Female contraception was legalized, abortions legally authorized, divorce made easier. Limited but unpopular measures were also taken to make life a little more bearable in French prisons. In all these measures, the President of the Republic took a keen and courageous interest: he annotated and amended the first divorce Bill sent to him by the Minister of Justice, and he had frequently to back the Minister of Health in her struggle against conservative Members of Parliament.

President Giscard d'Estaing's concern with environmental issues was dictated by both electoral pressures and by personal taste. He shared with a growing number of his compatriots an anxiety about the insensitive damage being inflicted on large parts of France. The beauty of major cities such as Lyons was being destroyed by massive rebuilding programmes in which good taste was not always the most striking characteristic. Uncontrolled industrial expansion had turned the outskirts of most major French towns into dreary, ill-equipped and crime-ridden dormitories. Paris and the Paris region was specially badly affected and the wave of speculative building was so uncontrolled and often so flagrantly illegal that one critic could describe the region as 'a Far West without a sheriff'. Elsewhere, building permits allowed the construction of barbarisms such as Basque villas on the Britanny coast and Alpine chalets in the Auvergne. Areas such as the Mediterranean coast became the particular targets for speculative and frequently illegal horrors. The President of the Republic acted quickly in this domain. In June 1974, barely a month after his election, he effectively sabotaged the extension of the Left-Bank motorway in Paris by withdrawing State aid for the project (the area affected is now being turned into gardens). This especially outrageous piece of urban vandalism had enjoyed the active encouragement of President Pompidou. Two months later, in August 1974, Giscard d'Estaing scrapped the plans for an International Commercial Centre in Paris, a huge slab of concrete nastiness which was scheduled to replace Les Halles, the old fruit and vegetable market in the heart of Paris: the Centre is to be replaced by a park. Later measures have revealed the President's continuing concern for environmental issues. In two open letters to the Prime Minister in September 1974 and January 1975, he clearly defined his objectives and priorities for Paris and the Paris region. In April 1975 an inter-ministerial council, chaired by the President, decided to limit the growth of the Paris region, to reduce the urban motorway programme and to develop the public transport system. The 1975 Land Act and the Law on Nature Protection of the same year (a project which had been gathering dust on the shelves of the Ministry of the Environment for the previous five years) were both presidential initiatives to limit environmental damage and to ensure greater public control over, and participation in, urban development. Later, in July 1975 and in June 1976, in open letters to the Prime Minister, the President clearly indicated his preference for a new urban policy and insisted on the introduction of new measures (such as limiting the height of new buildings) to prevent France from becoming 'uglier' (*l'enlaidissement de la France*). In a similar letter in October 1976, he insisted that fifty acres of La Villette be made into a public garden and in February 1977 he launched his 'ecological charter' in which he reasserted his concern for environmental issues.

Interventions of a sporadic nature

Apart from the above-mentioned areas in which presidential control is pervasive and constant, there are other areas in which the President may intervene on specific occasions. This may occur in a number of cases. The first case is when ministers have reached deadlock, as was the case in 1967 when de Gaulle decided to have paid advertising introduced on State-run television. The second case arises when the problem proves particularly intractable because of the interests at stake. It was President de Gaulle who swept aside the objections of a powerful network of pressure groups in 1959 and decided that the wholesale meat and vegetable markets should be moved from the centre of Paris to the wind-swept wastes of Rungis in the suburbs, and it was President Giscard d'Estaing who, in October 1975, personally took the final decision to move an unwilling École Polytechnique out of Paris to the suburbs. Such questions may seem minor, but decisions had been held up by powerfully entrenched groups (in the case of the renewal of Les Halles for nearly forty years!) and presidential authority was required to impose them.

The third case in which the President is likely to intervene in an area not normally belonging to his domain is when an issue becomes politically explosive. General de Gaulle's decisions, during the stormy events of May 1968, to reform the higher education system and to introduce regional reforms both fall within this category. In both cases de Gaulle was responding to what he considered to be a widespread yearning for greater participation in decision-making – a yearning he discerned in the protests, the demands and the slogans of those troubled days of May 1968. In the passage of the educational reforms the President of the Republic had to throw all his personal authority and support behind Edgar Faure, the Minister of Education, who was under constant attack from the Government's own parliamentary supporters. The regional problem has exercised successive Presidents of the Republic. President Pompidou sabotaged his own Prime Minister's ambitious regional plans, and the conservative and prudent regional law of July 1972 reflected the President's own sceptical views on the subject. His successor has been no more adventurous, and in spite of promises made during his election campaign, Giscard d'Estaing continues his predecessor's very conservative policy.

The fourth area of presidential intermittent intervention concerns issues which *threaten* to become politically explosive. Thus Giscard d'Estaing interfered in detailed fashion in the drafting of the June 1975 Secondary Education Act, even though, according to the Minister of Education, the President of the Republic was responsible only for the general guidelines of the Bill: in a nation where students can and do paralyse universities and where school children have a penchant for rowdy and sometimes violent street demonstrations, the country's chief political leader can scarcely afford to ignore what is going on in the field of education. Another smaller yet no less revealing example of presidential intervention in a politically delicate situation occurred in September 1976 when Giscard d'Estaing personally prevented the building of the controversial toll booths on the A4 motorway.

The fifth and final case of sporadic intervention is when the President wishes to satisfy a whim. Examples abound: General de Gaulle had the convicted murderer Gaston Dominici released from prison after seeing the sad old man on television, whilst Georges Pompidou protected the study of Latin and Greek in French *lycées*. Giscard d'Estaing's many whims have included an insistence on a change in the tempo of the Marseillaise, the French national anthem, when it is played on official occasions. He has also raised such vital questions as the evening dresses of women generals, the uniform of the female traffic wardens in Paris – the notorious *aubergines* – who exercise their authority with the mirthless malevolence worthy of the *tricoteuses* of revolutionary times, and the need to modernize the telephone directories.

Twenty years after the foundation of the Fifth Republic the Presidency has clearly emerged as the main centre of decision-making is France. The President may not be, as was asserted by one French writer, 'omniscient, omnipresent and omnipotent', but his power is considerable and his influence all-pervasive: he is now Head of State, head of the Government, head of a party coalition and the nation's chief policy-maker. Presidential intervention now affects all areas of public and private life, as roles assigned to others have gradually been usurped by the President, aided by his personal staff and his ministers. It was presidential encroachment upon the prime ministerial domain which eventually provoked the resignation of Prime Minister Jacques Chirac in the summer of 1976. But the concentration of power into presidential hands has had more serious consequences which will be explored at some length in the concluding chapter of this book Suffice to say at this point that the power of the Presidency, whilst very considerable, rests on precarious constitutional and political foundations. It has been forged by three men exploiting a set of circumstances which may not last, and it is an awareness of that fact that gives French politics its peculiarly obsessive nature.

3 The political instruments and agents of presidentialism

The tentacular growth of the Presidency under the Fifth Republic has been both the cause and the consequence of a growth in the number and the use of the instruments and agents at its disposal. In order that the presidential will may prevail many means (some of highly doubtful constitutional validity) have been employed, and in the pursuit of his policies each President has acted by either communicating directly with the nation or through his many aides – the President's men.

Presidential direct links with the nation

President Giscard d'Estaing, like his predecessors of both the Fourth and Fifth Republics, regularly visits the French provinces: General de Gaulle claimed that during his first seven-year period of office he made eighty visits outside Paris, going to every *département* and to more than 2500 towns. It is the most striking example of the President's direct contact with the people and a means of ensuring the physical presence of State authority. Giscard d'Estaing has even underlined the latter point by holding a small number of meetings of the Council of Ministers in provincial towns. The present President, also like his two immediate predecessors, regularly uses (some would argue *abuses*) television and radio to convey, over the heads of the 'intermediaries', his personal message to the nation or to explain Government policies.

The differences in the style of the three Presidents of the Fifth Republic may be seen in their press conferences. Giscard d'Estaing oscillates between a nervous ponderousness and a relaxed conversational style, whilst Pompidou after an early informality gradually lapsed into heavy solemnity. Their press conferences certainly lacked the sense of theatre which infused those of de Gaulle. To the English observer they could verge dangerously on Dr Johnson's view of an opera – 'an exotic and irrational entertainment' – in which the listener was expected to suspend belief, sit back and simply enjoy the spectacle. But they were more than that. They were great didactic exercises (it was said that de Gaulle's *conférences de presse* were really *conférences à la presse*), massive acts of presidential egoism, and some were major political moments of the régime.

The need for the present President to communicate directly with the people was highlighted by the publication in October 1976 of a short book, *Démocratie française*, in which he outlined his basic philosophy, ideals and ideas. Nearly a million copies were distributed or sold, and the publication of the book was accompanied by an unparalleled propaganda campaign on television and radio. The President is not only interested in establishing a direct link with the people but has always displayed a keen interest in the shape of that link. Like his two predecessors, he closely supervises any major policies affecting the television network (this was certainly true of the 1974 reform), and he has a full-time press officer who is in permanent contact with political journalists. He is also kept well informed of the prevailing state of opinion through prefectoral and police reports (analysed by the Minister of the Interior), through summaries of the press (prepared by his press officer) and through the opinion polls (analysed by an expert on the Élysée staff).

The final method by which the President establishes contact with the people is through elections. Presidential election campaigns are occasions for the candidates to give detailed accounts of themselves and their future programmes. The President sees his election as the basis of his legitimacy and a mandate for him to carry out his programme. Elections to the National Assembly have also been considered by successive Presidents as judgements upon themselves and their programmes, and Giscard d'Estaing, like de Gaulle and Pompidou, has directly intervened in successive campaigns to exhort the voters to back his candidates. The third type of electoral consultation which has been used by the President to make a direct and personal appeal to the nation is a referendum – the most Bonapartist weapon in the Presidential armoury. There is a tendency to exaggerate the significance of the referendum in the functioning of the present régime: Professor Prélot, for example, went as far as to describe the Fifth Republic as 'a plebiscitary democracy'. It is true that *every* general election and referendum has been turned into a plebiscitary appeal by the President of the Republic. Nevertheless, it should be emphasized that the referendum itself (the object of so much apprehension and criticism) has been used only five times since the beginning of the régime and only twice since October 1962. President

Pompidou used the device only once and his successor has yet to resort to it. In theory, the President cannot take the initiative in calling a referendum: that initiative lies with the Government or Parliament. Nor can he call a referendum on any reform which would be in conflict with the Constitution. In practice, however, de Gaulle and Pompidou both took the intiative in calling the five referenda and at least two involved major changes in the constitutional structure (Table 2).

Table 2   *Referenda of the Fifth Republic*

8 January 1961 ⎱ 8 April 1962 ⎰	Related to the Algerian war
28 October 1962	Direct election of the President
27 April 1969	Creation of regions and restructuring of Senate
23 April 1972	Ratification of the treaty relative to the entry of Denmark, Ireland, Norway and Great Britain into the European Community

General de Gaulle once claimed that the referendum was 'the clearest, the most honest and the most democratic' of political practices. But the experience of the Fifth Republic suggests that, whilst it may be democratic (by inviting the people to make a sovereign decision), it is also unclear and singularly dishonest as an instrument of government. If de Gaulle was so keen to elicit the public's sentiments on matters of great moment he should not have been so selective in the subjects he chose. De Gaulle called no referenda on important – and unpopular – policies such as his rejection of Britain's request to enter the European Community, his precipitation of a major crisis in the Common Market in 1965, or his policy towards Israel. Pompidou held his one referendum on a policy which manifestly commanded massive parliamentary and public support. The profoundly dishonest nature of the referendum also emerged in the presentation of the issues. The first two referenda on Algeria involved one reply to two distinct questions, whilst the fourth (that of April 1969) required a single response to a wide-ranging and complex package deal which included major innovations in local government, a radical reform of the Senate and a change in the interim Presidency (in the event of the death or incapacity of the incumbent President). The opinion polls showed that the electorate had different responses to each of the proposals: the regional reforms were popular, those involving the Senate were not, and those concerning the interim Presidency were largely unknown. Furthermore, it was clear that, as in the three previous referenda, the electors when casting their votes were motivated less by their views of the proposals than by their assessment of General de Gaulle and his Government. In a sense, this was perfectly understandable, since de Gaulle had deliberately turned the referendum into a vote of confidence in himself. Each of his referenda was preceded by a stern warning that in the event of a negative vote he would resign, a threat (or promise) he carried out after the failure of the April 1969 referendum. The dubious nature of the referendum emerged clearly in the April 1972 referendum: according to a British observer (Michael Leigh) the President's motives for holding the referendum were four-fold:

To claim credit for European policies which differed somewhat from those of his predecessor. He was attempting to mobilize opinion to strengthen his position against the hard-line Gaullists, just as de Gaulle, in January 1961 and April 1962, had mobilized opinion behind his Algerian policies to demonstrate the political isolation of the extremist supporters of *Algérie française*.

To increase the prestige of the Government and his power over it. This had also been a motive of de Gaulle in April 1969 when he attempted to buttress his own personal authority which had been so seriously undermined during the events of May 1968.

To exploit the conflicts of opinion on a subject which clearly divided the opposition Left-wing parties at a time of negotiations (for greater unity of action) between those parties.

To underline the extent of his popular backing for future diplomatic negotiations.

In other words, the President of the Republic was not attempting to sound public opinion on a contentious issue, but rather was bolstering his own domestic and diplomatic position.

The use of referenda under the Fifth Republic has not only been dishonest (and unconstitutional – a minor peccadillo in the catechism of the régime); it has also proved dangerous to the President. The failure of the April 1969 referendum led to de Gaulle's resignation, and the exceptionally low turn-out in the April 1972 referendum (the electors 'bristled with indifference', to use Michael Leigh's felicitous phrase, and only 53·4 per cent bothered to vote) severely damaged Pompidou's image as an effective political manager. The lesson of the last two referenda has not been lost on the present President of the Republic, and for that reason the referendum is likely to be used only sparingly – if at all – in the future.

The President's men

Presidential councils and committees

The President stands at the head of an extensive and complex network of political councillors and executants, some official and others less so, who enable him to carry out the task of deciding and implementing the major policies of the nation. The widening of the web of aides has been both a cause and consequence of the growth of presidential government. The nature of the relationship between the President and his aides may be institutionalized and formal or purely personal and informal, and it may be permanent or very transitory. The President may appoint a man to carry out a particular task or *mission* which, once accomplished, may put an end to the relationship. Thus, in 1975, President Giscard d'Estaing appointed Arpaillange, a judge, to study the reform of justice: Lecanuet, the Minister of Justice, was merely informed of the presidential decision. In the same year, he gave Pinot, another judge, the task of looking into the lot of French prostitutes, he asked Guichard, a Gaullist ex-Minister, to prepare a report on the problems of local government, he requested Monguilan, a financial expert, to report on the consequences of introducing a capital gains tax, and he invited Raymond Barre, not then a member of the Government, to examine the vexed problem of housing subsidies. In May 1977, he appointed Poniatowski, ex-Minister of the Interior, as a roving ambassador, and in the following month he invited Madame Pelletier to draw up a report on the increasingly controversial subject of drugs.

The President also acts through a network of councils and committees, the more important of which are mentioned in the Constitution. These include the powerful Higher Council and Committees of National Defence (it is there and not in the Council of Ministers that defence policy is decided). The President may also establish permanent councils or committees which are either presided by him or directly accountable to him. These include the Higher Committee for the Environment (created in 1970 by Prime Minister Chaban-Delmas but enlarged and reinforced by President Giscard d'Estaing in 1975), the Central Planning Council (created in 1974 with the task of laying down the guidelines of the French five-year Economic Plan and of ensuring co-ordination between government departments in the implementation of the Plan) and the Council for Nuclear Foreign Policy (founded in September 1976 with the task of examining all proposed exports of nuclear equipment). *Ad hoc* committees may also be created by the President to examine specific problems. One such committee was the Committee for Algerian Affairs which was established after the revolt in Algeria in January 1960 and which functioned until the end of the Algerian war in 1962. More recent *ad hoc* committees include the Commission for the Reform of the Tourist Industry which was created in January 1977. These major instruments of presidentialism are accountable to him alone and their importance cannot be overestimated, but they do not give the kind of continuous advice afforded by the next category of advisors – the Élysée staff.

The Élysée staff

The most immediate collaborators of the President belong to his personal staff who work at the *Château*, the name given familiarly to the Élysée Palace. Under the Fourth Republic this staff was very small (President Auriol never had more than eleven and President Coty never more than twelve), weak and concerned essentially with administrative tasks. This situation has changed under the Fifth Republic: the *services* of the Élysée have become bigger and more influential, thus reflecting and helping to perpetuate the power of the Presidency. The size and nature of the Élysée staff depend on the tastes and personality of each President, for it is his team, accountable to him alone and disbanded when he leaves office. It is not mentioned in the Constitution and has no formal status: its size, shape and membership are entirely dependent upon the will and whims of the President.

Since the beginning of the Fifth Republic, the *services* of the Élysée have comprised three basic elements, even though they have been officially fused under the authority of the General Secretariat since 1974: the General Secretariat; the *cabinet*; the Military Household.

A fourth element – the General Secretariat for French Community and Malagasy Affairs which was responsible for relations with countries of the French union – was created by de Gaulle and maintained by Pompidou but was abolished, in May 1974, by Giscard d'Estaing. For the entire period 1958–74 it was headed by the influential and shadowy Gaullist 'baron' Jacques Foccart. Of the three present elements, the most important is the General Secretariat. The Military Household has a limited sphere of competence, and the *cabinet* is involved in mainly administrative chores: it regulates the domestic arrangements of the Élysée, organizes presidential trips to the provinces, is responsible for the clerical and secretarial side of the Élysée, and arranges presidential audiences. The General Secretariat is the centre of decision-making at the Élysée. It is composed of a small group of men (never more than thirty since 1959 and presently only eighteen) drawn mainly (at present about three-quarters) but not exclusively from the upper ranks of the civil service, and headed by a General Secretary and a Deputy Secretary. Many are young (three of the present eighteen were recruited before their fortieth birthday) and most are the products of the *grandes écoles* (the highly competitive schools which recruit the nation's administrative elite).

Table 3   *Organizational structure of the Élysée in January 1978*

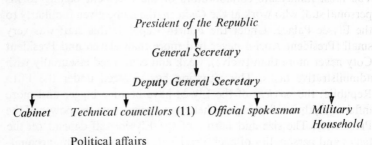

President of the Republic

General Secretary

Deputy General Secretary

Cabinet   Technical councillors (11)   Official spokesman   Military Household

Political affairs
Foreign trade
Financial matters
Economic affairs
Press
Social affairs and justice
French overseas territories
Education and parliamentary affairs
Public works and environment
Foreign affairs
Energy

Chargés de mission
Press
Political affairs
Foreign affairs

A majority were recruited from the *grands corps* and have thus proven ability, administrative experience and extensive contacts with the administrative machine. More than half the present Élysée staff belonged to Giscard d'Estaing's private staff when he was Minister of Finance, and a select few are known to be personal friends of the President. Each member of the staff is given a specific field to cover and his duty is to provide ideas for the President and also to supervise the work of the ministries.

At the head of the staff (Table 3) is the General Secretary who is responsible for co-ordinating the work of his subordinates and for making daily reports on their work to the President. Since 1959 there have been only seven General Secretaries (Table 4).

Table 4 *General Secretaries of the Fifth Republic*

De Gaulle	January 1959	De Courcel (Diplomat)
	February 1962	Burin des Roziers (Diplomat)
	July 1967	Tricot (Councillor of State)
Pompidou	June 1969	Jobert (Member of the Court of Accounts)
	April 1973	Balladur (Councillor of State)
Giscard d'Estaing	May 1974	Brossolette (Financial Inspector)
	July 1976	François-Poncet (Ex-Diplomat and Industrialist)

The General Secretary is not only an administrative co-ordinator. He may represent the President at official ceremonies or deputize for him at certain inter-ministerial meetings. He enjoys a privileged position, since he meets the President daily, and acts as the final screen between the President and the outside world. He is, in the words of J. Gicquel, 'the eyes, ears and arms' of an absent President. Yet the influence of the General Secretary depends a great deal on his willingness and capacity to use it. Under de Gaulle, successive General Secretaries, although influential, were diplomatic, discreet and self-effacing, and had a largely administrative view of their role. Of the two General Secretaries who served Pompidou, the first, Michel Jobert, was interventionist and political (he left the post to become Foreign Minister) whilst his successor was a quiet and efficient technician. President Giscard d'Estaing first appointed Pierre Brossolette, a close friend and collaborator of long-standing, but personal and political differences between the two men led to the resignation of Brossolette and to his replacement, in July 1976, by François-Poncet, another personal friend of Giscard d'Estaing who was also known to be more sympathetic to the President's reformist ideals.

The General Secretary may not be the most powerful man on the presidential staff. Under de Gaulle that position was held by Jacques Foccart, who, from 1959 to 1974, was officially in charge of France's relations with her colonies and ex-colonies in Africa, but who frequently intervened on the President's behalf in governmental and Gaullist party matters. The *éminence grise* of Pompidou's personal staff was the arch-conservative Pierre Juillet, who was the President's principal political advisor. Under Giscard d'Estaing three men are reported to be as influential as the General Secretary. They are Yves Cannac, the Deputy General Secretary, Jean Sérisé, the Political Councillor, and Victor Chapet, the *chargé de mission* for political matters. The former two have Left-wing reputations: Cannac, as a member of Mitterrand's entourage in the 1960s, was considered to be more than a trifle *gauchiste* and was known for his 'socialistic' tendencies whilst a member of Premier Chaban-Delmas' private staff from 1969 to 1972; Sérisé, an ex-member of the Socialist Party, belonged to the private staff of Mendès-France in the 1950s.

The power of the private staff is difficult to assess. It has certainly been claimed that they exercise power without responsibility, and it is true that they are strategically placed, through their direct access to the President and their contacts with the administration, to exercise great influence. It is equally true that certain members have exerted considerable power in particular circumstances: Foccart frequently by-passed ministers in shaping French policy in black Africa, whilst Juillet undoubtedly played a key role in the downfall of Prime Minister Chaban-Delmas in 1972. Similarly, Sérisé has been influential in determining the political strategy of Giscard d'Estaing and was one of the President's firmest supports in his conflict with Prime Minister Chirac. Generally, however, it would be more accurate to describe the position of the Élysée staff as one of discreet influence. They present the President with advice on policy options which may confirm, differ from or even conflict with those of the ministers. President Giscard d'Estaing has not infrequently asked both a member of his staff and of the Government to write reports on the same subject, and reserves for himself the right to make the final choice and decision. Members of the Élysée staff have neither the time nor the facilities effectively to supervise all the activities of the ministers and their civil servants. They also lack the political weight and the legitimacy to meddle too openly, too directly, too closely or too frequently in decision-making. It would be wrong to conclude that members of the presidential staff have become *véritable super-ministres* and represent 'a technocratic parallel government' or even 'the occult government of France'. President Giscard d'Estaing has described them as his 'grey cells', as members of his brains trust, and has insisted that they must not become a screen between him and his ministers, who remain his principal collaborators.

The Prime Minister

The Prime Minister has been described as the chief of the presidential headquarters (Capitant), as a Vice-President (Raymond Aron), and as the principal executive officer of the President (Marcel Prélot). Other observers have been less charitable. François Mitterrand likened the Prime Minister to a political strip-teaser who, under the greedy eyes of the President, steadily shed the prerogatives clearly conferred upon him by the Constitution. According to the 1958 Constitution 'the Prime Minister is in general charge of the work of the government': and to that end he is given an impressive list of powers, which include the right to appoint and dismiss ministers, to make appointments to certain top-ranking military and civil service posts, to replace, in certain circumstances, the President of the Republic as Chairman of the Council of Ministers and other important Committees, to be consulted by the President before the application of Article 16 (emergency powers), to ask the Constitutional Council to judge the constitutionality of a law or treaty. In practice, of course, many of the constitutional powers of the Prime Minister have been usurped by the President of the Republic. Nevertheless, the importance of the Prime Minister should not be under-estimated: in public press conferences, de Gaulle (in January 1964), Pompidou (July 1969) and Giscard d'Estaing (January 1977) all stressed the significance of the office.

The office of Prime Minister under the Fifth Republic has been criticized by defenders of parliamentary government as being weak and ineffectual. But in some important respects he is much more powerful than his predecessors of the Fourth Republic. First, the choice of a Fourth Republic Prime Minister was often as arcane, as subtle and as mysterious as the election of a modern Pope, with the role of the Holy Ghost being assumed by the very earthly President of the Republic. But the analogy goes no further. Even the present Pope can count upon the loyal support of most of his followers, the unquestioning backing of some and the querulous acceptance of the rest, whereas a Prime Minister of the Fourth Republic was always the prisoner of the forces that had brought him to power (or rather to office). He was the broker of often violently conflicting interests and of personalities who were united only in their desire for portfolios. He was viewed with envy by all, with suspicion by many (even by members of his own party), and with dislike or contempt by some. Rarely had any Prime Minister of the Fourth Republic any genuine following in the country: the exceptions were Pinay and Mendès-France. Gathering popular support could be construed as demagogy, and to the Republicans, creatures and victims of their own history, the demagogue inevitably concealed the future dictator. A Prime Minister of the Fifth Republic is stronger than his predecessors of the Fourth, for he is not constantly absorbed and even exhausted by the task of keeping his Government together, and can spend more time on policy-making: Edgar Faure, Premier from January to February 1952, claimed he lost four kilos in forty days in his struggle with the Deputies. Compared with his predecessors before 1959, he has been spared most of the persistent harassment of his ministerial, party and parliamentary colleagues. He is in a stronger position, too, because he enjoys a much longer tenure of office: under the Fourth Republic, a Prime Minister survived, on average, only six months, whereas since the beginning of the Fifth Republic there have been only seven Prime Ministers. The shortest lived Prime Minister of the Fifth survived longer than the longest lived of the Fourth, and each has been able to take a longer-term view of his task.

The role of the Prime Minister under the Fifth Republic has been the subject of a great deal of debate and controversy. When President Giscard d'Estaing declared that the President was responsible for what was 'permanent and essential' whilst the Prime Minister was in charge of 'contingency problems', he was clearly violating the letter and the spirit of the 1958 Constitution. But he was reiterating a doctrine preached and practised by his two predecessors. In practice, the tasks of the Prime Minister under the Fifth Republic have been essentially five-fold: the first is

to initiate in areas that do not interest the President, and to exercise a general influence in the formulation and implementation of presidential policies. Prime Minister Debré took a direct interest in all areas of policy: his tenacious, hard-working, authoritarian and meddlesome methods led to the resignation of at least two disgruntled and exasperated ministers, but they facilitated the pushing through of badly needed reforms in subjects as diverse as State aid to Church schools, the transfer of the Paris wholesale meat market from the centre of the capital to a more salubrious site in the Parisian suburbs, the reduction in the brewing of home-made alcohol, and the thorny problem of ex-servicemen's pensions, all subjects which had confounded previous administrations. Prime Minister Pompidou was more discreet, but he insisted on seeing all files. Pompidou, like Debré and Raymond Barre, played an important (arguably predominant) role in shaping French economic and financial policies during his Premiership. Other Prime Ministers have shown a keen interest in particular areas of policies. Chaban-Delmas, in the name of his 'new society', took a direct interest in forging better relations with the unions, and was directly responsible for the introduction of workers' educational and training schemes. Jacques Chirac always kept a keen eye on agricultural matters, and on at least one occasion (in June 1975) was able successfully to oppose the Minister of Agriculture. The remaining four tasks of the Prime Minister are

To ensure the overall co-ordination of governmental policy.

To provide a constant liaison with Parliament to ensure the smooth passage of governmental legislation.

To maintain friendly contact with the Gaullist party, the biggest party of the Government coalition.

To arbitrate between the conflicting claims of the parties of the ruling coalition.

The Prime Minister thus provides a two-way channel between the President on the one hand and, on the other, the Government, Parliament, the ruling party coalition and the administration. In short, he initiates, co-ordinates, arbitrates, conciliates and implements. In the pursuit of his many roles the Prime Minister is helped by a small group of junior ministers (there is always one, for example, for civil service affairs) who are attached to his office. He also has at his disposal a wide-ranging network of committees which embrace a variety of subjects, including regional planning, scientific and technical research, tourism and the affairs of the French overseas territories. The Prime Minister chairs a number of inter-ministerial committees and is generally represented by a member of his personal staff at any other important meeting of ministers. The purely administrative work of the Government is left to the General Secretariat of the Government, headed by a General Secretary and manned by about thirty other civil servants. The General Secretary, a high-ranking and politically neutral (but not hostile) civil servant, prepares all ministerial meetings (even those chaired by the President of the Republic), assists at such meetings and ensures that the decisions taken are translated into administrative action, guides their administrative passage into law and ensures their implementation.

The Prime Minister is also assisted by a private staff – his *cabinet*, composed essentially, but not exclusively, of young and able civil servants who act as the eyes and ears of the Prime Minister. The *cabinet* is usually small – about thirty members, although that of Chaban-Delmas was much bigger. Within the *cabinet* there are always several distinct elements: the purely political element (to look after parliamentary, party, electoral and constituency matters), the policy-making element (to initiate policies or merely supervise those of other ministers) the technical element (for instance, there is always a legal expert, normally from the Council of State, who advises on the legality or constitutionality of the proposed measures), and the secretarial element (which carries out all the clerical work and organizes the Prime Minister's timetable). Co-ordination between the various elements is ensured by the head – the *directeur* – of the *cabinet*. Prime Ministerial *cabinets* have varied greatly in their activity, style and reputation, and they have tended to reflect the personality and tastes of the Prime Minister. The *cabinet* of Debré was overtly and often ruthlessly interventionist and reformist in certain areas, whilst that of Pompidou was more conservative and more discreet but equally ubiquitous and reputedly very influential. Chaban-Delmas recruited a *cabinet* which quickly gained the reputation of being brilliant, creative, innovatory, active and reforming, and as such was regarded as dangerous, incompetent, meddlesome and socialistic by the President of the Republic and his private staff. By 1972 the Prime Minister's *cabinet* had grown in both size and prestige, and the emergence of this powerful group constituted a major institutional innovation of the Fifth Republic. Since the dismissal of Premier Chaban-Delmas, however, the power of the prime ministerial *cabinet* has declined. The *cabinets* of Couve de Murville and Messmer were lacklustre affairs, whilst that of Chirac, although undeniably very competent, was largely administrative and rarely innovatory. Prime Minister Barre appears to have modelled his *cabinet* on that of his immediate predecessor.

The power of the Prime Minister rests not only on his strategic position or on the ability and activity of his *cabinet* but also on a number of other factors. The first is his own political stature. He must have sufficient force of personality and prestige to enable him to impose his views or judgements upon his ministerial colleagues and his parliamentary and party supporters. He has occasionally to conciliate and arbitrate between the conflicting forces that compose his political backing: this task may involve him in delicate and difficult situations. For most of the Fifth Republic, he had, for instance, to arbitrate in choosing candidates who were to represent the Government coalition in the national and local elections, and he had to define both the strategy and the tactics of that coalition. Even Barre, who had openly declared his intention of devoting himself exclusively to economic and financial matters, was quickly drawn into the electoral arena, although with singular lack of success, as the Gaullist party rejected his leadership. To succeed, a Prime Minister requires a dominant relationship with the Gaullists, the principal party of the Government coalition, and a good working relationship with the other coalition parties: Pompidou had both, Debré and Chirac enjoyed the former but not the latter, Chaban-Delmas the latter but not the former, Couve de Murville and Messmer had neither, whilst Barre appears to have the latter but clearly lacks the former.

The second main factor which explains the power of a Prime Minister is the prevailing political situation. Whilst the President of the Republic, the Prime Minister, the majority of the Government and the dominant party of the *majorité* were all Gaullists, political friction between them, although sometimes real, was nonetheless limited. This situation prevailed until May 1974 when a non-Gaullist President appointed a Gaullist Prime Minister to head a Government dominated by non-Gaullists and to impose its policies upon a parliamentary group still dominated by Gaullists. The Prime Minister, Chirac, who was unquestioning leader of the Gaullist party, was quickly torn between his dual and conflicting loyalties, and resignation was eventually the only way out of the dilemma. The situation today is still conflict-ridden, with ex-Prime Minister Chirac leading a Gaullist party which continues to be the biggest force in Parliament, and is unfriendly towards the President, unhelpful in its dealings with the Prime Minister who is not a member of the party, and suspicious of a Government which it no longer dominates. The political role of the Prime Minister has always been important, time-consuming and exhausting: Chaban-Delmas described his period of office as 'two hundred weeks of work six days a week, fifteen hours a day'. It is also fraught with difficulties, and those difficulties have multiplied, since the political conditions which existed at the beginning of the Fifth Republic now no longer prevail.

The final factor which determines a Prime Minister's power is the extent of the support given him by the President of the Republic. The Prime Minister is, in conformity with the Constitution, chosen by the President, and the choice of Prime Minister has always been a highly personal affair: de Gaulle chose as his Prime Ministers an unpopular Senator (Debré), an unknown banker (Pompidou) and a professional diplomat, who had been Foreign Minister for the previous nine years (Couve de Murville). None had any previous experience in the National Assembly to which they were constitutionally responsible. President Giscard d'Estaing in his appointment in August 1976 of Barre, a university teacher and high-ranking civil servant with no parliamentary experience and no party links, publicly emphasized the personal nature of his choice. In spite of the constitutional provisions and the early assertions of General de Gaulle, the Prime Minister is also dismissed by the President. Indeed, the dismissals of Prime Minister Pompidou (who had just led the Government forces into a landslide victory at the polls) in June 1968 and of Chaban-Delmas (who had just received an overwhelming vote of confidence by 368 votes to 96 in the National Assembly) in July 1972 were brutal reassertions of presidential supremacy.

The President and the Prime Minister must have a good working relationship based on mutual confidence and what Pompidou described as 'a wide-ranging identity of views'. This does not mean that the President must always take the Prime Minister into his confidence: Debré was invariably kept in the dark over President de Gaulle's intentions in Algeria; Pompidou was not warned at all about de Gaulle's mysterious and dramatic trip to Germany in May 1968 when the country appeared to be on the verge of anarchy; Chirac was always kept in complete ignorance over foreign and European policy. Nor, as shall be seen, does this signify that there can be no differences of opinion on particular subjects. But if presidential support of the Prime Minister is seen to be *generally* lukewarm or hesitant the latter's position is seriously weakened and ultimately untenable. The suspicion felt by the highly conservative President Pompidou toward Chaban-Delmas' reformist ideas was public knowledge, and was exploited both by the Élysée staff and by the

Prime Minister's party adversaries. The resignation of Chirac in 1976 was motivated by his feeling that the President was 'depriving him of the means of carrying out his functions' (Chirac's own phrase) and was giving him insufficient backing in his struggle with his ministers: in the six months before his resignation, the President had reshuffled the Government without fully consulting him, had rejected his request for an early election and had backed the Finance Minister against him in a number of budgetary disputes.

So far, the President has been able to assert his ultimate supremacy over the Prime Minister, but the situation may dramatically alter if the Prime Minister, backed by a majority of the National Assembly, has views which conflict with those of the President, and insists on his constitutional right to impose them: such a situation, which may occur if the Left wins a general election, has exercised the imaginations of constitutional experts and haunted the minds of successive Presidents. The relationship between the President and the Prime Minister, even if they do enjoy 'a wide-ranging identity of views', is, in the very nature of things, complex and troubled. The *Canard Enchaîné*, a Left-wing satirical weekly, put it nicely:

A Prime Minister must have no merits. . . . He must take responsibility for all errors, especially if they are those of the President. He must not fail, otherwise he runs the risk of being sacked or being forced to resign for incompetence. Still more, he must not succeed, for to do so would be the ultimate impertinence, and his disgrace would then be even more terrible. . . . A Prime Minister must maintain himself in an honest, active and competent mediocrity, half-way between obvious failure which would harm the President and striking success which would put the President in the shadows.

The Prime Minister faces a number of dilemmas: if he succeeds he may be seen as a rival but if he fails he will be considered incapable; if, like Pompidou or Chirac, he is a strong personality (which is required for him successfully to carry out his many duties) then conflict with the President may prove chronic and even acute; on the other hand, if, like Couve de Murville or Messmer, he is a weak personality he will avoid clashes with the President but may lack the forcefulness successfully to pursue his many demanding duties. For the President of the Republic, the ideal Prime Minister must be omnipresent but self-effacing, powerful but discreet, forceful but conciliatory. In short, he must combine strength with subordination – a combination more readily found in saints than in ambitious politicians.

The ministers

Nowhere is the gap between constitutional theory and presidential practice greater than in the formation and functioning of the Government. According to the 1958 Constitution, the Government 'decides and directs' the policies of the nation, and has at its disposal the administration and the armed forces. Its members are proposed by the Prime Minister to the President of the Republic, who appoints them. In principle, the Government is a collective body of ministers, responsible to the National Assembly which is empowered to force it out of office. In practice, the Government has become yet another instrument of presidential government, with its members reduced to the role of presidential advisers. In that sense, the French Government has come to resemble the cabinet of the American President.

The control of the President over the Government may be seen in several ways:

The President appoints and dismisses its head, the Prime Minister.
The President openly fixes the agenda and timetable of the Government.
The President determines the size and shape of the Government.

Thus, the shape of the Governments formed under Giscard d'Estaing has reflected the current preoccupations of the President: in May 1974 he appointed Junior Ministers for Penal Reform, Feminine Affairs and Immigrant Affairs, three areas where he hoped to introduce reforms, and in December 1976, without informing the Prime Minister, he created a post of Junior Minister for Industrial Affairs in order to relieve the minister (a political friend who was totally absorbed in the Paris elections) of his heavy departmental duties.

The President intervenes directly and increasingly in the choice of individual ministers. President Giscard d'Estaing has made no attempt to disguise his direct interference in ministerial appointments and even goes so far as to comment upon them on television. But he has merely extended and made more open the practice of his two predecessors. There have been several recent instances of the President nominating ministers who were viewed with frank disapproval by the Prime Minister: the most recent cases include those of Jean-Jacques Servan-Schreiber, the *enfant terrible* of French politics, who was appointed to a newly created Ministry of Reforms in May 1974 against the better judgement of the Prime Minister, of Françoise Giroud who was made Junior Minister for Feminine Affairs in May 1974 even though she had openly declared her support for Mitterrand, the Left-wing candidate, in the previous presidential elections and whose public utterances on the Gaullists had always been less than flattering, and of Jean François-Poncet, a well-known anti-Gaullist, who was made Junior Minister at the Quai d'Orsay in January 1976.

The President determines the political balance of the Government.
President Pompidou always insisted on the political predominance of the Gaullist party, whilst his successor has clearly striven to reduce Gaullist representation in the Council of Ministers: in the first Government formed under Giscard d'Estaing's Presidency, only a third of the members belonged to the Gaullist party, compared with two-thirds in the last Government formed under Pompidou. In the Barre Government, formed in August 1976, the Gaullist party not only lost the Premiership but was given only five of the eighteen portfolios, and only four of the eighteen junior ministers were members of the party. The President has also clearly attempted to displace the political axis of the Government towards the centre Left.

The President treats the Government not as a collective body responsible to the National Assembly, but as a group of individuals responsible to himself. Indeed, General de Gaulle in his *Mémoires* was specific on that point: 'when one is a minister, it is to de Gaulle and to him alone that one is responsible'. And Pompidou and Giscard d'Estaing never failed to act upon that unconstitutional assumption.

Two recent studies of the Ministers of the Fifth Republic, by Pascale and Jean-Dominique Antoni and by William Andrews, note that they are predominantly male, married, middle aged, bourgeois (with a sprinkling of aristocrats), northern French and well educated (generally at the Paris Law Faculty and/or the Institute of Political Sciences) and they have many links with established political, administrative, financial and economic elites. Compared with their predecessors of the Fourth Republic they lack parliamentary experience: indeed, several had no parliamentary experience at all before becoming ministers. The first Governments of the Fifth Republic had a high proportion of non-parliamentary ministers although by 1974 such appointments were very rare. The practice seems to have been revived by President Giscard d'Estaing: in the Barre Government, formed in August 1976, six of the eighteen ministers and six of the eighteen junior ministers were chosen from outside Parliament. Another interesting fact to emerge from the studies is that half the ministers had started their careers in the civil service (hence the constant complaints of the *fonctionnarisation du pouvoir politique* in France).

Under the Fifth Republic, it would be misleading to refer to the power of the Government, since, in practice, it exercises no *collective* power at all. This has led certain commentators to dismiss ministers as 'the little toy soldiers of the President', and as sycophantic executants of presidential whims. Such a view would be equally misleading, since certain ministers exercise considerable power, and the extent of that power depends upon the interplay of several factors:

The degree of interest displayed by the President of the Republic in the affairs of the ministry. As already noted, the interest of the President of the Republic in certain areas is intense and continuous and precludes any initiative on the part of ministers. President de Gaulle could even keep a minister in the dark about matters concerning his own department: the Minister for Algerian Affairs learnt through the newspapers of the details of a secret deal which de Gaulle had concluded with the Algerian liberation fighters.

The extent of prime ministerial interference. As previously indicated, some Prime Ministers (such as Debré) meddled in all governmental matters, some (such as Pompidou and Chirac) were interested in specific areas of governmental policy whilst others (Couve de Murville and Messmer), by taste or necessity, left a great deal of discretion to ministers. Prime Minister Barre is too absorbed in economic and financial matters to have time to interfere too much elsewhere.

The support of the President of the Republic. Some ministers have clearly enjoyed a privileged relationship with the President. It was said by Prime Minister Pompidou of Malraux, who was Minister of Culture for ten years, that he was so little gifted for action that he was incapable of posting a letter without tying himself in knots. Malraux spent all his time in the Council of Ministers scribbling immensely elaborate and psychologically revealing doodles. Yet with the active and unflagging support of President de Gaulle Malraux was able successfully to pursue his policies of creating *Maisons de Culture* (cathedrals of enlightenment in the French provincial desert), defending ancient monuments and cleaning Paris. Chirac, as Minister of Agriculture and later as Minister of the Interior, clearly enjoyed a warm and close personal relationship with President Pompidou (who referred to him as his bulldozer) whilst Poniatowski – *le Prince* – enjoyed similar *rapports* with President Giscard d'Estaing. Presidential support may be vital: it enabled

Edgar Faure to push through his controversial Education Act of 1968, and was essential to the Ministers of Justice and of Health in 1974 and 1975 when the Government parties were clearly unhappy about their proposed reforms of the divorce and abortion laws.

The minister's conception of his role. Some ministers view their role as essentially technical and managerial, and become the faithful and faceless executants of the Presidential will. Since 1958 three professional diplomats (Couve de Murville, Sauvagnargues and de Guiringaud) have been promoted to the post of Minister of Foreign Affairs. Each was noticeable by making himself unnoticeable, carrying diplomatic discretion to the lengths of total self-effacement. Other ministers, however, have left reputations as able and active reformers: Edgar Faure at Education, Debré at Defence, Chalandon at Public Works, Ségard at Foreign Trade, Pisani at Agriculture. Finally, there have been ministers who closely resemble most of their predecessors of the Third and Fourth Republics in that they are less interested in the work of their ministry than in exploiting the prestige and politically strategic position it confers upon them. The personality, temperament, tastes and ambitions of a minister are important factors in determining his influence.

The political weight of the minister. Some ministers, especially the non-parliamentary ministers, lack the political influence and 'punch' of their colleagues. Much of Giscard d'Estaing's influence as Minister of Finance (a post he occupied for many years) sprang not only from his technical and financial expertise but also from his leadership of one of the parties of the governing coalition. Many ministers buttress their position (particularly within their own ministries) by acquiring political positions. And one of the more interesting political phenomena of the Fifth Republic has been the number of ministers of purely technocratic background who have sought local political office and party positions. It is eloquent testimony to the need for a minister to acquire political credibility and stature.

The minister's tenure of office. The longer a minister remains in office the more likely is he to be able to carry out his own policies. Malraux, Minister of Culture from 1959 to 1969, was clearly in a happier position to initiate policies than any of his successors who have survived, on average, for little more than a year. Under the Fifth Republic, certain ministries (notably Defence and Foreign Affairs) have been 'stable' whilst others have been much less so: during de Gaulle's Presidency there were only two Ministers of Foreign Affairs but twelve Ministers of Education and eleven

Ministers of Information. Between January 1959 and January 1978 there were no fewer than forty ministerial changes or reshuffles.

The prestige and power of the ministry. Certain ministries, notably Interior and Finance, enjoy a very high reputation and confer upon their political head an undeniable prestige. Other ministries, such as Education, are considered as 'the graveyards of political ambitions', whilst others, such as the short-lived Ministry for Feminine Affairs, suffer from a weak administration, lack of adequate financial resources, an ill-defined scope of action and the scepticism of other ministries.

The strength of the administrative services of the ministry. This factor raises the question of the autonomy of the administration and its power to resist the will of the politicians. The administrative services of the Quai d'Orsay are known to be fairly weak whilst those of Education, Finance and Public Works have the reputation of being very powerful. It requires a minister of ambition, ruse, ruthlessness and longevity to impose his policies upon these latter ministries.

The efficiency of his own private staff (cabinet ministériel). The minister's *cabinet* is composed of a small group of individuals, drawn increasingly from the civil service, whose task is to provide the link between the worlds of politics and administration. The *cabinet* is the minister's brains trust, advisor and negotiator. It ensures that the ministry is sensitive to the political exigencies of the minister and that the minister is not impervious to the requirements of the ministry. They also look after the minister's local responsibilities, provide a permanent liaison with Parliament and ensure a constant link (often through their personal relations) with other *cabinets*. *Cabinets* vary enormously: some are timid, self-effacing and dominated by the administration, whilst others are dynamic, interventionist and highly effective. Some see themselves as the provider of ideas whilst others view their role as essentially managerial. There is, in truth, an infinite variety of *cabinets* and it is difficult to generalize about them, but a well-organized, determined and sensitive *cabinet* may be a powerful support for a minister.

The power of individual ministers depends, therefore, on a large number of factors. Some may justifiably be described as 'little toy soldiers' whilst others are powerful and highly susceptible political figures. Yet all may rightly be considered as the 'President's men', and constant or profound disagreement with the President leads inevitably to resignation or dismissal. The President's view of the

Government is profoundly ambivalent: Giscard d'Estaing, like his two predecessors, insists that the Government is a team and he places a premium upon its 'unity, cohesion and harmony', yet he persists in treating it as an assembly of individuals, all beholden to himself alone.

The President of the Republic meets his ministers in a number of circumstances, and in ways which appear designed to emphasize their non-collective nature. For although he meets them at official Councils of Ministers, these tend to be formal and ritualistic occasions for rubber-stamping decisions made elsewhere. And if President Giscard d'Estaing allows a freer flow of discussion than under his predecessors, a minister still speaks only when invited and generally only on his ministry's affairs. The President also meets ministers at inter-ministerial councils held at the Élysée (*conseils restreints*) which are chaired by himself and attended by the Prime Minister and a selected number of ministers and their top civil servants. These *conseils restreints* have often been seen as the real decision-making bodies of the Fifth Republic, and they have certainly been used to discuss major problems: in 1976, for example, the subjects considered included the annual budget, housing finance, factory legislation, school transport and the economic problems of small firms. Decisions made in these *conseils restreints* are later presented to a Council of Ministers for formal acceptance. The President may also meet his ministers at working lunches, such as that which took place in September 1976 when he met three ministers to define French policy in Africa. In April 1975, the President also held a governmental seminar with most of the ministers in 'an exercise of collective reflection' on the major policies to be pursued: the experiment was such a success that it has been repeated only once since that date. Finally, the President meets members of the Government individually: almost once a week he has a working session with the Prime Minister, the Foreign Minister, the Finance Minister and the Minister of the Interior. President de Gaulle in an impressive calculation noted that in his first term of office (1959 to 1966 he held 302 Councils of Ministers, 420 inter-ministerial Councils, he met the Prime Minister 605 times and other ministers, individually, on nearly 2000 occasions. A breakdown of the President's timetable in 1975 shows that he held 53 Councils of Ministers, 72 *conseils restreints*, 77 working lunches and 195 individual audiences with ministers. President Giscard d'Estaing frequently uses the telephone directly to contact his ministers (a device rarely resorted to by his predecessors). The President is also represented (generally by the General Secretary of the Élysée) at inter-ministerial committees held at Matignon, and a member of his personal staff is present at any important gathering of ministers. Thus the President is informed either directly or indirectly of the activities of all the ministers, and is thus well placed for supervising their work.

The President's men: some concluding remarks

The President of the Republic has at his disposal a large group of advisors, which include his private staff and his ministers and junior ministers led by the Prime Minister. All are the creatures of his patronage, and disagreement with him over major issues can lead only to resignation or dismissal. It is questionable, however, whether the presidential advisors constitute in any real sense, a team. Indeed, it may be argued that there has emerged around the President a system of institutionalized tension, a system encouraged, either actively or tacitly, by successive Presidents. This tension manifests itself at different levels:

Between the President and the Prime Minister. There have been several well-publicized differences between the two men. Even the ever faithful Debré was known to be hostile to President de Gaulle's Algerian policy, and voiced private disquiet about the President's somewhat cavalier interpretation of the Constitution (in March 1960 and August 1961). Prime Minister Pompidou, who, in de Gaulle's own publicized phrase, practised 'the art of temporizing', had a quiet and effective capacity for shelving some of General de Gaulle's 'wilder' schemes, such as workers' participation. He successfully prevented the execution of a General involved in the 1962 army putsch in Algeria, and in May 1968 he dissuaded the President from holding a referendum on participation. Later, as President, Pompidou clashed with Chaban-Delmas, his Prime Minister, over the latter's proposals to reform the regional and communal structure of France, to liberalize the French television network, to introduce limited measures of worker participation, to restructure the social security system, and to negotiate a limited incomes policy which guaranteed an automatic increase in the standard of living. On all these issues the President took a prudent, sceptical and very conservative line. The differences between Prime Minister Chirac and President Giscard d'Estaing revolved round policy (the Prime Minister disliked the President's flirtation with social democracy and his pro-European ideas), strategy (Chirac wished to reassure the traditional conservative electors of the *majorité* whilst Giscard d'Estaing was (and remains) intent on attracting the votes of the moderate Left) and tactics (the President refused the Prime Minister's request for an early election). The differences were such that one observer (Viansson-Ponté) could describe the Prime Minister as 'the chief of staff of a general whose strategy he disapproves'.

Between the Élysée staff and the Government. It is well known that relations between Chaban-Delmas' Government and Pompidou's private staff were far from cordial. In his Memoirs (*l'Ardeur*) the Prime Minister recounts how he fell foul of the 'terrible tandem' of Pierre Juillet and Marie-France Garaud (a gallic version of Marcia Williams) of the Élysée staff: he was accused of 'bringing socialism to France'. The *rapports* between the Leftist-leaning staff of Giscard d'Estaing and Prime Minister Chirac were characterized by mutual suspicion; the public wrangle in 1975 over the purchase of telephone equipment for modernizing the French network and which opposed the Industrial Councillor of the Élysée and the Minister of Posts and Telecommunications was noticeable only because of its acrimony.

Between the Prime Minister and the ministers. The history of the Fifth Republic has been punctuated by unseemly squabbles between the Prime Minister and his 'subordinates'. When at his last Council of Ministers in August 1976 Chirac accused certain ministers of not having made his difficult task any easier, he was merely making known the sentiments that must have been felt by many of his predecessors. The disputes take place over three sorts of problems. First, there are conflicts over defining respective spheres of competence: this is especially true over settling budgetary disputes, with the Finance Minister disputing the Prime Minister's right to exercise (normally with electoral considerations in mind) an ultimate control. There are, secondly, frequent altercations over specific policies: even the mild-mannered Messmer was moved in January 1974 to rebuke Charbonnel, the Industry Minister, whom he accused of showing too much leniency towards the workers who were then occupying the Lip watch factory. Finally, disputes may take place over the political line of the Prime Minister: the last year of Chirac's Government was marked by real friction between the Prime Minister and some of his more 'reformist' ministers.

Between individual ministers. As has been previously underlined, the Government under the Fifth Republic has not created any tradition of collective solidarity and responsibility. Clearly, if a Minister disagrees with an official major policy of the Government he will resign (several ministers resigned over de Gaulle's Algerian and European policies) or will be dismissed (the most recent example was the sacking of Servan-Schreiber in June 1974 after he had publicly exposed the folly of French nuclear policy). But there is a surprising amount of latitude allowed to ministers in airing their quarrels in public: in 1975, for example, it was no secret that the Minister of the Interior and the Finance Minister disagreed over the reform of local finance, that the Minister of Finance opposed the views of the Minister of Labour over the financing of the social security system, and that the Industry Minister and the Foreign Minister were at loggerheads over the restructuring of the French computer industry (or what remained of it). The disputes in 1959 between the Ministers of Education and of Defence over national service deferment and in 1960 between the Industry and the Finance Ministers over the freedom of industry and trade were matched by much later squabbles between the Ministers of Justice and of Feminine Affairs in 1975 over proposals to pay salaries to mothers with very young children, and between the Finance and the Justice Ministers in 1976 over the latter's reluctance to start judicial proceedings against unnamed petrol companies suspected of illicit price-fixing. Between the Minister of the Interior and his colleagues at Justice friction is endemic: as early as 1959 the two Ministers clashed over the seizing of *La Gangrène*, a book which depicted the spread of torture in Algeria. Sixteen years later their successors were indulging in a bout of public mutual recrimination: in November 1975, the Minister of Justice, in a public speech, rebuked his colleague for his attacks on the country's judges (whom he had accused of pusillanimity). As recently as December 1976 another public dispute broke out between the two Ministers over Interior's expulsion of the workers who were occupying the offices of the *Parisien Libéré*, a Right-wing newspaper.

Between ministers and their junior ministers. There have been several well-publicized disputes at this level. Amongst the most recent were those which involved the Minister and Junior Minister of Agriculture (all relations were carried on by laconic notes) in 1974–5, the Minister of Infrastructure (*Équipement*) and his Junior Minister for Housing in the same period, the Minister of Education and his Junior Minister for University Affairs in 1975 and in 1976. The disputes have revolved around differences of personality, of policy or over the vexed question of their respective areas of competence – the political demarcation lines.

It may be that institutionalized tension or even friction between the President's men enables him better to control them, on the age-old principle of dividing and ruling. Or the President may be simply elevating an inevitability into a virtue. Constant tension and dissension may easily produce vacillation and even paralysis. It is certainly detrimental to the cohesion and to the image of the governing team as well as damaging to policy co-ordination. It is nonetheless true that successive Presidents have been able to retain their general control over their many advisors who have been divided over principles, policies and personalities. And in so doing they have generally avoided that obsessive and stultifying search for consensus which characterizes the operation of executive government in Great Britain. The problem arises, however, that a changed political situation may radically change things, for the divisions between the President's men (many of whom would reject the title) may prove too great. And some of the men (the Prime Minister and his ministers) who have been the willing agents of presidential government may well become the instruments for trying to dismantle it.

4 The administrative state: myth and reality

In popular demonology, the administration looms as large in France as the trades unions do in Britain. The French administration is seen as a modern Leviathan condemning man to an existence which is becoming more nasty and more brutish because it is getting longer. Its 'dictatorship' was described as both 'arrogant and inhuman' by President Pompidou who added his voice to the all-party chorus of vilification. Such criticism is not new, but it has rarely been so persistent, so widespread, so strident. The Fifth Republic, it is argued, has become 'a technocrat's paradise', 'a régime dominated by officialdom', 'an administrative State': the Deputy-centred régime of the Fourth Republic has been supplanted by the civil servant-dominated régime of the Fifth. Several arguments have been forwarded to buttress the claim.

The myth

The power of the French State has been further strengthened under the Fifth Republic

The State has become omnipresent, invading all areas of private and public life. Already in the nineteenth century there were eloquent denunciations in France of 'the all-invading' nature of the State, and these were multiplied as State intervention increased with the impact of three major wars (1870-1, 1914-18 and 1939-45), with the increased demands for social welfare and for full employment, and with the increasingly technical and costly nature of economic policies. Since the advent of the Fifth Republic, the economic and social transformation of France has been accelerated, and massive State intervention and aid has been required to coax France into 'marrying her century', to use President de Gaulle's phrase. More than ever, the State has become an employer of men, an owner of property, a manager and modernizer of the economy, a protector of the nation's boundaries, a guarantor of its social welfare: its agents, who now constitute a tenth of the total work force, regulate the citizenry from before the cradle to beyond the grave.

State interventionism is particularly apparent in the economic sphere: at present, the State controls two-thirds of all credit and, either directly or indirectly, more than half of all French industrial investment. The principle of interventionism evokes no primitive antagonism (although its implementation by the administration does) either from the public or the business community. It is exercised through a variety of methods:

The directives and 'indications' of the Five Year Plans (see pp. 89–90).

The policies and general level of activity of: (*a*) the *nationalized industries*, which include coal, gas, electricity, the railways, the civil aviation industry, an important part of the car industry (Renault), the tobacco and matches industry. There is no doubt that successive Governments (as in Great Britain) have abused their positions *vis-à-vis* of these industries: they have complained about their deficits (the State propped them up to the tune of 30000 million francs in 1976 or nearly 8 per cent of total State expenditure) but have insisted, for example, that Air France continue to use the loss-making Concorde and Caravelle and unpopular Roissy airport, have told the mining industry to work old and unprofitable mines in areas of high unemployment and have insisted that the Electricity Industry give preferential rates to industry; (*b*) the *semi-public corporations* such as the giant petrol companies Elf and Total. The French Government exercises the kind of control over their activities which would cause a revolt in BP if a British Government were to do likewise; (*c*) *the network of firms which have been brought under State control by the use of secondary share-holding.* It was calculated in 1975 that there were more than 800 firms in which the State owned, indirectly, at least 30 per cent of the shares.

The control of credit through the Bank of France, the nationalized banks and insurance companies.

The far-reaching but generally ineffective system of price control: in the short period of rigid price control in 1976–7 over 300000 checks were carried out.

Loans, investment and research grants facilitated by bodies such as the Crédit National (a semi-public organ which is the principal dispenser of long- and medium-term loans to private industry), the Caisse des Dépôts and the Caisse de Crédit Agricole which have branches in the provinces.

State orders, which are now massive. The State can effectively protect any industry by guaranteeing orders over a number of years.

The sectoral investment funds such as the FDES (the Economic and Social Development fund), the FIAT (the Regional Intervention fund used for promoting industrial decentralization), the Rural Renovation fund and the FORMA (used for restructuring the agricultural marketing system).

Involved in the process of State economic intervention is an army of officials from the nationalized banks, industries, and insurance companies, the semi-public corporations, the INSEE (the National Institute of Statistics), various specialized divisions and subdivisions of the Finance Ministry (notably the Budget Division, the Forecasting Division and the Economic Intervention Service which vets requests for loans and whose advice on marketing prospects may be decisive), and of sponsor ministries (which may intervene in the siting and detailed regulations of an industry). There is no doubt that the French Government has fully exploited all the means at its disposal: the *Plan Calcul* (designed to create a powerful French computer industry), the creation of the vast petrochemical complex at Fos, the policy of encouraging industrial mergers in the 1960s, and the massive loans decided in 1977 to restructure and modernize the motor-car and the iron and steel industry of Lorraine are but four examples of direct State interventionism.

State interventionism has not only increased *quantitatively* but it has also changed *qualitatively*, and in ways that invariably strengthen the administration. Nowadays, the State is involved in imparting a certain sense of direction to groups, firms and individuals: this is especially true in urban and industrial planning. The increasingly complex nature of decisions places a premium upon technical expertise and esoteric knowledge, and the administration, imbued with the sense of its own permanence, has the time, the stability and the facilities for acquiring both.

The present régime had the clearly declared intention of expanding the role of the administration

The founders of the Fifth Republic, in their search for a strong and respected State, stressed that political and constitutional reform had to be complemented by administrative reforms. The constitutional and political reinforcement of the Executive led to a corresponding reduction in the powers of Parliament, and the regulatory power and discretion of the administration was increased by Articles 34 and 38 of the Constitution which severely restrict the realm of law-making (areas where Parliament is necessarily involved). Moreover, many of the important laws passed in Parliament are so-called *lois d'orientation*, laws which present the general outlines and guidelines of legislation and which leave the details to the administration. Under the Fifth Republic, civil servants are also much less harassed by prying Deputies (pursuing a constituency or pressure-group interest) and their projects are more likely to survive unscathed. The administration may exercise its influence *before* a piece of legislation is presented when it helps in drafting, *during* its presentation when it advises ministers on the desirability of concessions to Members of Parliament, and *after* the passage of the legislation when it supervises its implementation. Its obstructionism can be very powerful: for instance, the Nature Protection Act of April 1976 emerged from the *bureaux* of the Environment Ministry only after five years of savage mauling. Obstructionism is generally most evident at the stage of implementing a law – and especially if Parliament had had the temerity to insist on concessions. The Agricultural Act of December 1968 was still waiting full implementation by the end of 1977. These powers in the formulation, the drafting, the passage, the implementation and the supervision of legislation are traditional: under the Fifth Republic they have been constitutionally extended to encompass a greater number of subjects.

The views of the founders of the present régime on the administration involved not only a strengthening of its traditional powers, but also another related objective – the increasing of its efficiency. This objective emerges from the utterances of Michel Debré, the first Prime Minister of the Fifth Republic and the constitutional *alter ego* of President de Gaulle. Debré was one of the few politicians to recognize the importance of the administration, and in 1945 had been responsible for the creation of the École Nationale d'Administration. In his book, *La Mort de l'État Républicain*, written in 1947, he insisted that 'a new type of political power must be accompanied by a new kind of administration'. Underlying the need to strengthen the administration was the desire to 'rationalize' decisions, to 'depoliticize' them, and to reject the incrementalism practised by the politicians of the previous régime. Since 1958, the efficiency of the administration has been the object of countless and constant reforms. In 1963, a Ministry for Administrative Reform was created to complement (the critics said duplicate) the work of older bodies such as the Central Committee on the Cost and Efficiency of the Public Services, and later a Permanent Mission for Administrative Reform was founded. New bodies at national, regional and local level have mushroomed forth with astonishing regularity, all intent on solving the crucial problem of administrative co-ordination, but most resulting in rendering the original problem that shade more intractable. Economic decentralization was placed essentially (but not exclusively) in the hands of the DATAR (the *Délégation Générale à l'Aménagement du Territoire*), the co-ordination of scientific and technical research to the DGRST, the economic development of certain regions was confided to horizontally organized *missions* (those of the Languedoc–Roussillon and Aquitaine are the two best known) and the tackling of specific problems (such as the growing threat to the Côte-d'Azur from pollution and property speculation) was confined to other *missions* which were to cut through the entanglements of the traditional administrative jungle. On other occasions, *ad hoc* commissions were given the role of co-ordinating administrative activity in a specific domain: the Barre commission on housing finance of 1975 was one such commission. At the local level, new regional institutions have been created to co-ordinate the social and economic policies of the provinces, and an attempt has been made to ensure some degree of policy co-ordination in the growing urban conglomerations through the creation of urban communities and districts (see pp. 208–9). The régime's obsession with administrative co-ordination and efficiency also explains the major restructuring of the Paris region, the creation of super-ministries, the founding of new ministries, the appointing of co-ordinating general secretaries in certain ministries, and the internal reform of almost all ministries. This constant flurry of administrative change has been motivated by the régime's desire for greater efficacity. So, too, has the introduction of RCB (the French equivalent of PPBS) in the mid 1960s which also attempts to introduce 'rationality' into public policy making.

The civil service has permeated all levels of social and economic decision-making, both public and private

Civil servants, the agents of State control, have infiltrated all aspects of public and private decision-making through their membership of:
  (i) *The presidential staff, and the private staffs of the Prime Minister*

and other ministers: they now constitute 90 per cent of those staffs.

(ii) *The numerous inter-ministerial committees* which bring together ministers and their senior civil servants concerned with particular policy areas or specific policies.

(iii) *The* ad hoc *and permanent specialized bodies* which have proliferated since the war. It was calculated in the mid 1960s that there were no fewer than 500 councils, 1200 committees and 300 commissions linking the organs of State with the major pressure groups. These 'instruments of administrative pluralism' have been increasing at all levels, both national and local, giving rise to mounting disquiet about 'government by commission' and the accompanying effacement of the traditional representative institutions.

(iv) *The French Planning Commissariat,* which is considered by many as the lynchpin in the French system of *concertation.* The Planning Commissariat is headed by a Planning Commissioner, the best known of whom was Jean Monnet, the first to hold the post. It is a small and high-powered brains trust of civil servants, a permanent, administratively autonomous and intellectually independent body which forms an integral part of the present machinery of government, and has access to all levels of government from the Presidency (through the Central Planning Council) to the local administration. Its task is to form committees which associate business, trade unionists, civil servants and other industrialists and economic experts: the membership of various committees was nearly 5000 in the Sixth Plan (1971-5), and a half to two-thirds were appointed by the pressure-groups. By linking the groups within the State, it is able, in theory, to transmit the State's general directives, by providing, through a five-year Plan, a framework which 'indicates' the medium-term economic and social priorities of the Government: hence the term 'indicative planning'. It is within the Plan's framework that the social and economic 'partners' (a word frequently employed) are asked to collaborate. Pierre Massé, a previous Planning Commissioner, described the objectives of the Plan as reducing the areas of economic uncertainty (by issuing forecasts of the likely evolution of various economic sectors) and as providing a 'framework of social justice'.

The French Plans have become increasingly ambitious, technical, complex – and suspect. The planning process is clearly under a shadow and has lost a great deal of its prestige: it encountered the jealousy and hostility of the Finance Ministry (which even established 'parallel' functions such as its own Forecasting Division); the main unions have boycotted its work because they feel, not unjustifiably, that they are under-represented; the Left-wing parties emphasize the timidity of its proposals in key areas such as income distribution, suspect it as a tool of governmental propaganda and claim that it is insufficiently discussed in Parliament. Its reputation for political neutrality and impartiality – one of the props of its power – has, therefore, been badly shaken. Moreover, its vulnerability to outside events (such as the Algerian war, the May events in 1968, the explosion in petrol prices after 1974) has been all too apparent. It has twice been sacrificed to short-term anti-inflationary packages, and it is abundantly clear that the Barre anti-inflation Plan of 1976 has already basically destroyed the present, Seventh Plan (1976–80). Perhaps the most serious blow to the Plan is that few people now believe in it: even most of the planners are plainly discouraged about its inefficacy.

(v) *The boards and management of many private firms and public industries* through the process of *pantouflage*: top civil servants often take up lucrative posts either in the public sector (in 1972, thirty of the forty-four key posts in the twenty largest public enterprises were in the hands of civil servants) or in the private sector. Of the four most important civil servants involved in industrial affairs in 1972, one (from the presidential staff) went to Crédit Lyonnais (one of France's biggest banks), one (from the Prime Minister's staff) joined Hachette (the publishing empire), a third (from the Industry Ministry) took up a key post with Peugeot (the car firm), and the fourth became a junior minister. Of the three predecessors of the Prices Director at the Finance Ministry in 1977, one became head of the Crédit Industriel et Commercial (the biggest private bank in France) before becoming a Minister, one was put in charge of the GAN (a giant public insurance group), and the third moved to be head of the SEITA (the nationalized tobacco industry). Such examples are not exceptional. In 1976, for example, there were only 560 French firms employing more than 1000 workers, but they completely dominated the French market, and a majority of them were headed by ex-students of the prestigious École Polytechnique (familiarly called 'X') who then became State-trained mining or highway engineers or by other civil servants. Almost all of those firms had ex-civil servants on their boards of directors. The result of *pantouflage* is to establish a widespread network of personal relations which enables the State to transmit, on a purely informal basis, its wishes.

There has been an increasing politicization of the civil service which has become increasingly docile to the directives of the ruling Right-wing coalition

There is no doubt that under the Fifth Republic there has been an increased tendency for civil servants to colonize politically sensitive positions and even the major political institutions of the country. As already noted, the presidential staff, the Prime Minister's staff and other ministerial *cabinets* are composed almost exclusively of civil servants. These posts invariably involve – and often directly – some of those civil servants in areas which are intrinsically political: party, parliamentary and constituency affairs are all sensitive and overtly political, and all are dealt with by members of presidential or ministerial private staffs. The politicization of the administration may also be seen in the number of civil servants who stand in parliamentary elections and who are elected: in the 1956 general elections thirty-five civil servants were elected to the National Assembly, a figure which rose to forty-three in 1958, fifty-six in 1962, sixty-three in 1967 and seventy-nine in 1973. These figures exclude members of the armed forces and of the teaching profession, who are technically civil servants in France, and it should also be noted that they also exclude ex-civil servants. In local politics, too, the influence of civil servants (especially of those based in the capital) is quite astonishing. Amongst the 38 000 mayors of France, members and ex-members of the *grands corps* and the central administration are well represented.

What has also struck many critical observers is the increasing identification of the civil service with the ruling Right-wing coalition. The contact of the régime's top politicians with the civil service appears to exemplify this: *all* the Prime Ministers of the Fifth Republic had spent part of their career in the civil service; Debré and Pompidou had both been members of the Council of State, Chaban-Delmas and Couve de Murville started their careers in the Financial Inspectorate, Messmer emerged from the colonial administration, Chirac started his professional life in the Court of Accounts whilst Barre, after teaching, became a prominent 'Eurocrat'. A study of the ministers of the Fifth Republic shows that more than half those who served de Gaulle and Pompidou were recruited directly from the civil service or had been civil servants. That proportion has increased since 1974. In January 1976, the Prime Minister, the Finance Minister and the Foreign Minister were amongst the thirty-one (of the forty-three) members of the Government who had previously been civil servants. At the end of 1977, the President of the Republic, the Prime Minister and no fewer than thirty-one of the thirty-six ministers and junior ministers had had previous experience in the civil service. It is not surprising, therefore, that it is contended that there has been a clear *fonctionnarisation du pouvoir politique* under the Fifth Republic, and that it is difficult to know where the civil service starts and the government ends. At the parliamentary level, too, the identification of the civil service with its political masters is striking: in the 1967 elections, thirty-eight of the fifty-three civil servants who were elected belonged to the Government coalition, and in the 1968 and 1973 elections fewer than a fifth of the elected civil servants belonged to the Left-wing opposition.

Evidence of the politicization of the civil service in a pro-governmental sense may also be gleaned from a study of the appointments to the key posts of *directeurs* (who head the divisions of the central administration) and to ambassadorial and prefectoral posts (which are largely at the discretion of the Government). Even the *grands corps* have been penetrated by political appointees through the judicious use of outside appointments: the Government has the right to appoint a certain proportion – usually about a quarter – and it has used this right to place politically sympathetic men. It is further argued that successive Governments have not hesitated to harass vocal Left-wingers within the civil service: in 1976 the transfer of Blache, a tax inspector, and the attempted transfer of Ceccaldi, a judge at Marseilles, to a Siberian waste in the north of France, gave rise to charges of McCarthyism.

The reality

The growing power of this ubiquitous and apparently highly political civil service has caused grave disquiet in all circles: *L'Administration au pouvoir* was the title of a popular book, a title which contained a warning, confirmed a popular prejudice and purported to state a fact. But to claim that the administration is running the country is grossly to oversimplify the real situation. It is true that it exercises considerable influence: that influence is ensured by its strategic position in the drafting, the passage, the implementation and the supervision of legislation. It is equally true that certain parts of the civil service and certain civil servants exercise a discretion which borders on the autonomous exercise of power: such civil servants would include Jérôme Monod, head of the DATAR from 1968 to 1975; Pierre Massé, the Planning Commissioner from 1959 to 1966; Pierre Dreyfus of the nationalized Renault for most of the Fifth Republic; Bloch-Laîné, the Head of the Caisse des Dépôts from 1952 to 1967; Pierre Guillaumat, managing director of the State-owned petrol empire; Jacques Calvet, the head of the private office of Giscard d'Estaing when he was Finance Minister; Claude Villain, the Prices Director at the Finance Ministry from 1974, who was accorded great discretion in negotiating price deals with industry and private firms. Yet a close look at the French administration raises nagging doubts about its so-called omnipotence.

If the administration is so powerful, why do so many of the more able and more ambitious civil servants forsake it for politics? Why do so many depart so precipitously for other posts in the nationalized industries or in the private sector? For so many to deny themselves the exercise of power would constitute a collective act of self-abnegation rarely paralleled in French history. If the civil service is so powerful why are so many civil servants so disgruntled and disenchanted? Why do so many complain of their impotence? Why *'la crise de la fonction publique'*? The picture of the Fifth Republic as 'an administrative State' requires serious reservation, and for the following reasons.

The founders of the Fifth Republic were intent not only on strengthening the administration but also ensuring its subordination

They were determined not to tolerate what they thought to be the administration's unchecked exercise of power during the Fourth Republic. It was one of the axioms of students of the Fourth Republic that the administration was the real centre of decision-making, but like most axioms in politics, the claim represents but a half-truth, and half-truths on close examination are rarely even half-true. . . . According to the claim, there lay behind the chaotic and pusillanimous behaviour of short-lived Governments the unchanging, the omnipresent and omnipotent administration. This *sottogoverno* was the steadfast guardian of the national interest against the politicians and the pressure groups. For the Gaullists, this 'administrative State within the State' clearly had to be dismantled, and the loyalty and subordination of civil servants ensured.

The Government's determination to ensure the subordination of the administration was emphasized in the 1958 Constitution, in the

1959 revision of the civil service charter and in the 1964 decree regulating relations between the State and the French radio and television network personnel. Limitations were placed on the right of State employees to strike, governmental control of the nationalized industries was tightened, the police were brought into line, and the prefectoral corps' professional association was informed that its open complaints about working conditions would no longer be tolerated. In attempting to ensure the subordination of the civil service, conflict with the civil servants was inevitable. The latter, imbued with a keen sense of their own permanence, their stability, their technical competence and their disinterested guardianship of the national interest, view the politicians as transient and personally ambitious, their vision of the national interest frequently blurred by parliamentary, party, pressure-group or purely electoral considerations. The politicians, keenly aware of their democratic legitimacy, of their responsibility for decisions taken, and of their own self-importance, see the administrators as antediluvian, lethargic and generally obstructive, their guardianship of the national interest normally manifested in an implacable and unhealthy attachment to the *status quo*. For the politician, the administration is a kingdom where precedent reigns supreme, where habits are sacrosanct, where innovation is frowned upon and where imagination is treasonable. In such circumstances conflict is always near the surface. There have been some epic struggles under the Fifth Republic between the civil servants and politicians: the ferocious clashes between Debré, when Minister of Defence, and his officials led to the suspension of the General Secretary of National Defence and the *Ingénieur général des armées* in December 1969, and to the 'resignation' of the naval Chief of Staff in March 1970. The battle between Quermonne, Director of Higher Education and the Junior Minister responsible for Higher Education in 1975 and 1976 was infused with all the intense academic malice of which those two ex-university teachers were capable, and was settled only by the resignation of the civil servant. There have also been several instances of the civil servants resorting to their favourite blocking tactics to combat unpopular policies. The obstructionism of the *ingénieurs de l'équipement* of the Environment Ministry is legendary; the minister who first held the post described it somewhat dolefully as the *Ministère de l'Impossible*.

Yet relations between ministers and civil servants under the Fifth Republic generally conform neither to the Gaullist wish nor to the popular stereotype. First, there are often areas of broad agreement

between the administration and the politicians: for example, the
financially orthodox Giscard d'Estaing, when Finance Minister,
ruled over a ministry most of which was dedicated to financial
orthodoxy. Secondly, there are areas where the administration has
been passive, weak or largely managerial and has not actively
opposed the minister: the civil servants of the Quai d'Orsay were
often opposed to French foreign policy but they were unable or
unwilling to modify it. Thirdly, a skilful minister will always get his
own way even against a powerful administration: Edgar Faure
imposed his mildly liberal educational reforms upon an administration which considered them as positively Maoist; the construction of
the Rhine–Rhône canal was given the go-ahead in spite of the
animosity of large parts of the Ministry of *Équipement*; France
withdrew brutally from NATO even though the Defence Ministry
was violently opposed to the policy. Finally, many ministers enjoy
a symbiotic relationship with their civil servants: they are, after all,
condemned to live together. For the civil servants, a strong minister
may be a nuisance but he is more likely than a malleable minister to
fight for some of their projects at the political level. Amongst the
factors that shape the relationship between the civil servants and
ministers are the determination, skill and political weight of the
Minister, the strength of his private staff and the cohesiveness of the
administration.

The régime has been inconsistent in its administrative practice

No one would dispute the quantity of administrative reforms under
the Fifth Republic. But the lack of internal logic and coherence of
those reforms has frequently struck observers. Indeed, it would be
no exaggeration to say that there has been a total lack of system,
since the reformers have sought to reconcile or to juxtapose or even
to superimpose basically conflicting ideals. The reformers could not
make up their minds whether the fundamental purpose of their
measures was to render the administration more efficient, more subordinate or more democratic. By some mysterious alchemy it was
hoped to fulfil all three objectives. Nowhere was the confusion more
apparent than in the 'reform' of the local administration. Ministers
involved in the reforms were divided amongst themselves about their
nature and even their desirability. Michel Debré, the first Prime
Minister, viewed any concession to the provinces as the thick end
of the wedge, as a dangerous step in the dismemberment of a fragile

nation, whilst Pompidou, first as Prime Minister and then as President of the Republic, continually cast a prudent electoral eye on the reaction of the established local *notables*. Jeanneney, a Left-wing Gaullist, who was responsible for the ill-fated regional reforms proposed in the 1969 referendum, was primarily concerned with the problem of increasing public participation in decision-making. The administrative advisors of the ministers were no less divided in their attitudes, with some (notably in the prefectoral administration) becoming the vociferous defenders of the interests and the privileges of the *corps* to which they belonged. The consequence of the divisions of opinion was a series of compromises which were ill-digested, incoherent, unhappy and uninspiring, designed to satisfy everyone but failing to please anyone.

Contradictions emerge in other reforms of the administration. The declared intention of Louis Joxe, the Minister of Administrative Reform, was 'to simplify, to co-ordinate the structure of administration, to reduce duplication and to reorganize the already too numerous public services'. Certain reforms have undoubtedly achieved that end: the 'harmonization' of local public services within the context of the regions and the 'rationalization' of administrative services within the regions, the restructuring of certain ministries and the creation of new ones must be counted as successes. There are many areas, however, where the problems of co-ordination and of duplication have not been tackled and have even been made worse. For instance, the policy of industrial decentralization was confided to a newly created *délégation* – the D A T A R – but other administrations which continue to be involved include the staffs of the President of the Republic and of the Prime Minister (for electoral reasons), the appropriate officials of the Ministry of the Interior (since its implementation involves the local prefects), of the Finance Ministry (since it has financial implications), of the Ministry of *Équipement* (which analyses any technical aspects) and of any other affected ministry (for example, Housing or Transport). The D A T A R has thus become yet another cog in a very large and badly functioning machine.

The power of the administration is weakened by its internal divisions

Much of the critical literature on French 'technocracy' rests on the assumption that the administration is one coherent entity. Most of the evidence, however, points to its diversity and fragmentary nature and suggests that it is especially prey to internal tension and dissension.

Moreover, the interplay of divergent interests is often open, unlike in Britain where differences are masked behind a screen of courteous yet apprehensive anonymity.

Internal divisions are manifested in various ways. First, like most large organizations, the administration is not spared personal and generational conflicts which sometimes transcend professional and ideological similarities. Second, there are deep-seated ideological cleavages within the administration, even within the top elite. Most studies emphasize that top civil servants come largely from the Paris bourgeoisie, tend to be the sons of civil servants, are generally educated in the better State grammar schools (often in the select group of Paris *lycées*) and then either attend the Paris Institut d'Études Politiques (or *Sciences Po* as it is familiarly known) to prepare for the highly competitive examination to the École Nationale d'Administration (ENA) or they prepare for the no less competitive examination to the École Polytechnique. Students from the ENA (often referred to as *Énarques*) take another competitive examination at the end of their studies at the School, and the result of that examination determines the students' career prospects. The well-placed *Énarques* choose the highly prestigious *grands corps* (the Financial Inspectorate, the Court of Accounts, the Council of State and to a lesser extent the prefectoral and the diplomatic *corps*). Students from the École Polytechnique also have a competitive examination at the end of their studies, at which time many go to another specialist school – the École des Mines (for mining engineers), the École des Ponts-et-Chaussées (for highway engineers), the École de Génie (for military engineers) are three of the better known – before entering the appropriate State technical corps which are no less prestigious than the administrative *grands corps*. Members of the State administrative and technical elite issue, therefore, from a narrow social and educational base, and their exclusiveness is heightened by their belonging to the small yet powerful professional *corps*. It is contended that family, educational and professional socialization produces an administrative elite which is remote, cut off from the bulk of the nation and insensitive to its aspirations: hence the critical allusions to its 'arrogance' and 'inhumanity'. It is further contended that socialization tends to produce amongst the elite certain shared attitudes, a common language and technocratic outlook, a widely accepted mystique. A profile of the typical French civil servant emphasizes his attachment to the values of pragmatism, efficiency, scientific rationalism and apoliticism. He believes in the strong State, the purveyor of social justice and of progress, and lauds the virtues of State interventionism which prevents public poverty amidst private affluence.

Such generalizations must be treated with scepticism, for it is questionable whether the top civil servants share a common *weltanschauung*. Social and educational backgrounds may be powerful socializing agents, but they may push towards diversity as well as uniformity: the essence of the training at the ENA and the École Polytechnique is that it fosters amongst the students both a certain uniformity of approach (if not of outlook) and a sense of rivalry (if not of enmity) which is rooted in the mercilessly competitive nature of the schools. Moreover, social and educational influences may be offset by professional pressures: the *Énarques* tend to become generalists whilst most 'X' (as students of the École Polytechnique are called) become technical experts (at least initially) and they are distributed amongst the *corps*, each of which has its own peculiar rites, norms and prejudices. Other variables also complicate the picture. The attitudes of a one-legged Protestant transvestite bourgeois *Énarque* may be shaped as much by his physical deformity, his religion or his sexual abnormality as by his social origins or his professional training. Furthermore, even if it were possible to extrapolate from an analysis of social, educational and professional background to the construction of a syndrome of shared beliefs, it would still be necessary to demonstrate that shared *beliefs* lead to shared *behaviour*. There may be no relation between the two, because top civil servants (like members of every other group) differ in courage, ambition, assiduity and a whole range of other personal characteristics. Sociological determinists too readily confuse backgrounds, beliefs, attitudes and conduct in a comforting, yet dangerously misleading, general equation. Ezra Suleimann has shown that attitudes amongst top civil servants *do* differ, and that one of the determining factors is the function or role they perform. Furthermore, a change of function may lead a top civil servant to adopt different attitudes: a member of a *grand corps* who takes up a position in a ministry frequently adopts the norms and prejudices of his new home (indeed it may be an essential prerequisite of success to do so); prefects who are promoted to the Council of State are often zealous – and knowledgeable – critics of the administrative malpractices of their erstwhile colleagues; a member of the litigation (*contentieux*) section of the Council of State who joins a ministerial private staff may shed his professional obsession with legal niceties to become usefully inventive in circumventing the tiresome supervision of the Council (he is often recruited to the *cabinet* to do precisely that). In short, the *role* played by the civil servant may be as important as his family, class, educational and professional background in fashioning his behaviour and conduct. Finally, it should be added that too often top civil servants are seen as representative of the whole administration. In fact, they represent a small and admittedly decisive part of the administration, but there are many influential civil servants further down the hierarchy who come from totally different social and educational backgrounds.

In truth, the French civil service is riddled with cleavages, which is scarcely surprising given its highly fragmented nature. It is possible to discern four main groups involved in decision-making: the *grands corps*; the technical *corps*; the top-ranking civil administrators; the middle-ranking bureaucrats.

Members of the *grands corps* and the technical *corps* are often very mobile: they move in and out of their *corps* to man key posts in the ministries and the ministerial *cabinets*. Members of the other two groups generally remain in one ministry, frequently in the same division, forming veritable administrative closed shops. Whilst it is generally possible to pinpoint the level of *responsibility* for decisions it is not always possible to identify the *effective* points of decision-making. Top-ranking civil servants are often like politicians: they are absorbed in presiding the work of others, in arbitrating between the ideas and views of subordinates, and in time-consuming ceremonies. They are also like politicians in that they tend to spend only relatively short times in particular posts: divisions are seldom headed by the same man for more than three years.

Cutting across hierarchical divisions are the differences between the generalists and the specialists, the bureaucrats and the technocrats. The four main decision-making groups are distributed among different ministries (and different divisions within those ministries) and their local field services, the *grands corps* and the technical *corps*, and the so-called missionary administrations such as the Planning Commissariat and the DATAR. Between the various administrative organs there is plenty of scope for conflict, and the evidence suggests that such conflict exists. Conflicts *between* the ministries are inevitable, as each tries to defend its own interests and departmental viewpoint. There is continuous struggle between the Finance Ministry, the watchdog of the nation's wallet, and most of the spending ministries. Conflicts between other ministries arise over specific issues which crystallize deeper commitments. The Ministry of the Interior has clashed with the short-lived Ministry of Penal Reform (which it accused of wanting to build 'three-star hotels' instead of prisons to house delinquents), with the Ministry of Justice over the use of the law as an instrument of political repression, and with the Ministry of Health over the treatment of drug addicts. There have also been conflicts between the Ministries of Education and of Defence over the deferment of national service for *lycée* students, between the Ministries of *Équipement* and of Cultural Affairs over the destruction of ancient monuments, between the Ministries of the Environment and Industry over river pollution. Disputes between the ministries can paralyse action: the law of 30 December 1968 on the exploration of the continental shelf emerged only after two years of acerbic wrangling between the Ministries of Posts and Telecommunications, of Transport and of the Navy.

Conflicts *within* the ministries are no less frequent, for most ministries resemble the Education Ministry which has been likened to a highly compartmentalized and hierarchical 'monstrous machine' (Catherine Arditti). The Finance Ministry has been described as 'a federation of autonomous divisions' often physically separated (there are no fewer than thirty-four annexes of the Ministry in Paris): 'it is easier to turn a soldier into a sailor than it is to transfer from one of the Finance Ministry's divisions to another' (Jean Monthen). Conflicts within a ministry may be muted and courteous, disguised by affable courtesy: such is normally the case in the Foreign Office which is said to be divided between a pro-Gaullist 'clan' – nationalist, in favour of *rapprochement* with the Soviet bloc and pro-Arab – and an anti-Gaullist 'clan' – more Atlanticist, pro-American, pro-European and pro-Israel. Conflicts between the *grands corps* and the technical *corps* and the rest of the administration often spring from resentment when the latter see the former being appointed to key administrative posts outside their *corps*. The administration also dislikes the pettifogging supervision (and condemnation) of its activities by the Council of State, the Court of Accounts and the Financial Inspectorate. Between the missionary administrations and the rest of the administration there is frequent dissension. Many of the missionary administrations were formed originally to solve specific problems requiring urgent action, but they have tended to become permanent bodies and have taken on many of the character-istics of traditional administrations. The traditional administration not unnaturally resents having lost many of its interesting tasks to the missionary administrations, and professional rivalry is often compounded by policy differences. The Finance Ministry has always cast a jaundiced eye on the work of the Planning Commissariat whose policies it suspects as financially dubious and intrinsically inflationary. It has done much to undermine the faith in the Five Year Plans, and where it has been unable to beat the planners it has duplicated their work: the Economic Intervention and Forecasting Services were founded at the *rue de Rivoli* (the home of the Finance Ministry) to parallel those of the Planning Commissariat. The work of the DATAR also elicits an obstructive animosity in certain administrative quarters. In 1976, for example, it came into conflict with the Ministry of Industrial Affairs over allowing Digital Equipment Corporation, an American computer firm, to set up a factory at Annecy. The DATAR was in favour, arguing that it would bring jobs to an area of high unemployment, but the ministry was against, since it supported a policy of protecting the home computer industry. In December 1976, the Government found in favour of the ministry. The firm decided to install its factory in Germany.

Rivalries between the *corps* are a normal feature of French administrative life, and they sharpen when there are disputes over respective areas of influence and competence. Particular *corps* believe that certain sectors or posts or policy areas are their 'reserved domains' (for instance, the Financial Inspectors view the banking sector and the *corps* of Mining Engineers the energy field as preserves), and 'driven by the monopolistic logic' (Jean-Claude Thoenig) do all they can to protect their domain against the marauding activities of other *corps*.

The French administration is fragmented and stratified and is riddled with internal tensions and dissensions. Some co-ordination is introduced by the highly mobile *grands corps* and technical *corps* which, through their corporate links and personal friendships overcome some of the compartmentalization of the administration. Co-ordination is also attempted by the ministerial *cabinets*, by the horizontally organized missionary administrations and by the interministerial committees which bring together politicians and their principal administrative advisers. But such methods are clearly inadequate, and their inadequacy has been often demonstrated: the notorious inability to control the money supply or the equally notorious ability to build science faculties for non-existent students are but two examples. Corporate, functional and ideological fiction often hampers effective co-ordination, prevents the administration from acting as a corporate entity, and singularly diminishes its power.

The weakness of the administration is accentuated by its inability to carry out its many tasks

Paradoxically, the greater the area and depth of administrative intervention the more difficult may it be for the administration effectively to intervene. It is not only the poor *administrés* but also the administrators who are inundated with endless streams of laws, decrees, circulars and instructions. The local social security services, for example, received no fewer than 180 detailed texts from the ministry in Paris in the first two months of 1974: like the rest of the administration it is overworked and undermanned. In theory, the implementation of laws and decrees gives the administration wide discretionary powers. In practice, however, the administration is often so overwhelmed by the sheer magnitude of its tasks that it is incapable of doing anything but keeping a minimum of administrative order. Ehrard Friedberg has shown that the economic intervention service of the Finance Ministry, which is at the very centre of French economic decision-making, is so overburdened with work that it is materially impossible for it to deal in any depth with the mass of matters which clamour for its attention. The rest of the Finance Ministry – the favourite target of the administration-haters – is so weighed down by its purely managerial and administrative tasks that it has little time to take initiatives or think creatively. And Thoenig's perceptive study of urban development policies in France confirms that, whilst the State administration has numerous weapons at its disposal, it is often physically incapable of wielding them. The administration – the modern Leviathan – on closer analysis resembles a land-locked whale: impressive, yet more dangerous in appearance than in reality.

The French civil service is undoubtedly very politicized but the nature of that politicization has been over-simplified

The civil service in France has always been more overtly 'political' than those of other European States. It is equally true, as Guy Drouout shows in his study of the *député-fonctionnaire*, that there has been a steady increase in the number of Deputies issuing from the civil service – from 17 per cent at the end of the Third Republic to 20 per cent at the end of the Fourth to 35 per cent at present But his study also reveals that the proportion had been higher in earlier régimes: a majority of the Deputies of the July Monarchy (1830–48) also held civil service appointments.

The phenomenon of politicization is not peculiar to the present régime. Nor should its extent be exaggerated: many Deputies may be ex-civil servants, but the vast majority of civil servants never become Deputies. Nor is it true that the politicization always works in favour of the Government: the administration is no docile creature manipulated by an unscrupulous Right-wing coalition. It may be conceded that the Government appoints no declared political opponents to politically sensitive civil service posts (such as Prefect or Ambassador) and it must be admitted that most civil servants appreciate the general stability of the Fifth Republic (although so, too, do most Frenchmen). However, most officials who presently hold politically compromising posts are not necessarily friends of the Right: there are well-known Left-wingers in the prefectures, the diplomatic corps and the ministerial *cabinets*. Even amongst those who are amicably disposed towards the Right, sympathy is tempered by prudent scepticism. In a country which has seen so many political upsets (and administrative purges) it is scarcely surprising that an expectant opportunism suffuses the entire civil service.

Civil service sympathy for Governments of the Fifth Republic has not always been apparent. The leaking of confidential and damaging reports (the Lamoureux Report on the Côte d'Azur, the Albert Report on Paris, the Report on the progress of the Five Year Plan which was leaked during the 1974 presidential election) and of ministerial tax returns reveal a degree of animosity on the part of certain civil servants. The Council of State opposed General de Gaulle's unconstitutional referenda of October 1962 and April 1969, and added insult to injury by leaking its hostile – and 'secret' – comments to the press. As a result it earned the reputation in opposition circles of being 'a bastion of Republican defence', a severe and televised rebuke from the irritated President of the Republic, an official Government protest, two venomous paragraphs in General de Gaulle's *Mémoires* and the lasting enmity of diehard Gaullists. Sympathy and even support for the Left is widespread in the top civil service and predominant in the lower echelons (where the decisions are often made and where the scope for obstruction is unlimited). Jean-François Kesler has shown that the *Énarques* are more likely than the rest of the population to vote for the Left, whilst a poll taken just before the second ballot of the 1974 presidential elections amongst the 600 students of the École Polytechnique gave Mitterrand a slight majority against Giscard d'Estaing (an ex-student of the School). Whilst the Communist Party attracts few civil servants (although there is a small group of Communist *Énarques*), the Socialist Party of Mitterrand has drawn widespread and often active support: amongst Mitterrand's close lieutenants is a bevy of young, able and ambitious civil servants.

Government supporters have constantly complained about the political malevolence of the civil service. A Right-wing Deputy, Destremeau, claimed that during the early years of the Fifth Republic there was 'a semi-sabotage of governmental decisions in several ministries', and in 1976 several ministers, including Poniatowski, the Minister of the Interior, denounced politically motivated tax inspectors who were wrecking the Government's electoral chances by excessive zeal in collecting taxes. Whilst admitting that an element of paranoia underpins most politicians' assessments of civil servants, it must be conceded that the suspicions harboured by successive Governments of the Fifth Republic about the political sentiments and fidelity of the civil servants are not totally unfounded.

Controls on the administration of the Fifth Republic have remained intact and in some respects have even been strengthened

The barrage of internal control mechanisms includes a network of Administrative Tribunals, headed by the Council of State and the Mediator's Office (founded in the autumn of 1972 and a pale version of the Ombudsman), which are judicial bodies with the task of judging alleged administrative abuses against the citizen. The Court of Accounts and the Financial Inspectorate look into the financial irregularities of the administration. The efficacy of such controls has frequently been called into question. The Court of Accounts, for example, has displayed extreme timidity in enquiring into politically explosive affairs. Concorde, the creation of the petrochemical complex, at Fos, the *Plan Calcul* which was supposed to give France an independent computer industry, and the building of the giant meat-marketing complex at La Villette in the Paris outskirts were all examples of extraordinary financial profligacy: Concorde is a commercial disaster, Fos is an economic and ecological catastrophe, the *Plan Calcul* collapsed completely, and La Villette – one of the great scandals of the régime – cost the State ten times the original estimate and is now an unused desolation. Yet the Court of Accounts contented itself with criticism only after the scandals broke: like the army of Offenbach, its courage was restored when it was clear that it could reach the battlefield only after the battle was over. The Council of State is also under a cloud because many civil servants treat its judgements with casual disdain: at present, a third of its decisions are never executed by culpable officials. Nevertheless, the significance of internal controls should not be understated. The average civil servant dislikes the quibbling enquiries of the *corps de contrôle* and fear the adverse publicity given to his administrative peccadillo.

Perhaps even more important than the *post hoc* internal control mechanisms are the external political controls over the administration. Parliamentary control of the Executive has undeniably weakened, but Members of Parliament still keep a keen eye on the activities of the administration. It may also be argued that with the reinforced Executive power of the Fifth Republic the power of the administration should, logically, decline. Governments of the Fifth Republic, unlike those of the previous régime, can count on a strong and disciplined majority in Parliament, and ministers are no longer obliged to spend most of their time in purely political activities, shoring up Governments that are fated to early collapse. In spite of a few notorious exceptions, ministers of the Fifth Republic have much more time to run their departments and, with the help of their *cabinets*, more closely to supervise the administration. Nor has the vigilance of the pressure groups weakened under the present régime. The complex relationship between the State and the groups is dealt with in a following chapter, but it is a banality worth underlining at this point that the administration is dependent upon others to ensure the drafting, the smooth passage and the implementation of policies. The administration often needs the groups not only for their expertise but also because they help to legitimize decisions. Paradoxically, increased State interventionism makes the administration both more potentially powerful and more vulnerable to strategically placed monopolistic groups: ultimately, the danger for the French administration may spring not from its overweening power but from its exposure to powerful groups which sap its moral integrity.

The administrative State: some concluding remarks

The administration, as the principal agent of a State which has permeated most sectors of life, enjoys great *potential* power in the formulation and the implementation of social and economic policies. That power is, however, less great than the critics contend. In the first place it should be remembered that the State may be ubiquitous but it is not omnipresent: there are areas of decision-making which the administration is unable or unwilling to penetrate. These 'political no-go areas' are discussed in Chapter 8. In many other areas the administration may obstruct policies, but not indefinitely, and it is rarely either able or willing to adopt an initiating or creative role: it reacts rather than acts, it is passive rather than active. Its power is also limited by its unwieldiness and its proverbial inefficiency, and its effectiveness is impaired by its fragmented and divisive nature. Moreover, internal administrative controls and external political pressures circumscribe its freedom of action. Between its *potential* and *alleged* power and its *effective* power there is a gulf, and it is perhaps the realization of that gulf which explains 'the crisis and the malaise of the civil service' which is so frequently referred to in France. The Fifth Republic has altered very little in its attempts to reform the administration: it is no more coherent, no more efficient, no more co-ordinated and no more subordinate to the political masters of the régime than the administration of the Fourth Republic. The intentions of the reformers have been subverted by the weight of traditional habits and prejudices. Many top civil servants continue to take refuge in a passive and prudent careerism and are characterized by unhealthy susceptibilities about personal and corporate privileges. Their subordinates cling to entrenched habits, deify precedent, resist change and obstruct the inconvenient: an epic lethargy and a legendary inefficiency marks the lower ranks of the administration. Certain officials in parts of the administration do enjoy considerable influence but they are by no means alone in the complex tissue of decision-making, and the price of their power is dependence upon, and cooperation with, the other decision-makers.

5 The French Parliament: impotence and potential power?

One of the most striking characteristics of the Fifth Republic has been the rapid decline of Parliament. Indeed, it is argued that from its omnipotent position during the Third and Fourth Republics Parliament has now been relegated to a position of total impotence. Such a view is, however, misleading. On the one hand, the decline of the French Parliament dates not from 1958 but from well before that date. On the other hand, whilst not denying the continuing decline of the French Parliament, its weakness should not be exaggerated. Moreover, whilst the body may have been weak since the commencement of the present régime, its power in changed political circumstances may prove to be very great

Most French historians distinguish four phases in the evolution of parliamentary power in their country. The first period, from 1814 to 1877, from the Restoration of the Monarchy to the establishment of 'the Republican Republic', was characterized by the sporadic but apparently inexorable extension of parliamentary power: Parliament asserted itself with increasing success against the Executive. During the second phase, from 1877 to 1914, parliamentary supremacy was firmly entrenched, and established as an integral and essential ingredient of the Republican tradition. The Government during this period was reduced to the role of a mere committee whose main task was the implementation of decisions made in Parliament. Within Parliament individual members exercised great power, and because of weak party discipline were able to create havoc with Governmental proposals; at budget times they would harass unstable governments into concessions in favour of their constituencies. Parliamentary initiatives delayed the adoption of the budget and all too often compromised the balance between revenue and expenditure. It was small wonder that one critic (Gaston Jèze) could describe the parliamentary assemblies as 'wasteful, incompetent and irresponsible'.

The third period, from 1918 to 1958, from the victorious conclusion of the First World War to the collapse of the Fourth Republic, was marked by the progressive decline of Parliament. The impact of foreign and colonial wars, of military occupation, of the growing weight and technicality of legislation, and the rise of well-organized pressure groups all had their impact in reducing Parliament's capacity to initiate or effectively to control legislation. After the First World War, important policies in foreign affairs, defence and economic planning often completely escaped parliamentary attention. A significant step in the demise of Parliament dates from 1934, when Parliament formally granted the Government the right to legislate by the use of decrees. Unfortunately, whilst recognizing a Government's right to legislate in its place, Parliament nonetheless persisted in calling into question the political responsibility of the Executive. Powerful and highly specialized parliamentary committees harassed hard-pressed ministers, thus earning themselves the reputation of being 'alternative' or 'counter' Governments. A number of ingenious constitutional devices were introduced in 1946 to reinforce governmental authority but proved ineffective: the habits of generations proved stronger than the machinations of the well-intentioned framers of the Constitution.

During this period 1918–58 Parliament slowly abdicated many of its rights and was increasingly by-passed in significant policy areas. Yet parliamentary sovereignty continued to be recognized in a number of important ways: Parliament had complete control over its own timetable; it decided its own rules and own agenda; it had the right to legislate in any domain it wished and that right was, in theory, exclusive to itself (although it did, in practice, often delegate its right); it enjoyed a monopoly in supplying ministerial personnel; its members enjoyed a position of power and prestige at the local level. Moreover, Parliament constantly paralysed Governments by frequently denying them its support: in other words, Parliament was a declining yet ultimately all-powerful body, whilst Governments could be powerful in certain circumstances but were generally short-lived. In those conditions neither Parliament nor the Government was really powerful. It was said that by 1958 government was being carried out not *by* Parliament but essentially *through* Parliament.

The fourth and final phase in the decline of Parliament began in 1958 when the framers of the Constitution put Parliament in its largely subordinate place. That decline has been accelerated as the result of several political and personal factors. The Constitution of the Fifth Republic places the French Parliament in an ambivalent position, since it enunciates the principle of governmental responsibility to Parliament and at the same time very seriously reduces the power of Parliament. In other words, Parliament is constitutionally weakened yet the Government remains dependent upon its goodwill for its survival. The weakening of the French Parliament corresponded to the Gaullists' wish to put an end to the *régime d'assemblée* which they had so persistently criticized during the Fourth Republic. The principal architect of the French Constitution was Michel Debré, the intransigent and inflexible Minister of Justice, whose basic constitutional philosophy was outlined in his books *Refaire la France* and *Ces Princes qui nous gouvernent* and in his important speech to the Council of State in August 1958. His analysis was rooted in a somewhat obsessive reading of French history. This unrepentant Jacobin believed that France was profoundly divided on a large number of problems and that those divisions were reflected in an unstable multi-party system. As a result, no Government could ever rely on stable and disciplined party support in Parliament. It was essential, in those circumstances, to create institutional mechanisms capable of protecting the Government in its relations with Parliament: new constitutional arrangements should, therefore, compensate for the traditional absence of a parliamentary majority. Hence, the notion of *rationalized parliamentarianism*. In place of the *régime d'assemblée* of the Fourth Republic would be constructed a 'true' parliamentary régime, on British lines, in which Parliament could control but not destroy or supplant executive power. As a result, the Constitution of the Fifth Republic contains several provisions which deliberately seek to reduce the powers, the prerogatives and the prestige of the French Parliament.

The constitutional assault upon Parliament: the provisions

The framers of the Constitution wished to underline the new situation by a rigorous separation of executive and legislative powers

This separation was clearly inspired by General de Gaulle himself, and included in the Constitution against the advice of Michel Debré. De Gaulle had always insisted:

It goes without saying that executive power should not emanate from Parliament . . . or the result will be a confusion of powers which will reduce the Government to a mere conglomeration of delegations. . . . The unity, cohesion and internal discipline of the French Government must be held sacred, if national leadership is not to degenerate rapidly into incompetence and impotence.

But how, in the long run, can this unity, this cohesion and this discipline be maintained if executive power is the emanation of the very power it ought to counter-balance. . . .?

The result was Article 23 of the Constitution, which makes membership of the Government incompatible with that of Parliament. If a Member of Parliament is appointed to a ministerial post he must give up his parliamentary seat to a replacement (*suppléant*) who is elected at the same time as himself. Moreover, the minister gives up his seat for the remainder of the legislature: thus if he is appointed minister just after a general election he may have to wait another five years before entering Parliament again. It was hoped that this provision would put a brake on the undignified scramble for ministerial portfolios which had characterized previous Republics, for, it was argued, Deputies would think twice before sacrificing their parliamentary seats. It was also felt that temperamental ministers would hesitate before resigning (thus causing a government crisis) if they had no seat in Parliament to go back to. This so-called 'incompatibility rule' was seen, therefore, as a factor which would make Governments more stable. But the rule has been too much for most ministers. After officially resigning from Parliament they still keep both feet firmly in their constituency which they continue to visit and assiduously to nurse. A member of their private staff is always given the task of keeping a keen eye on constituency affairs. Many ministers (and not the least, since they include such men as Chaban-Delmas and Chirac) on quitting the Government have insisted that their replacements resign which then leaves the seat empty. In the ensuing by-election the minister stands as a candidate in the hope of being re-elected. It has even been claimed that certain replacements provide their Members of Parliament who are possible ministers with un-dated letters of resignation. Those rare replacements who have obstinately refused to resign have been denounced for their treasonable behaviour. The spirit if not the letter of the Constitution has been constantly violated; Article 23 has become a constitutional absurdity, and the present President of the Republic is not alone in wishing to abolish it. The breakdown of the incompatibility rule was inevitable, since French politicians feel deprived without a local power base. It is instructive that even most ministers chosen from outside Parliament strive to find a constituency in the following general election (only André Malraux, Minister of Culture, translated his disdain for Parliament into a wish never to become one of its members). They feel, not without justification, that a parliamentary seat gives them added political prestige and weight in negotiating with their ministerial colleagues and with their own ministries.

If the attempt to separate legislative and executive powers has been less than a success, the same cannot be said of the panoply of other constitutional measures which were designed to ensure the docility of Parliament.

There are now severe restrictions on the time Parliament is allowed to meet

Previous Republican constitutions guaranteed a *minimum* period for parliamentary sessions, whilst that of the Fifth Republic imposes a *maximum* period. Parliament now meets only twice a year in ordinary session, for a total of not more than five and a half months a year. Special sessions are limited to a fortnight, and only on the basis of a specifically defined agenda. The purpose of these provisions was to put an end to the lengthy parliamentary sessions of the Third and Fourth Republics. But parliamentary sessions are now so short that the Government often has difficulty in pushing through its own legislation, and the end of each session is characterized by an undignified scramble to complete governmental business. As a result the efficacy of parliamentary control has diminished as the disgruntlement of Members of Parliament has grown, and the quality of legislation has undeniably suffered.

Severe restrictions have been imposed on law-making by Parliament

Article 34 of the Constitution defines the area of law (i.e. legislation which has to be passed by Parliament) in two ways:

Parliament determines the rules on a range of specified subjects, which include fundamental liberties, civil status and civil rights, liability to taxation, conscription, penal procedures and electoral laws.

It also lays down the general principles and the framework of laws relating to another range of subjects, comprising local government, education, property rights, trade union law, social security and finance Bills. The detailed implementation of such laws is left to the Government.

Any area not specified in the above two categories is left entirely to the discretion of the Government. The constitutional restriction of the law-making domain represents the most important single breach of the principle of parliamentary sovereignty, and contrasts sharply with the British situation which Michel Debré was apparently trying to emulate.

The Government has been given effective control of the timetable and agenda of both Houses of Parliament

The Government can thus give priority to its own measures. In fact, it is now the President of the Republic who informs the Government, by letter, of the legislative programme of Parliament. The Executive has not been very generous in its dealings with Parliament, especially in allowing time for full-scale debates on politically important or contentious issues: between 1959 and 1974, for example, the National Assembly, the major political forum of the Fourth Republic, held full-scale debates on an average of only ninety-one days a year. Again, unlike the British situation the Opposition to the Government has absolutely no right at all to have time in which it can determine the nature of parliamentary business.

The committee structure of the National Assembly has been drastically altered

During the Fourth Republic there were nineteen permanent highly specialized committees, each composed of forty-four prominent members (although, in practice, they were often controlled by a much smaller group) and each zealously controlling the activities of a particular ministry (a zeal which was often heightened by the Chairman coveting the portfolio he was controlling). Ministerial bills were often savaged beyond recognition at the committee stage. These 'permanent anti-governments' of the Fourth Republic have now been replaced by six much larger committees:

Four committees of 61 members
Defence
Finance
Foreign affairs
Legal and administrative matters

Two committees of up to 121 members
Production and trade (which includes agriculture, fishing, public
    works, town planning)
Cultural, social and family affairs

These parliamentary committees are much less specialized and more unwieldy than the smaller committees of the previous régime, and are far less capable of detailed interference in governmental legislation. They were further weakened by another important innovation: under the Fifth Republic, Parliament has to debate the text of the Government's bill and not the one emanating from the appropriate committee. The present situation is recognized by many to be totally unsatisfactory. There is too much legislation for too few committees, and there have been demands recently (including one from the Speaker of the National Assembly) to increase their number.

The financial powers of Parliament have been severely curtailed

Article 40 of the Constitution and the Organic Law of 2 January 1959 stipulate that, without the consent of the Government, Deputies may propose no increase in expenditure or reduction in taxation through a private member's Bill. Governments under the Fifth Republic have also been given tight control over finance Bills: this is to prevent the previous practice of Deputies holding up the Budget in order to extract concessions from a desperate and precarious Government. Parliament is now given a total of seventy days to debate and vote the Budget, and after that the Government has the right to impose it by Ordinance. In fact, no Government has invoked this provision since the foundation of the Fifth Republic, although it might prove to be a useful weapon in the future.

Parliament's power to force a Government from office has been severely limited

In fact, the Government has to resign in only three sets of circumstances:

If a vote of censure is carried in the National Assembly. The means by which such a motion must be passed were clearly designed to help the Government. A motion of censure has to be moved by a tenth of the Members who, if the motion fails, are then precluded for the remainder of the parliamentary session from moving another motion of censure. This can be a severe restriction: from 1968 to 1973, for example, Opposition Deputies represented only three-tenths of the total membership of the National Assembly. Deputies have to wait for forty-eight hours before voting on the motion: during this interval tempers may cool and the Government may make promises or threats to convince the waverers. In the vote of censure, only votes in favour are counted, abstentions being considered as favourable to the Government, this provision being based on the dubious yet convenient assumption that those not against the Government are for it Finally, for a motion of censure to be carried it must be voted by a majority of the total membership of the House and not simply a majority of those present: thus absentees join the abstainers as being considered to be not against the Government. The vote of censure is thus difficult to carry; in the eighteen years between January 1959 and January 1978 only twenty-five were moved, with only one, in October 1962, being successful.

The Government must also resign *if Parliament rejects its statement of general policy*, but only when it has specifically pledged its responsibility. A simple majority of the National Assembly suffices in these circumstances. The only time a Prime Minister is likely to pledge governmental responsibility on a statement of general policy is when it is sure of its majority or when it may wish to provoke Parliament into forcing its resignation. Debré (October 1959), Pompidou (April 1962) and Chirac (June 1974) pledged the responsibility of their Governments, but Pompidou (April 1966), Couve de Murville (May 1968), Chaban-Delmas (June 1969) and Barre (October 1976) refused to do so.

The Government may be forced from office *by the rejection of any Bill which it has made an issue of confidence*. But once the Government has made it an issue of confidence, the Bill is automatically carried unless a censure motion can be prepared and carried in the circumstances outlined above. This device, which was used by President Giscard d'Estaing when pushing through his Bill on direct elections to the European Parliament in June 1977, had been employed on eleven previous occasions since 1959.

Although Deputies and Senators may propose amendments to any Bill the Government may, at any time, insist on a single vote on its own text

'Its own text' is the whole Bill with only such amendments as the Government has proposed or accepted. In other words, the Government can insist on Parliament making a package vote (*vote bloqué*), thus preventing the latter from destroying the coherence of a Bill by amendments related to specific points. This provision was invoked regularly in the early years of the Fifth Republic (twenty-three times between 1959 and 1962, and sixty-six times between 1962 and 1967), but the procedure has been losing favour because Deputies of the Government coalition have expressed their intense dislike of it.

The Government has the right, under Article 38 of the Constitution, to ask Parliament to authorize it to legislate by ordinance for a specific period on any subject normally requiring laws voted in Parliament

The Constitution thus formalizes the traditional practice of Parliament allowing the Government to legislate by way of *décrets-lois*. Since 1959, this right has been requested and accorded on nine occasions, although its use is increasingly infrequent (only twice since April 1967). The legislation concerned involved the maintenance of order in Algeria, the implementation of provisions of the Treaty of Rome, agricultural problems, social security, and social problems such as alcoholism and prostitution.

The constitutional measures outlined above constitute a powerful combination of constraints – what has been described as a 'rigid constitutional corset' which highly restricts parliamentary initiative and control. As Professor Goguel points out, the framers of the Constitution created a form of parliamentary régime without parliamentary sovereignty. But the constitutional weakness of Parliament has been aggravated by other factors which will now be considered.

The decline of Parliament: factors unconstitutional and extra-constitutional

The constitutional provisions outlined above have generally been interpreted in a highly restrictive manner. The Constitutional Council, which has the task of deciding disputes between the Executive and the Legislature over their respective rights, has generally been much more friendly towards the former than the latter. The Constitutional Council has been particularly ungenerous in defining the competence of Parliament to make law and in interpreting Parliament's financial powers, particularly during the early years of the Fifth Republic. On occasions, the powers of Parliament have been outrageously limited. For instance, in March 1960, following unrest in certain rural parts of France, a majority of the National Assembly requested a special session of Parliament to debate the agricultural policy of the Government. The Constitution seemed clearly to indicate that the President of the Republic was obliged to convoke Parliament. Yet General de Gaulle flatly refused, arguing, in essence, that the Deputies were acting out of fear and under pressure from rowdy and politically irresponsible pressure groups. The March 1960 incident was an exceptional, yet revealing incident: it demonstrated the first President's contempt for an institution to which he had never belonged and to which he attributed many of the errors of the previous régime.

A second factor which has led to a further weakening of Parliament has been the attitude of certain Prime Ministers towards it: Michel Debré treated it with barely disguised disdain; Georges Pompidou generally affected a benign detachment; Messmer was apprehensive whilst Chirac was petulant and impatient and Barre is patronizing, didactic and irritable. Only Chaban-Delmas (who had been a Member of Parliament for many years and President of the National Assembly for ten years before his appointment to the Premiership) showed any real sensitivity for the feelings of the representatives of the nation, but he improved merely the form rather than the substance of the relationship between the Government and Parliament. All Prime Ministers have displayed a steady determination to maintain the subordination of Parliament.

A third factor which helps to explain parliamentary weakness relates to the technical incompetence and physical incapacity of Parliament to deal with present legislation. The weight of modern legislation is daunting, and given the shortness of its sessions Parliament rarely has the time to control the Government's legislative programme. In the nine weeks of the spring session of 1975, for example, Parliament 'examined' 106 texts (sixty Government Bills, twenty-two private members' Bills and twenty-four treaties or international conventions). Important Bills are given only cursory attention; an important change in the rules governing the election of the President of the Republic was debated at one meeting – during the night – in April 1976. The problem is particularly acute in the financial field. Each year a Member of Parliament receives from the Government more than 120 separate documents relating to the annual budget: according to one exasperated Deputy the budgetary documents of 1977 weighed more than twenty kilos. If he is conscientious he would also have to wade through the hundreds of amendments proposed by private members as well as the reports of the Finance Committee. The problem is rendered worse by the technical and intricate nature of financial legislation. The budget, with all its far-reaching and complex financial and economic consequences and implications is increasingly based on a rationally quantifiable model (although the 'rationality' is often used to disguise some very irrational political choices), a set of forecasts (which have the genius of being invariably wrong) and a nice calculation of party and pressure group interests. The annual budget is a prodigious act of balancing, and if Members of Parliament upset one part of the structure the rest may collapse: in the words of Professor Lalumière, parliamentary amendments may 'disturb the internal coherence of the whole [budgetary] system'. In such circumstances, no Government is likely to look kindly upon parliamentary amendments.

The fourth extra-constitutional explanation for parliamentary ineffectiveness must be sought in the acceptance, toleration or indifference shown by Deputies towards certain abuses committed by the Government which have the effect of reducing parliamentary control. For instance, they have grumbled but have done little about the Government sending them badly drafted Bills well after the date officially allowed. Nor have they taken any action against last-minute changes in the parliamentary agenda which were made to suit the Government. They have also done little to insist on prompt answers to parliamentary questions. In the period 1970 to 1974 only 14 per cent of the questions requiring an oral reply from a minister were answered within the stipulated period. A question about the disgraceful Ben-Barka affair (a leader of the Left-wing opposition of a foreign country was kidnapped in broad daylight in Paris and then 'disappeared') which was put down in November 1965 received an answer (as the Government euphemistically described it) in May 1967. All too frequently Deputies have accepted, albeit with ill grace, that their questions will be treated with little respect. On 28 November 1975, for example, the Junior Minister for *Housing* gave perfunctory replies to parliamentary questions concerning atomic energy, the French car industry, the crisis in the textile industry, and the speed limits of heavy lorries. The appropriate ministers were not in Parliament, even though the rules stipulated that they should be.

It is in the all-important financial and economic domain that Parliament has not asserted the rights that belong to it. It is not only that Parliament's control over the numerous (over 600) public and semi-public enterprises is largely fictitious. That has always been the case. Nor is it that the Government seems totally unconcerned about keeping Parliament well informed about the nation's economic affairs: while Parliament was piously debating the aims of the Seventh Economic Plan in 1976 the Government was simultaneously taking other measures which ensured that many of those aims would not be realized. More disturbing is what the French call the process of 'debudgetization' which has steadily increased since 1963. That ugly but useful gallicism means that the Government has placed important items of public expenditure outside the official budgetary process (which is examined, however inadequately, in Parliament) and has transferred the responsibility for financing such items to bodies which, in practice, completely escape parliamentary control.

The fifth major source of the extra-constitutional weakness of Parliament is that body's inability or unwillingness to exploit the meagre means which remains at its disposal. Examples abound. Parliamentary questions requiring written replies are fully exploited (in 1973, for example there were more than 6500), but the potentially more interesting question times in Parliament are treated with disrespect by ministers and indifference by Deputies. Parliamentary debates only rarely atttact a good attendance: most debates are ill-attended and ineffective. On one afternoon during the debate on the very important regional reform of July 1972 only fourteen Deputies were in attendance.

Constitutional experts have pointed out that there exists a battery of devices which may seem very complex and over-ingenious but which would increase parliamentary control over financial legislation – if effectively used. Parliament has also been timid in setting up special *ad hoc* committees to examine designated public economic and financial corporations: although many such corporations badly need examination, Parliament has exercised its right to do so only twice since 1959. *Ad hoc* commissions of enquiry or control are rarely established if the subject proposed is likely to prove politically embarrassing to the Government. In 1975, Parliament itself refused requests to investigate, amongst other things, the exorbitant profits of the pharmaceutical industry, the creation of nuclear energy plants, and the pollution of the mouth of the Seine.

The sixth major source of weakness of the French Parliament lies in the scope of the subjects it considers. In foreign, European, colonial and defence matters, parliamentary control is derisory: in May 1977 even the very Gaullist Deputy Le Theule was moved to protest that Parliament was not even informed of vast changes in the organization of the French army. Even major domestic matters of great political sensitivity (such as the situation in Corsica, the agricultural riots in the South of France or the economic effects of the terrible drought of the summer of 1976) were not debated. It is depressing, yet revealing, to consider the role of Parliament during two of the great political crises of the Fifth Republic. The first was the Generals' *putsch* of April 1961, when Parliament was reduced to listening to a fifteen-minute message from the President of the Republic. The second was in May 1968, when Members of Parliament were the helpless spectators of events far beyond their control and comprehension.

Even in areas which fall within the law-making field of Parliament control is often derisory. Parliament is frequently by-passed, as the Government enters into direct contact with the pressure groups. Again, there is an embarrassing number of examples. One such occurred in November 1971 when the Government and the main civil service trades unions agreed a salary structure for the following year. Parliament which, in principle, fixes the expenditure on civil service staff was not associated with the agreement: it merely ratified the agreement when the 1972 budget was voted. Similarly, the financial compensation given to farmers badly hit by the summer drought of 1976 was agreed between the Government and the main agricultural interest groups: Parliament was left with the ungrateful ritual of ratifying the *fait accompli*.

The seventh extra-constitutional reason for the ineffectiveness of Parliament lies in its inability to control the implementation of even those measures which are voted in Parliament. In France, most laws are, in principle, implemented by a series of decrees (*décrets d'application*). In some cases (such as the law on early retirement benefits for ex-servicemen) the decrees have been so restrictive in their interpretation that they subvert the intentions of the framers of the law. In other cases, the decrees are promulgated very late. It was reported by Prime Minister Barre that, on average, six months after the promulgation of a law half the statutory instruments had still to be issued. Two years after the passage of the 1975 Handicapped Persons Act only ten of the expected forty decrees had been promulgated, and more than a year after Parliament voted the Secondary Education Act of June 1975 not one decree had been issued. Many decrees are never promulgated at all: certain parts of the Higher Education Act of 1968 remained, happily, a dead letter. Even when decrees are promulgated they are frequently ignored by the people responsible for implementing them. The Neuwirth Contraception Bill (so called after the Deputy responsible for guiding it through Parliament) was passed in December 1967, but it took seven years for it to be put into effect. Certain anti-pollution measures voted in Parliament in the

1960s are still awaiting implementation. Professor Debbasch has recently calculated that about a quarter of all laws passed in Parliament are never implemented.

It is in the economic and financial field that the gap between the texts voted in Parliament and the ensuing practice is most glaring. Ministries frequently change their budgets (voted in Parliament) in the light of changed circumstances or new pressures, and blandly ignore the criticisms made against them by the Court of Accounts, a worthy but toothless animal. Parliament has occasionally expressed its dissatisfaction and has recently made an official protest about the practice. But the protest was more symbolic than real: the practice is but another example of a widely tolerated abuse.

The final and most important reason for parliamentary submissiveness towards the Executive has been the existence, since 1959, of a pro-governmental majority in the National Assembly. For the first time in Republican history the Government has been able to count upon the support of a reasonably cohesive and disciplined party coalition with a majority in the National Assembly. And until the election of Giscard d'Estaing to the Presidency, there was a basic identity of views between the Presidency, the Government and the party which dominated the parliamentary coalition, since all three were Gaullists. The basic premise on which the Constitution was framed has proved totally unfounded: the elaborate institutional procedures devised by Michel Debré to compensate for the *lack* of a parliamentary majority, although ruthlessly exploited, have been rendered superfluous. The 'constitutional corset' was placed upon a body determined to diet on the political equivalent of grapefruit and grated carrots. The Government's majority in the National Assembly since 1959 has ranged from the uncomfortable (1959–62) and the precarious (1967–8) to the comfortable (1962–7, 1973–8, 1978—) and the massive (1968–73).

The parliamentary groups within the presidential coalition are co-ordinated by a liaison committee comprising the leaders of the constituent groups. Until mid 1976 the Prime Minister occasionally intervened within the committee to impose presidential directives. Since then, however, the Gaullists, who constitute the biggest single group in the pro-governmental coalition, have refused prime ministerial arbitration.

The Government not only enjoys a comfortable majority in both Houses, but it has used its majority to colonize all the key posts in the parliamentary committees: all the chairmanships and vice-chairmanships are now in the hands of Government supporters. Moreover, the ousting of Giscard d'Estaing from the chairmanship of the Finance Committee of the National Assembly in 1968 showed clearly that the Government would not tolerate even moderate opposition.

Some concluding remarks

The demise of the French Parliament may be attributed to a combination of factors – the constitutional restrictions, governmental ill-will, the obstructionism of the administration, the indifference of individual Members of Parliament, and the domination of Parliament by a disciplined pro-governmental coalition. Members of Parliament are reasonably well paid, and they enjoy free travel and free postal and telephone facilities. In 1970 they were granted an allowance to employ a secretary, in 1974 they were each given an office, and in 1976 they were each awarded a grant to employ a research assistant. But the facilities, although infinitely better than those at Westminster, do not compensate for the political frustration of parliamentary life: absenteeism, which is rife, is both a consequence and a cause of the decline of Parliament. That frustration has been expressed in all sections of Parliament: in July 1971, the chairmen of the six permanent committees of the National Assembly, all of whom belonged to pro-Government parties, formally and publicly protested about the way the Government treated Parliament.

The question arises: does Parliament serve any useful purpose at all? Is Parliament, as many critics have claimed, merely 'a talking-shop', an elaborate and costly institution whose main function is to rubber-stamp and legitimize Executive decisions? The claim needs to be modified somewhat. First, Parliament, however weak, continues to define the general parameters of Executive action: the President and the Government are aware of what is and is not acceptable to Parliament. So, too, are the leaders of the Opposition. When Prime Minister Chaban-Delmas announced his famous programme for liberalizing French society, François Mitterrand, the leader of the Socialists, expressed a justifiable scepticism: for Mitterrand, it was not the will of the Prime Minister which was in question but the willingness of his parliamentary supporters to back him. Those supporters who had been elected in the 'elections of fear' of June 1968 were deeply conservative and fearful of many of the reforms proposed by the Prime Minister: they had been elected not to reform society but to protect society against subversion. The President of the Republic, Pompidou, was more in tune with the political sentiments of the National Assembly, and his opposition combined with parliamentary reticence was sufficient to prevent the realization of the Prime Minister's programme. It is also clear that the reforming zeal of the present President of the Republic has to be tempered by an appraisal of what an essentially conservative Parliament will tolerate.

There have been several cases of a President of the Republic having to drop cherished ideas because of the probable opposition of Parliament. These include Pompidou's wish to reduce the presidential mandate from seven to five years, and Giscard d'Estaing's plan to modify the 'incompatibility rule' which debars ministers from retaining their seats in Parliament. The Government has also been forced by Deputies to withdraw proposed legislation before it even reached Parliament. In October 1968, for example, Prime Minister Couve de Murville had to abandon his plan to increase estate duties because of the hostility of prominent Gaullist Members of Parliament, and in November 1976, Prime Minister Barre withdrew a Bill designed to increase the powers of the European Assembly in Strasbourg because of Gaullist opposition.

The second way in which Parliament continues to control the Executive is through parliamentary questions and through amendments to the Government's Bills. In the two sessions of 1974, over 10000 questions (demanding written or oral replies) were put down by Deputies and Senators, and they proposed over 2000 amendments to the Government's proposed legislation. Recent changes which they demanded and obtained from the Government relate to matters such as the independence of the Comoro Islands (May 1975), the retirement age of high-ranking civil servants and judges (June 1975), the protection of forests in the neighbourhood of big towns (April 1976), the modification of the electoral law proposed by the Minister of the Interior (July 1976). In June and July 1976 they rendered an already anodyne capital gains tax, inspired by the President of the Republic, even less noxious to the capital gainers, and in May 1977 they extracted from the Government important concessions in the major Bill relating to local finances. In all these cases, the Government was forced to give ground to its backbenchers: the concessions in question are normally negotiated before the legislation in question reaches the floor of the House.

The third check on the Executive provided by Parliament is through its role as pedagogue and exposer of scandals. The permanent parliamentary committees have been responsible for sensitizing or mobilizing public opinion on issues as varied as civil service salaries, conscientious objection and conscription. The *ad hoc* Parliamentary Commissions of Enquiry and Commissions of Control have uncovered scandals relating to illicit publicity on television, the wholesale marketing system of meat in Paris, property speculation, the lucrative but unpatriotic practices of the major petrol companies in France, the notoriously inadequate telephone network, and some of the doubtful financial practices of the Dassault aircraft company in early 1977.

Parliament may be weak, and it may be, and frequently is, ignored by the Government, the administration and the pressure groups. Yet it remains one of the recruiting grounds for the political elite, the breeding ground of ministers. It is also a major forum for political debate. Furthermore, a major constitutional fact remains: the Government is responsible to Parliament. The passage of its programme is dependent upon the good will or tolerance of a majority of the National Assembly. Since 1958 that good will has existed, although the belligerent obstreperousness of the Gaullists, especially since mid 1976, is a reminder that an assertive Parliament can be very disruptive. A future victory of the Left (which is not totally inconceivable) would create a totally new situation. The President of the Republic would no longer be able to count upon the docility of Parliament, and in spite of all the elaborate constitutional devices he would be faced with a series of alternatives all fraught with political danger. Presidential primacy might well be imperilled by a body which, since the beginning of the Fifth Republic, has been one of its principal props. The apparently powerless Parliament might well become destructively powerful.

6 Presidential coalition-building

A President of the Republic must build two coalitions – one to elect him and the other to sustain him for the seven years following his election. Both require the mobilization of party support. If the founder and first President of the Republic had an especially jaundiced view of the parties – the propagators and perpetrators of French divisions – the effective functioning of his régime came increasingly to depend on their co-operation, good will and organizational capacity, especially after his departure in 1969. This chapter will examine the electoral support of the Presidency and will outline the party realignments which were provoked by the presidential elections of the Fifth Republic and then consolidated, not without difficulty, during the ensuing period of presidential office.

The electoral bases of presidentialism

The French electorate decided in the referendum of October 1962 to accept President de Gaulle's proposal that henceforth the President of the Republic be directly elected by universal suffrage. The new system requires a candidate to win more than half the votes cast at the first ballot in order to win; otherwise there is a second ballot two weeks later between the two best placed candidates of the first ballot. The conditions to be fulfilled in order to stand are surprisingly unrestrictive, and in May 1974 there were no fewer than twelve candidates. But a candidate to have any realistic chance of winning must have some backing, however reluctant or begrudged, from one or more of the major political parties. Candidates such as de Gaulle, Pompidou, Giscard d'Estaing and Mitterrand always entertained the fiction that their candidacies were 'above' the parties, but none ever spurned their official backing and organizational support.

In the December 1965 presidential elections General de Gaulle enjoyed the support of the Gaullist party and of the Independent Republicans, led by Giscard d'Estaing. Georges Pompidou's election in 1969 was facilitated by the backing given him by the Gaullist party, the Independent Republican Party and a small group of Centrists led by Jacques Duhamel who were shortly after to form a party called the Centre Démocratie et Progrès. His successor elected in May 1974, Giscard d'Estaing, won at the second ballot with the support of the three parties of Pompidou's coalition and also that of the Centre National des Indépendants et Paysans, the Centre Démocrate of Jean Lecanuet, the Radical Party of Jean-Jacques Servan-Schreiber and the Mouvement Démocrate Socialiste de France (a small group of anti-Communist Right-wing Socialists) – all the parties which form the basis of his present coalition.

Giscard d'Estaing was elected President of the Republic in May 1974 in the highest poll since the introduction of universal suffrage in 1848, and by only the narrowest of margins: at the second ballot he won 50·8 per cent of the votes against 49·2 per cent for Mitterrand, his Left-wing opponent. The high turn-out bore witness to the popularity of the contest and to the electorate's perception of its importance and significance. Traditional electoral geography was not upset as the result of the election: as expected, Giscard d'Estaing had his best results in the Catholic west (in the seven *départements* of that area he won more than three-fifths of the votes), in parts of the Massif Central (his native region of the Auvergne gave him a very comfortable majority), in the Catholic east (Alsace was his most single important bastion) and in the French capital where he won a majority in sixteen of the twenty *arrondissements*. His opponent carried the Mediterranean region, most of the south-west and all but one of the Pyrenean *départements* – the Midi Rouge lived up to its name – as well as in the densely populated 'red-belt' which almost encircles Paris, and in the arc of industrialized *départements* to the north-east of the capital. Not unexpectedly, Giscard d'Estaing won most of his support from those Right-wing electors who previously backed Pompidou (Table 5).

Table 5 *Voting in May 1974 by political preference*

Political preference	Giscard	Mitterrand
	(per cent)	
Communists	5	95
Non-Communist Left	12	88
Centrists	75	25
Pompidou's coalition	88	12

The break-down of the voting by socio-economic categories revealed no great surprises (see Appendix 9).

Compared with the electorate of Mitterrand that of Giscard d'Estaing was more feminine, older, more rural. Other polls revealed that it was better educated, wealthier and much more religious. The social and economic boundaries of the new President's electorate were also not only smaller than those of his two predecessors (General de Gaulle was elected with 55·2 per cent of the votes at the second ballot and Pompidou with 58·2 per cent also at the second ballot). It was also socially and economically more narrowly based: whilst a quarter of the working class voted for him it was a much smaller proportion than had voted for Pompidou and especially for de Gaulle. Compared with the population as a whole, Giscard d'Estaing enjoyed the support of a disproportionately large number of women, of elderly, upper-managerial, professional and commercial groups and of farmers. The accusation of the Left that his victory was that of 'elderly, wealthy and pious widows' was, of course, monstrously simplistic and morally suspect (for the democrat some voters are not more equal than others . . .). But it contained a grain of comfort for a Left which claimed the overwhelming backing of *la France jeune et travailleuse.*

The present President of the Republic is not only the leader of an electoral coalition. He is also, in part, its prisoner. If General de Gaulle often pointedly ignored his electorate (although his domestic policies did little to upset it) Pompidou ensured, by temperament and calculation, that his policies coincided with the conservative aspirations of his electoral base. Giscard d'Estaing is, however, faced with a dilemma. His electorate is even more conservative than that of Pompidou whilst he proclaims the need for creating a more socially just and more egalitarian society. The nature and composition of his electorate – what the French refer to as *les pesanteurs sociologiques* – is not conducive to reform, especially if that reform involves any redistribution of income. Faced with the reality of his electoral position this self-styled 'progressive conservative' has become progressively conservative – a tendency which has also been encouraged by most of the Deputies belonging to his party coalition.

The party bases of presidentialism

The Fifth Republic has seen a marked clarification of party politics, in spite of apparent complexity and confusion. New parties such as the United Socialist Party (PSU) have appeared, some – such as the MRP (an important Catholic centre party of the Fourth Republic) – have disappeared, some – the Radical Party, for instance – have dramatically declined, others – the Communist Party is the best example – have stagnated, whilst others – notably the Socialist Party – have grown. Matters have not been simplified by the constant changes of nomenclature (the Gaullists have changed their official party title no fewer than ten times since 1947 and five times since the beginning of the Fifth Republic), by the appearance of short-lived alliances and ephemeral coalitions and by proposed yet abortive fusions and federations, all with their own and often bewilderingly similar epithets. In the especially murky waters of centrist politics men have swum in and out of parties with the ease of experienced dolphins (or sharks as the uncharitable might contend). Finally, political dissensions within each party and highly publicized squabbles (often of a simulated nature) between coalition partners have added to the confusion. Yet behind the apparent confusion there lies one major trend – the almost inexorable pressurizing of the parties into a choice of one of two great coalitions. This process of so-called bi-polarization involved the emergence of a reasonably coherent and disciplined party coalition of the Right with the purpose of promoting, maintaining and defending governmental policies in the country and especially in Parliament – an essential prerequisite for the smooth functioning of the political institutions of the régime. This situation contrasts sharply with that of the Fourth Republic, which was plagued by the absence of a large and disciplined Right-wing party or coalition. The parties of the Left responded – albeit slowly – by creating their own uneasy alliance, based on electoral agreements and a legislative programme. The nature of the Left-wing alliance is the subject of the following chapter.

The parties of the centre tried for most of the early period of the Fifth Republic to avoid being squeezed into coalition with either the Gaullists or with the Left, hoping to remain an independent and autonomous force, but they have been progressively forced to make unpleasant choices. Most have gradually been converted to, or been absorbed by, the presidential coalition. Political mavericks – those independents who eschewed party labels and party discipline – have virtually disappeared from French politics. To save their parliamentary seats they, too, have moved into the presidential orbit.

Bipolarization of French political opinion may be seen in a number of ways, but especially at the electoral level: the parties of the presidential coalition used to present only one candidate, in most cases (405 of the 473 constituencies of metropolitan France in 1973) as from the first ballot; since 1967 the parties of the Left have negotiated a binding agreement which involves in every constituency the withdrawal for the second ballot of all but the best placed candidate of the Left at the first ballot. The number of straight fights between the presidential coalition and the Left-wing coalition at the second ballot is now always very high: in the 1967 elections, of the 398 seats contested at the second ballot, 335 (or 84 per cent) were straight fights, in 1968 269 of 316 (or 85 per cent) second-ballot contests were straight fights, in 1973 there were straight fights in 84 per cent (360 of the 430) constituencies, and in 1978 in 409 of 423 (or 96 per cent). At the local level, too, the pressure of bipolarization have been felt: at the first ballot of the March 1977 local elections, for example, the presidential coalition presented a single list in 200 of the 221 biggest town (over 30000 inhabitants) and the Left in 204 of those towns (compared with 60 of the 159 in 1965 and 124 of the 193 in 1971). Increasingly, too, as Bruce Campbell has shown, elections are *perceived* in polarized terms by the voters, and particularly by the younger voters whose experience has been shaped exclusively by the Fifth Republic.

The second manifestation of bipolarization is at parliamentary level where, in spite of some spectacular exceptions, each coalition of the Right and of the Left acts with greater unity. Finally, bipolarization may be seen at the doctrinal level: each coalition remains divided on some important questions but each, however unsuccessfully, has made an attempt to elaborate a programme acceptable to all the partners.

The reasons for the bipolarization of French politics under the Fifth Republic are many, and are related in a dynamic and dialectical fashion.

Bipolarization: the institutional factor

With the emergence of the Presidency as the focus of political power in France, it was imperative that political support be marshalled to provide it with the necessary underpinning at both electoral and parliamentary level. In a modern state, parties are essential for effective and democratic government. Their task is to fulfil two ultimately irreconcilable aims: first, they must reflect, articulate, sharpen, exploit and mobilize political differences rooted in social and economic cleavages, and, secondly, they must also strive to transcend

those political differences by aggregating political support to pro-
mote a measure of consensus, without which effective government is
difficult. Parties must also provide the political elite of the nation
and attempt to give some form of organized, coherent and disciplined
support for their Government once elected. During the early years of
the Fifth Republic, President de Gaulle, who claimed to be 'above
parties', excelled in disparaging remarks about them and spurned
their overt support. But both he and his successors soon recognized
that organized party support was vital to their own success.

The second important institutional change pushing towards bipolarization has been the diminution in the prestige and power of
Parliament and the corresponding decline in the efficacy of its
members. Voters are less obsessed with the individual effectiveness
of their Deputy (since his room for manoeuvre has been somewhat
reduced) and are more concerned about his willingness to play a role
as a defender or opponent of the Government. It is instructive that
Deputies who break with a party under the Fifth Republic are
invariably penalized in the following election.

Bipolarization: the electoral impetus

Each election of the Fifth Republic, with the notable exception of the
1969 presidential election, has become, to use Jean Charlot's expression, 'a great simplifying duel' between two well-organized coalitions.
The bipolarizing pressures are evident at presidential, legislative and
local level. The presidential system which allows only the two best-
placed candidates of the first ballot to proceed to the second has the
obvious consequence of polarizing choice. The effects of the legislative electoral system, whilst less obvious, have also provided an
impetus to bipolarization. The present two-ballot electoral system
based on single member constituencies requires a candidate to win
over half the votes cast to be elected at the first ballot, but only
more than any other candidate to win at the second. In most constituencies there is a second ballot: in 1978, for instance, only 68 of the
491 Deputies were elected at the first ballot. To go forward to the
second ballot a candidate must win at least $12\frac{1}{2}$ per cent of the votes
at the first ballot – a stipulation which eliminates a great number of
candidates, and automatically clarifies choice at the second ballot:
in 1973, when there was a 10 per cent barrier (it was raised to $12\frac{1}{2}$ per
cent in 1976), 1334 of the 3092 candidates were automatically eliminated from the election, and in 1978 over a third of the candidates.

The underlying principle of the system is that 'at the first ballot the voter chooses and at the second he eliminates': in other words, at the second ballot the electors are often being squeezed into voting for the candidate they find the least undesirable.

The present system can be grossly distorting and can lead to some very curious results: in 1958, for example, the Communist Party with 18·9 per cent of the votes cast at the first ballot won only 2 per cent of the seats in the National Assembly whilst the Gaullist party with only 1 per cent more of the votes than the Communists won 41 per cent of the seats; in 1958 the Socialist Party with 15·5 per cent of the votes won 39 seats whilst in 1962, when its share of the poll *dropped* to 12·7 per cent, it *increased* its number of seats to 64; in 1967 a Gaullist Deputy was elected with an average of 27 959 votes, a Socialist Deputy with an average of 47 756, a Centrist with 74 531 and a Communist with 119 466; in 1968 the presidential coalition won 358 seats with 46 per cent of the poll (or more than two-thirds of the seats with less than half the votes) whilst the parties of the Left shared only 91 seats in spite of polling 42 per cent of the votes. The distorting effects of the electoral system are due not only to the different sizes of constituencies (the biggest is nearly four times bigger than the smallest) but also to the prevailing state of party alliances. *The system undeniably penalizes isolated and unpopular parties.* At the second ballot, when most of the seats are at stake, a party needs friendly allies. This may best be illustrated by summarizing the performance of the Communist Party (Table 6).

The electoral impetus to coalition-building has also been felt at the local level. According to the rules of the electoral system in the major towns (those with over 30 000 inhabitants), a successful list of candidates for the local council must win half the votes at the first ballot or a plurality of the votes at the second. Moreover, in 1964 the law was altered to prevent *panachage*: lists cannot be altered between the ballots as the result of negotiated compromises between parties. A party has thus every interest in entering into a coalition to present a single list from the first ballot. If, for example, the Socialist Party and the Communist Party each presents its own list at the first ballot, they are precluded from presenting a joint list at the second. This clearly reduces the Left's chances of winning, particularly if the Right has been united since the first ballot: it is possible for the two parties of the Left to win 66 per cent of the second ballot votes – 33 per cent each – and still lose to a single Right-wing list winning only 34 per cent of the votes. The result of the system is to accentuate the tendency towards bipolarization resultant upon the functioning

Table 6 *The electoral performance of the Communists during the Fifth Republic*

Election	per cent votes on first ballot	Number of seats	Comment
November 1958	18·9	10	Very isolated and very unpopular. No electoral agreement with other parties of the Left.
November 1962	21·8	41	Party less isolated. Limited number of agreements with Socialists.
March 1967	22·5	72	Party less unpopular and less isolated. Agreement in all constituencies with non-Communist parties of the Left.
June 1968	18·8	33	Similar agreement to 1967 but Party feared and unpopular as result of May 1968 'events'.
March 1973	22·5	73	Similar agrement to 1967 and 1968 and Party less feared and unpopular than in 1968.
March 1978	20·6	86	Similar agreement to three previous elections.

of the presidential and legislative systems. As already noted, in the March 1977 local elections, the Left and the Right each presented coalition lists at the first ballot in more than 90 per cent of the major towns.

Finally, it should be noted that joint electoral activity has its own dynamic: it creates habits and forms attitudes. The more elections are fought by a coalition of parties the more credible that coalition becomes: it was clear, for example, that until the breakdown of negotiations between the parties of the Left in September 1 1977 that first ballot Socialist voters were becoming less and less reticent about voting Communist at the second ballot, and that was not surprising, for since 1967 they had fought several election campaigns together. But as the result of the strained relations after September 1977 as many as one Socialist voter in three refused to give their second-ballot vote for the Communists. Whilst electoral systems may be a factor which powerfully contributes to coalition-building, their effects cannot be divorced from the political context in which they function: they do not operate in a political vacuum. The presidential electoral system not only did not prevent the dislocation of the Left in June 1969 but may have exacerbated existing divisions. Nor, for example, did the legislative or local electoral systems dictate to the vacillating Socialists what kind of alliances should be contracted. The shape of party coalitions during the Fifth Republic has been determined not only by electoral pressures but also by party politicians with often conflicting perceptions of what constituted a credible, a winning or even a morally tenable coalition, and those perceptions have been formed by both rational and calculated assessment and by unconscious fears and prejudices. Furthermore, viable political coalitions can only be rooted in a deeper economic and social reality: no form of electoral system is likely to induce friendly and enduring co-operation between rural Catholic conservatives and urban atheist Communists. For a fuller appreciation of the nature of bipolarization under the Fifth Republic it is essential, therefore, briefly to examine the changes in French society.

Bipolarization: the societal factor

The existence of an unstable multi-party system during the Third and Fourth Republics was attributed to the effects of the electoral system (often some form of proportional representation which did little to discourage the proliferation and fragmentation of parties), to the workings of a parliamentary system (which gave power to individual Deputies who could flout party discipline and even break with his party in order to obtain constituency interests in the knowledge that he would not be penalized in the following election) and, most importantly, to the nature of cleavages in French society. France was viewed as a fragmented and 'conflictual society', rent by bitter ideological divisions. Its schismatic political culture was contrasted with the integrated, homogeneous and consensual political culture of its neighbour across the Channel. The title of an influential book by Jacques Fauvet, written during the Fourth

Republic, *La France déchirée*, summarized the views of most observers.

What were the nature of the basic divisions in French society? The first related to the nature of the régime itself: quite simply, there were many determined opponents not only of successive Governments but also of the régime itself. This was nothing new: no previous régime in French history had received anything approaching unanimous support. The Third Republic had to fight off challenges from monarchists, from imperialists, from the supporters of General Boulanger and from the followers of later Fascist and other extreme Right-wing movements, as well as from the Communists. The parliamentary democracy of the Fourth Republic was also under constant challenge from the extreme Left and the extreme Right. The first organized Gaullist mass movement, the RPF (Rassemblement du Peuple Français), presented a serious Right-wing threat to the régime from 1947 to 1952. And from the mid 1950s the régime was again under attack – this time from the Poujadist Movement (the UDCA), which in the 1956 general elections won more than $2\frac{1}{2}$ million votes and had 53 Deputies elected. The Movement was against the State, against Paris, Parliament, big business, industrialization, French withdrawal from Algeria and (especially) taxes. By 1958 it had collapsed, victim of the incompetence of its leaders and the incoherence of its programme. The Fourth Republic, whilst contending with these challenges from the Right, had also to combat an equally serious threat from the Left. The French Communist Party, after its withdrawal from Government in 1947, never ceased to be a threat to the stability and indeed the survival of the régime. Well organized and well supported (it always captured about a quarter of the votes in general elections), its tactics (at that time mostly dictated from Moscow) towards the Republic ranged from violent and bloody opposition (in the great political strikes of the winter of 1947–8) to a resentful truce.

French political society was, therefore, divided between the opponents and supporters of the parliamentary democracy of the Fourth Republic. But there were other important divisions in French politics. First, there was the clerical/anti-clerical dispute, a dispute which had overshadowed all others during the early years of the Third Republic and which continued to complicate and embitter the politics of the Fourth. The issue of State aid to Church schools crystallized deep-seated and ancient antagonisms, and rendered difficult co-operation between political parties which might have reached compromises on other issues. Many Socialists and Radicals, guardians of a long secular tradition, still viewed any deal with the Church as incompatible with the Republican ideal, and it is instructive that when the Socialist Prime Minister Guy Mollet entered into preliminary negotiations with the Vatican he had to do so by employing secret intermediaries. The liberal and often leftish Catholic MRP leadership was obliged on many issues to follow its less tolerant, less compromising and less leftish electorate.

The class conflict was as present in France as in other countries. Indeed, it has been argued that it was particularly acute in France, where trades unions were weak, bitterly divided and politically motivated (this was certainly true of the Communist-dominated CGT) and where there was a long tradition of anarcho-syndicalism. The absence of highly representative, well organized, united and disciplined trades unions deprived France of institutional channels which have the general effect of moderating the debate (by canalizing specific and conflicting demands into generalized and negotiable packages), and thus ensured a more acrimonious dialogue between workers and employers. Moreover, the class war in France spilled over, in certain instances, into the specifically political domain, and deserted the safer territory of negotiable issues such as wages, working-conditions and holidays. In short, it frequently seemed that the working class was not only interested in its share of the national cake but was also keen to determine its ingredients, control its cooking and supervise its eating. Complicating the class equation was the presence in France of a large agricultural community: although rapidly decreasing in numbers, it still represented by 1958 nearly one in every eight Frenchmen. There were in France major differences of outlook and interests between industry and agriculture, between town and country, between producers and consumers.

To these divisions must be added a legacy of bitter strife: it is revealing that the dates which figured (and continue to figure) most prominently in the French historical consciousness – 1789, 1793, 1830, 1848, 1871, 1936, 1940 and 1944 – were all periods when Frenchmen were at their most bitterly divided. When a British politician invokes history it is normally to buttress an unconvincing appeal to national unity, whereas a French politician normally cites historical examples to illustrate the perfidy of his adversaries. And no dispute in French politics is complete without constant recourse to history. The political battles of the Fourth Republic were infused with a peculiar venom, as each released the accumulated rancours of generations. The great political battles of the Fourth Republic – over, for instance, the European Defence Community, over Indo-China and Algeria or over State aid to Church schools – were all rendered more intractable by constant and emotional appeals to history.

Finally, it was argued (not without some justification) that compromise in French political society was rendered difficult to attain by two other factors. The first was the tendency of the French to intellectualize problems: concrete problems were generally raised to the level of abstract and universal principles which much reduced the possible area of bartering: after all, the Pope is, or is not, infallible. The second factor lay in the nature of French political language which was so excessive and so emotionally explosive: no British politician since the war has even approached the level of personal vilification used by Pierre Poujade and some of his supporters against Pierre Mendès-France, or the intense vituperation employed by *Humanité*, the Communist Party newspaper, against anybody or anything not conforming to the orthodox Stalinist line, or the sheer nastiness of Michel Debré in his fulminations against any 'capitulation' in Algeria (that he was Prime Minister when that country was granted its independence was but another touch of the tragic irony so characteristic of the Algerian affair).

What emerges from this short outline of the nature of French political society during the Fourth Republic was that the country was heterogeneous, fragmented and divided. These characteristics were reflected in the number of parties and the nature of the relationship which existed between them. Some parties (the extremist anti-régime parties) were totally excluded or excluded themselves from dialogue with the others, whilst between the pro-régime parties there existed deep and, on some issues, unbridgeable cleavages. Moreover, political parties in order to retain their electors felt obliged to emphasize their distinctiveness and declare their resolution to have no dealings with the others. But many of the parties, from the moderate Right to the moderate Left, whatever their differences, were forced into wary intercourse, in order to defend the Republic itself against its enemies. The gulf between the lofty ideals proclaimed and the baser compromises negotiated served merely to reinforce the contempt felt by many towards the politicians and the régime.

France was pictured, therefore, as a country divided into warring and irreconcilable political camps, each camp forming its own party.

Hence, big, durable and stable coalitions were impossible. But it was clear that such a picture was simplistic even during the Fourth Republic and that it had become grotesquely so under the Fifth Republic. It could be argued that even during the Fourth Republic some of the social cleavages (notably the religious one) were no longer intensely felt and for the electorate were decreasingly salient. Political parties were giving expression to, and helping to perpetuate, outmoded cleavages. Paul Warwick, writing about the Popular Front Government, refers to 'the structural incongruence of French party politics' in the late 1930s: the same description seems equally fitting for the years of the Fourth Republic. It should also be noted that many of the bitter disputes between the parties were frequently more rhetorical than real: ideological slanging matches in public did not prevent peaceful accommodation in Parliament.

French society from the 1950s has rapidly undergone a transformation under the impact of the traumas of military defeat and occupation, of a rapid population increase, of massive industrialization and urbanization with their consequences for population mobility and the occupational structure of the country, and of widespread and increasing economic prosperity. After 1962 the poisonous and divisive problem of decolonization was largely over, and the thaw in the Cold War in the 1960s rendered the 'East–West' conflict in French politics less acute. Finally, the régime/anti-régime cleavage has virtually disappeared. A small group of Right-wing fanatics of *Algérie française* from 1960 to 1962 made, and certain extreme Left-wing *groupuscules* continue to make, the régime itself one of the objects of their hate, but all the major political parties are happy to function peacefully within the régime, even though some are bitterly critical of some of its aspects. Opinion polls are unanimous in indicating widespread satisfaction with the Fifth Republic – a striking contrast with the situation under the Fourth Republic. This does not mean that France is not plagued with economic and social problems: increasingly marginal groups like small farmers and shopkeepers are treated insensitively, the country's new wealth is unevenly distributed between regions and social groups, social services are inadequately provided for, universities are ill equipped to meet the massive intake of students. The explosion of May 1968 represented a concatenation of many and often violently conflicting protests, frustrations, yearnings, ideals and aims – economic, educational and political. But they were rarely related to the divisive issues of the Fourth Republic.

The evidence of the polls and of the elections in the 1950s and

1960s suggests not that political opinion in France was lined up into warring camps, each impregnated with a hatred of the others. It indicates rather *considerable fluidity in electoral choice*. Even the Communist Party was affected: in 1958 it lost more than a fifth of its supporters to the Gaullists and suffered particularly in its working-class bastions, and a quarter of the Communist Party voters of 1962 voted for other parties in the following election of 1967. Such fluidity of electoral behaviour may be attributed to many factors, including the relative weakness of family and environmental political socialization in a country in the throes of great economic, demographic and social change and where groups affiliated to political parties were weak and therefore unable to reinforce innate political sentiments. Moreover, the attitudes of the parties seemed to encourage political fluidity by their attitudes and recommendations. The Socialist Party, for example, asked its first-ballot supporters to vote at the second ballot for the Gaullists in 1958 and for the Communists in 1962. The same party saved its towns in the 1959 and the 1965 local elections with anti-Communist support but its parliamentary seats with Communist support in the 1962, 1967 and 1968 legislative elections. Linked with great fluidity of electoral behaviour was the *low degree of party identification* which characterized French party politics. Professors Dupeux and Converse, writing at the beginning of the Fifth Republic, showed that in France there was no widespread or intense psychological attachment to particular parties. Fluidity of electoral behaviour weakened party identification, and weak party identification facilitated great fluidity of electoral behaviour. The circle was closed. But both the fluidity of behaviour and the weakness of party identification were essential ingredients in the political realignments of the Fifth Republic.

In conclusion, during the Fifth Republic the conditions were ripe for a major restructuring of the French party system: the traditional cleavages of French society had never been as sharp or as salient as the party system implied and were becoming less intense and less salient as the result of changes in French society; the Presidency provided an institutional focus for a new party or new coalition or both; the presidential, legislative and local electoral systems placed a premium upon coalition-building; the electorate was susceptible to realignment as the result of weak party identification. But it required the will, leadership and ability of successive Presidents of the Republic to exploit this situation and to mobilize electoral support behind them in new political form. This was achieved by superimposing upon the existing cleavages a new cleavage which transcended the others in salience and intensity. The polarization of opinion into two great coalitions implies a division over one basic issue: de Gaulle presented it as a choice between himself and his régime on the one hand and 'chaos' on the other; under Pompidou the electors were asked to choose between 'peaceful change' and 'revolutionary adventurism'; in no less manichean fashion, Giscard d'Estaing confronts the electorate with a choice between his pluralistic, liberal, democratic, socially just and quietly reformist régime and the revolutionary, collectivist, bureaucratic, illiberal and undemocratic régime threatened by the Left. In fact, there was mounting evidence to suggest that the French were divided less over a fine and idealistic sensitivity about the political requirement of the country than a crude and reassuring calculation of materialistic self-interest: an analysis of the electoral support of the Right and of the Left coalitions underlines the increasing importance of class as a determinant of voting.

The parties of the presidential coalition

The growth of the presidential coalition has been the result of the steady absorption into the governmental camp of the so-called parties of the centre. This absorption took place by distinct stages (Table 7). In almost all respects the most important party in the coalition is the Gaullist party.

The Gaullist party

Since the beginning of the Fifth Republic the Gaullists have changed their official party title no fewer than five times: Union pour la Nouvelle République (UNR) in October 1958; UNR–UDT (Union Démocrate du Travail) in December 1962; Union des Démocrates pour la Ve République (UDVe) in November 1967; Union pour la Défense de la République (UDR) in June 1968; Union des Démocrates pour la République (UDR) in 1971; finally, Rassemblement pour la République (RPR) in December 1976. For the sake of convenience the party will be referred to throughout the chapter as the Gaullist party – even though at no stage does there appear in its official name the word 'party' – a dirty word in the Gaullist vocabulary.

It is one of the ironies of the Fifth Republic that its founder,

Table 7 *The emergence of the presidential coalition 1958–1978*

Legislative elections 1958	Gaullists (UNR)
Legislative elections 1962	Gaullists (UNR–UDT) + Independent Republicans (RI)
Presidential elections 1969	Gaullists (UDR) + Independent Republicans (RI) + Centre Démocrate et Progrès (CDP)
Presidential elections 1974	Gaullists (UDR) + Independent Republicans (RI) + CDP + Centre Démocratie (CD) + Radicals + Centre National des Indépendants et Paysans (CNIP) + Mouvement Démocrate Socialiste de France (MESF)
Position in April 1978	Gaullists (RPR) + Republican Party (except Independent Republicans + Centre des Démocrates sociaux (CDS, the fusion of CDP and CD) + Radicals + Fédération des Socialistes Démocrates + Centre National des Indépendants Paysans + Centre Républicain

General de Gaulle, who despised the parties, should endow France with its first great organized, well structured, cohesive and well disciplined party of the Right. The Gaullist party has confounded the fears of its founders and defied the hopes of its adversaries by proving to be no transient phenomenon: it survived the resignation of de Gaulle (June 1969) and his death (November 1970) and the death of Pompidou (April 1974).

There have been four distinct phases in the history of the Gaullist party under the Fifth Republic.

1958–62: the search for identity
It was during this period that the party acquired a centralized organization, internal discipline and cohesiveness, especially after the purge of pro-*Algérie française* elements, and a privileged relationship with the President of the Republic by being the subservient instrument of his policies.

1962–72: growth, consolidation and hegemony
This is the period of the *Gaullist phenomenon* which involved the following:

The propagation of a set of doctrines based on (i) the primacy of national unity and a denial of the Marxist notion of class war, (ii) the need for order and authority in all branches of public and private life, (iii) the defence of a powerful State and strong Executive authority as expressed in the new Constitution, (iv) the creation of a modern industrial economy and (v) the assertion of national independence in foreign and European affairs.

The consolidation of a powerfully organized party with the task of defending presidential policies in Parliament and in the country, especially at election times: much of the power of the Gaullist party resided in its symbiotic relationship with the President of the Republic. It was the principal buttress and guardian of the Presidency, the dispenser of unconditional and even obsequious support; its subservience was total and was demonstrated in 1971 when President Pompidou refused to allow it to elect its own leader. It was rewarded with the lion's share of *investitures* at elections: it was given the sole right to represent the presidential coalition in a number of constituencies which opinion polls suggested was disproportionate to its real strength in the country. Thus, in 1973, in the 403 constituencies in which there was only one pro-governmental candidate presented at the first ballot the Gaullists were present in 281 (or 70 per cent) even though the opinion polls gave them only the same number of votes as their coalition partners. During this period the Gaullist party grew in importance and in influence. Its electoral growth was spectacular (Table 8).

Table 8   *The rise of the Gaullists in Parliament 1958–1968*

Election	Votes	Percentage of votes cast
November 1958	4 165 505	20·3
November 1962	6 507 828	35·5
March 1967	8 448 982	37·7
June 1968	9 667 532	44·5

The rise of the Gaullist party was such that Professor Jean Charlot, the leading expert on Gaullism, could contend that it had altered the régime in a *qualitative* or *structural* manner: the multi-party system which had predominated in France since the beginning of the Third Republic had been transformed into a 'dominant-party system', with the Gaullists as the dominant party. That dominance was especially marked in Parliament: in the 1968 elections, the party won a majority of seats (296 of the 487) in the National Assembly – the first occasion since 1870 that any party had achieved such a feat – and was no longer even dependent on the support of its allies. The nature of Gaullist support was likened by André Malraux to 'the rush-hour crowd in the underground', that it represented a cross-section of the French population in general. That claim was never quite true, since the party always enjoyed the disproportionate support of the elderly, of women, of the higher income groups and of practising Catholics.

The domination of an electoral and parliamentary alliance, first with the Independent Republicans of Valéry Giscard d'Estaing and then, after 1969, with the Independent Republicans and the Centre Démocratie et Progrès, a centrist group led by Jacques Duhamel.

The penetration of the State apparatus. Key posts in the administration, the nationalized industries and the para-public corporations, the radio and television network were given to political sympathizers. The extensive network of political patronage bordered on the scandalous, and it was this unsavoury aspect of the régime which led to Michel Poniatowski's wounding denunciation of *'les copains et les coquins'* who sullied the reputation of the régime.

By 1970 the Gaullist party provided France with a vague yet pervasive set of doctrines, its President, its Prime Minister, a majority of its ministers, and it dominated Parliament (and all the parliamentary commissions) and the presidential coalition, and its sympathizers were well placed in key sectors of public activity. Its dominance was such that Jean-Jacques Servan-Schreiber could refer to the *État-UDR* – the Gaullist State. Some observers argued that the Gaullist party had become progressively 'Radicalized', that it came to resemble the Radical Party of the Third Republic in a number of important respects: it had become the major force in Parliament; it provided most ministers; it was a clientele party, distributing patronage to gain or consolidate political support; it was slowly putting down local roots; it was gaining seats in the traditional Radical areas south of the river Loire; it was divided into many and often conflicting currents of thought. There were, however, important differences between the two parties: unlike the Gaullist party, the Radical Party had an almost obsessional suspicion of strong leaders, even those from its own ranks; decision-making in the Gaullist party was (and remains) centralized and hierarchized whereas in the Radical Party it was diffused amongst a large number of independent-minded provincial and parliamentary notables; the Gaullist party was (and is) a disciplined organization which never hesitated to expel recalcitrant Deputies, whilst the Radical Party was always plagued by the endemic indiscipline of its leaders; ideologically, the two parties differed considerably – for example, the anti-clericalism of the Radicals found no echo in the doctrines of the Gaullists, whilst the chauvinistic posturings of the Gaullists in foreign policy were largely absent in the foreign policy of the Radicals.

1972–6: decline and disarray

There were clear signs in the early 1970s that the Gaullist party was in decline. In the 1973 elections it suffered a severe electoral setback: compared with 1968 it lost 2300000 votes and polled only 25·5 per cent of the votes, and it also lost seats and was deprived of its majority in the National Assembly. It lost its crushing predominance in the presidential coalition (in 1968 82 per cent of the presidential coalition Deputies were Gaullists and in 1973 this proportion dropped to 61 per cent). Moreover, the opinion polls indicated that the Gaullists enjoyed no greater support in the country than their coalition partners. In other words, the real extent of the Gaullist decline was effectively masked in the elections by their having been granted the lion's share of the *investitures* for the presidential majority. It was the death of Pompidou and the subsequent presidential election which was fully to expose the extent of the decline.

The electoral base of Gaullism was not only becoming smaller, it was also becoming socially more conservative: it was older, more rural, more female and more Catholic.

The death of President Pompidou in April 1974 dealt a severe blow to the Gaullists, since it left leaderless a party already reeling under the impact of its recent electoral setback and a series of property and tax scandals. The party's candidate in the May 1974 presidential elections, Chaban-Delmas, won only 15 per cent of the votes at the first ballot. The party was also badly split by the election, since an important minority, led by Jacques Chirac, refused to back Chaban-Delmas and favoured Giscard d'Estaing, and a small Left-wing element of the party supported Mitterrand at the second ballot. The election of Giscard d'Estaing to the Presidency also spelled trouble for the Gaullists since the new President was determined to dismantle the 'Gaullist State'. He chose Chirac – 'the traitor' – as Prime Minister, drastically reduced the number of Gaullist ministers, appointed

Table 9 *Socio-economic breakdown of Gaullist voters*

	Election of March 1967	*Election of March 1973*	*Election of Mareh 1978*
	(Percentage of each category voting Gaullist)		
Sex			
Men	34	32	21
Women	41	43	22
Age			
21 to 49	37	34	18
Over 50	40	44	27
Professions			
Farmers and farmworkers	45	50	31
Liberal professions	44	39	24
Businessmen	44	43	29
White-collar workers	35	35	19
Working class	30	26	14
Retired and not working	43	46	26

notorious anti-Gaullists to key ministerial posts, and purged key parts of the administration of Gaullist sympathizers. The party was also weakened by the departure of some Left-wing leaders (see page 153) and by the schism of a small group led by Michel Jobert (Pompidou's Foreign Minister) who formed his Mouvement des Démocrates in March 1975, for he could not stomach the party's subservience to the overtly European and Atlanticist Giscard d'Estaing. Equally alarming to the Gaullists were the opinion polls which suggested the collapse of their support in the country. The Gaullists who lost the Presidency in May 1974 suffered another blow when they lost the Premiership after the resignation of Chirac in August 1976. The structural bases of the Fifth Republic which had been based on the close and symbiotic relationship which bound the President, the Prime Minister and the dominant party of the National Assembly were thus undermined.

Since 1976: renovation and the quest for independence
The period since the resignation of Jacques Chirac from the Premiership has been characterized by a not unsuccessful attempt to breathe new life into the declining party and also to assert its independence *vis-à-vis* of the President of the Republic. On 5 December 1976 the

party changed its name to the Rassemblement pour la République (RPR) and altered its statutes in a way designed considerably to strengthen the leader of the party. Chirac, effective leader of the party since December 1974, was elected to the presidency of the party with Soviet-like ease (96·5 per cent of the delegates voting for him). The party organization has been strengthened: in spring 1978 the RPR claimed over 500000 members compared with the 285000 of the UDR, active federations in each of the ninety-six *départements* and even 200 factory groups. Whist the figures and the claims must be treated with some scepticism, the party has undoubtedly received a new lease of life. Furthermore, its standing in the electorate has improved since the dark days of 1974, when the opinion polls gave it only 14–15 per cent of the votes: in the March 1978 election the RPR won 22·8 per cent of the votes cast.

The attempt to renovate the Gaullist party has been accompanied by its increasing assertion of independence *vis-à-vis* of the President of the Republic. After the summer of 1976 the Gaullists opposed Giscard d'Estaing in a number of areas:

Institutional issues. The Gaullists forced Poniatowski, the Minister of the Interior and close friend of the President, to modify his Bill designed to change the electoral law, and they adamantly rejected the President's insistent claim that the Prime Minister was the sole co-ordinator of the presidential coalition.

Electoral strategy. They wanted the President to take a more resolute part in the 1978 election campaign as the effective head of his coalition and insisted that as such he should resign from the Presidency if he was beaten – a proposal categorically rejected by the President. They requested that he show less soft-heartedness in denouncing the Left and its policies. At bottom, many Gaullists suspect that the President harbours secret sympathies for the Socialists and that he would like to make a deal with them at their expense.

Economic matters. In the summer of 1976 they opposed the new system of local taxation proposed by the Government and they severely mauled the Bill on capital gains and during the 1978 election they demanded a change of economic strategy in order to combat unemployment.

International and European affairs. They opposed the extension of the budgetary powers of the European Assembly at Strasbourg and expressed serious reservations about the election of the European Parliament by universal suffrage. They also criticized the proposed ratification of the new statutes of the International Monetary Fund agreed at the January 1976 meeting in Jamaica and which envisaged a reduction in the role of gold and increased French participation in the fund.

The Gaullist leader's decision to reject the President's nominee for the mayor of Paris in the elections of March 1977 and his defiant gesture in presenting himself as a candidate for the post was only the most spectacular manifestation of the discord which reigned between the Gaullists and the President of the Republic. But the tension was not new. Gaullists remembered Giscard d'Estaing's acerbic remarks about President de Gaulle's autocratic tendencies and also his opposition to de Gaulle's referendum in April 1969. Those of historical inclination might trace the source of that tension to the distinct and, in some respects, antagonistic political traditions of the Gaullists and the *Giscardiens*: the former are heirs to a long Bonapartist, populist and nationalistic tradition whilst the latter trace their ancestors to the liberal, parliamentary, elitist and moderate conservatives who served any régime which served them.

Whatever the source of the conflict between the President of the Republic and the Gaullists, the implications are far-reaching. With the President of the Republic unable to count on the unquestioning support of the dominant partner of his party coalition – a support enjoyed by his two predecessors – the structural bases of the régime have been altered. Nor can he expect a major split in the Gaullist party in his favour, in spite of that party's heterogeneous nature. Within the party there have always been a number of fairly distinct chronological strata: the historical Gaullists who were bound by idealism, patriotism and fidelity to General de Gaulle, 'the man of 18 June 1940'; the RPF Gaullists of the Fourth Republic who were fired by a virulent anti-Communism and an equally virulent hatred of the régime; the UNR Gaullists of the early Fifth Republic who were linked by many and often conflicting motives; the governmental Gaullists of the UDR for whom the conservatism and cautious pragmatism of Pompidou and the prospect of patronage exerted an irresistible attraction; the *Chiraciens* of the RPR who prefer the muscular resolution of Chirac to the disingenuous waverings of the President of the Republic. There is no real unity over basic policies within the party: the party harbours economic liberals and economic *dirigistes*, social liberals and social conservatives, protagonists and adversaries of military conscription, pro- and anti-Europeans. Furthermore, there have always been opportunists in the Gaullist party ready to sacrifice their principles for the greater good of their own ambitions: in May 1952 an important group of Gaullist Deputies defied orders from the leadership and voted for the investiture of Prime Minister Pinay (the spiritual father of Giscard d'Estaing) and in the May 1974 presidential elections Chirac led a group of forty-three Gaullist Members of Parliament in refusing to support the party's official candidate. But in spite of the various currents of thought and the differences of generations and despite the temptations of office, the party generally acts and will probably continue to act as a reasonably united organization. The dilemma of the President of the Republic is rendered more acute by the weak, divided, disunited and dispirited state of the parties which are more sympathetic to his cause.

The non-Gaullist parties of the presidential coalition

The most important party after the Gaullists in the presidential coalition is the Republican Party. 'Party' is perhaps a misnomer for this badly organized, lightly structured collection of parliamentary *notables* (69 Deputies and 58 Senators), who dominate what little life it has. The Republican Party was founded in May 1977 as the direct heir to the Independent Republican Party, itself founded in 1962 by Valéry Giscard d'Estaing when he and several other Members of Parliament broke away from the conservative CNIP (Centre National des Indépendants et Paysans) in protest against that party's growing anti-Gaullism. The CNIP was destroyed as a viable national political force in 1962, although it still limps along on the local level as a home for conservative councillors with an aversion to both party labels and rigid principles. It is a party with a few leaders and fewer troops, no organization, no defined policies and no illusions. It was replaced by the Independent Republican Party which became, in Malcolm Anderson's words, 'a focus for conservatives who wished to rally to the new régime and to gain access to political power'. But it was never more than a *centre d'accueil* (the description of Poniatowski, one of its leaders) for conservatives who were prepared to back the Government but who had no wish to join the Gaullist party.

The present Republican Party is headed by Jean-Pierre Soisson, the young Secretary General of the party, who is a close political ally and friend of the President of the Republic. He has expressed the hope of transforming the party into a movement with mass electoral support and a heavy contingent of activists. In his attempt to emulate the Gaullists, Soisson wishes to forge 'an effective instrument of political action' at the disposal of the President of the Republic. Linked with the Republican Party are two pro-Giscardian movements – the Mouvement Génération Sociale et Liberale, a movement of well-bred youths founded in September 1974 and claiming an implausible 35000 members, and the political clubs Perspectives et Réalités founded in 1965 by Giscard d'Estaing and which in May 1976 claimed 228 clubs with 20000 members. Both movements spawn ideas and suggestions for a party leadership which solemnly shelves them.

The second party of the non-Gaullist presidential coalition is the Centre des Démocrates Sociaux (CDS) founded in May 1976 and presided by Jean Lecanuet. It was created by the merger of the Centre Démocrate (CD) of Lecanuet and the Centre Démocratie et Progrès (CDP) of Jacques Duhamel which had split away from the Centre Démocrate in 1969. The latter was founded in October 1966 following Lecanuet's relatively successful candidacy in the December 1965 presidential elections, but it never achieved the electoral success anticipated by its leaders, and it was also seriously weakened by the departure of the *Duhamelistes* in 1969. The *Lecanuetistes* and the *Duhamelistes* came together again at the second ballot of the 1974 presidential elections when they both supported Giscard d'Estaing, and shortly after they joined forces to create the CDS. The CDS is the direct descendant of the now defunct Catholic centre party, the MRP, which in 1946, with 28 per cent of the votes, was the biggest party in France. And it is the spiritual heir to a long social Catholic tradition which had sought to reconcile French Catholics to the ungodly Republic.

The third non-Gaullist element in the presidential coalition is the Radical Party, which, from being the most important party of the Third Republic and one of the influential pivotal parties of the Fourth, has been reduced to a marginal and insignificant force during the Fifth. It has been seriously weakened by the departure of its opportunists to the Gaullist party and of its Left-wingers who, in 1972, created a separate party which entered into alliance with the other opposition parties of the Left (see pages 153–4). Since October 1969 it has been dominated by its leader, Jean-Jacques Servan-Schreiber. J.J.S.S., as he is familarily known, is a man of unquestionable courage and ferocious intellect but of highly questionable political judgement: he is a politician who is totally unaware of the virtues of occasional silence and temporization. In spite of his undeniable energy (often expressed in unseemly tantrums), his genius for self-publicity and his gift to the party of a far-sighted manifesto (it was read with apprehensive consternation by some of the party's leaders and by bland disapproval by others), he has been unable to instil any real life into the largely moribund carcass of the Radical Party. The Radical Party rallied to the presidential camp in May 1974 when it backed Giscard d'Estaing at the second ballot of the presidential elections.

Apart from the Republican Party, the CDS and the Radical Party there are several other very small parties which belong to the presidential coalition: these include the Fédération des Socialistes Démocrates (founded in June 1975 by a motley collection of anti-Communist socialists who deserted the Socialist Party of François Mitterrand), the Centre Républicain (a *groupuscule* of *notables* who left the Radical Party in 1956 because its policy in North Africa was considered dangerously liberal), and the Centre National des Indépendants et Paysans (described above).

The non-Gaullist parties of the presidential coalition are all small and organizationally weak: the party with the biggest membership, the Republican Party, claimed 80000 members in August 1977 and even that figure seemed the product of a wildly imaginative optimism. They are also divided over personalities and principles, for each party represents a distinct current of thought which has been nourished by a distinctive historical tradition: the CDS has a social Catholic past whilst the Radicals are the historical champions of the anti-clerical secular Republic: the Republican Party has a moderate and opportunist conservative heritage whilst the Fédération des Socialistes Démocrates, as the name indicates, is wedded to the concepts of social democracy. Several attempts have been made or projected to wield them into a united and effective force: the Reformist Movement of November 1971, the still-born 'great federation of the Centrists' envisaged by Poniatowski in August 1971, the Movement of the Reformist Left founded in January 1975, the Federation of Reformists created in March 1975 and the projected 'great liberal party' have quickly collapsed even when they managed to struggle into life. In February 1978 they managed to forge a common electoral alliance for the first ballot of the elections: this alliance – the Union pour la Démocratie Française (UDF) – decided to present a single candidate in the elections, fared surprisingly well (with 21 per cent of the votes cast), and formed a single parliamentary group after the elections. It is not easy to envisage the lasting impact of a single movement of the non-Gaullist parties, since within it their divisions may well be compounded and their weakness accentuated. However, even in politics, the amalgamation of the weak, the unimportant and the plain derisory may produce something more than the insignificant.

Presidential coalition-building: some concluding remarks

The smooth functioning of the institutions of the Fifth Republic during the Presidencies of General de Gaulle and Pompidou reposed on the harmonious relationship which existed between themselves and their Governments on the one hand and, on the other, a party coalition which enjoyed a majority in the National Assembly and which was dominated by a Gaullist party totally subservient to presidential directives. Since 1976 that happy situation no longer prevails, and the President of the Republic is now faced with a number of very real problems. The first problem concerns the electoral decline of the coalition: the so-called *majorité* has clearly become a minority in terms of the votes won in the elections. Elections to the departmental councils in March 1976 and to the local councils in March 1977, successive by-elections and all the opinion polls revealed the extent of the decline and augured badly for the March 1978 elections to the National Assembly. Only the stupidity of the Left saved the Right from defeat. The second problem facing the President is the imbalance within his coalition: the Gaullist party, the least sympathetic towards him, continues to dominate the coalition. In the National Assembly it forms the biggest and most coherent group of the coalition; it has, unlike the other parties of the coalition, a mass membership; in contrast with those other parties, it has a centralized, disciplined, effective and well-financed, electoral machine; finally in Jacques Chirac it has a dynamic, audacious, autocratic and effective national leader.

The third major problem relates to the constant tension within the coalition, the inevitable result of the struggle between the component elements for preponderance and even predominance. That tension is maintained by fractious and susceptible party leaders and also by memories of past battles between the coalition partners. For instance, Jean-Jacques Servan-Schreiber, leader of the Radical Party, has an almost visceral hatred of the Gaullists: when President de Gaulle resigned after his defeat in the April 1969 referendum Servan-Schreiber publicly declared that it was 'the happiest day of my life'. Dissension within the coalition raises real problems of co-ordination at parliamentary and electoral level. President Giscard d'Estaing has described the basis of his party coalition as one of 'tolerant and organized pluralism', although the coalition frequently presents the spectacle of intolerant and disorganized anarchy. Chirac when Prime Minister was unable effectively to co-ordinate a coalition which he likened to 'a basket of frogs all jumping in different directions', and Prime Minister Barre is proving even more ineffective: Chirac was constantly defied by the Centrists and Barre has little control over the Gaullists. Finally, it is not only the Gaullists within the presidential coalition who display limited enthusiasm for the timorous reforms of the President. In the vote on the abortion Bill in November 1974 only 55 of the 173 (or 32 per cent) Gaullist Deputies, 17 of the 65 (or 26 per cent) Independent Republican Deputies and 27 of the 52 (or 52 per cent) of the Centrist Deputies voted in favour, and the Bill was carried only because of the support of the Socialists and the Communists. The June 1975 Bill liberalizing the grounds for divorce was also given a very lukewarm reception (many pro-Government Deputies voted against or abstained). In June 1976 during the passage of the Bill introducing a timid capital gains tax the Government's nominal supporters were diluting the impact of the proposed measures so much that François Mitterrand, the Left-wing leader, could quip that if they continued in the same way the Bill would ultimately cost the State a great deal of money! Yet the three Bills on abortion, divorce and capital gains tax were all known to enjoy presidential blessings. There is clearly a gulf between a President who proclaims the need for a tolerant liberalism and for greater social justice and equity, and most of his parliamentary supporters who, pushed by their conservative electorate, pine for the traditional values of social responsibility, family, order, work and religion.

The presidential coalition, however divided and however unenthusiastic about presidential policies, is likely to remain intact for the forseeable future. Admittedly it is a shaky ideological edifice, but the cracks are filled by the cement of fear and hatred of the Left, electoral self-interest and the prospect of office – a powerful if unattractive combination. Nevertheless, the coalition is unlikely to afford President Giscard d'Estaing the unswerving support it gave his two predecessors, so that in spite of the outcome of the election of March 1978 the President's task in finding the necessary support for his policies in Parliament proves delicate and difficult.

7 The Opposition Left: the quest for identity, unity and office

The bipolarizing pressures of the Fifth Republic, which squeezed the parties of the Right and Centre into coalition, have also made themselves felt on the Left. The two major parties of the Left – the Socialists and the Communists – have been forced to respond to the success of the Right-wing alliance, and each has done so by concerting tactics with the other whilst jealously guarding its own autonomy. Unlike the parties of the Right, they responded only very slowly to the challenges of the new régime, believing (and hoping) that Gaullism and presidentialism were but transient phenomena.

During the first years of the Fifth Republic the Left was profoundly divided and hence very weak: President de Gaulle could well have reversed the famous aphorism and proclaimed that with enemies like that who needed friends? The first stage of Left-wing unity took place in October 1962, when Socialists and Communists came to a limited number of second-ballot electoral agreements. Three years later, in December 1965, both supported François Mitterrand in the presidential elections, even though he belonged to neither party, and in the March 1967, June 1968 and March 1973 legislative elections they concluded a nationally binding second-ballot electoral agreement. Those agreements were cemented by a 'common platform' in February 1968 and the Joint Programme of Government signed in June 1972. But the path to unity during the Fifth Republic has been far from smooth: from 1958 to September 1962, from June 1968 to the end of 1969, from October 1974 to January 1976 relations between the two *partis-frères* were strained and occasionally embittered. From September 1977, the two parties were once again locked in angry confrontation after the failure of negotiations designed to update the Joint Programme of Government. Their relations are not as violently antagonistic as during the period following the foundation of the Communist Party in December 1920, from 1928 to 1934 when the same party was wedded to a strategy of 'class versus class', or from 1947 to 1953 at the height of the Cold

War. Nevertheless, the intensely and intrinsically conflictual nature of the relationship has been constantly revealed. Before looking more closely at that relationship it is worth looking at the constituent elements of the French Left.

The fragmented Left

For the sake of convenience, the Opposition Left may be divided into four main categories: the extreme and revolutionary Left; the centre Left; the Socialists; the Communists.

The extreme and revolutionary Left

The extreme Left in France is characteristically splintered into many warring factions, clans and *groupuscles* and it is perpetually torn between its centrifugal aspirations and its centripedal practices: unity is proclaimed as vital yet eschewed as opportunist.

The major element is the PSU (Parti Socialiste Unifié), which, since its foundation in 1960, has been the object of constant schisms. It was seriously weakened in October 1974 with the departure of many of its leaders (including Michel Rocard) and members who joined the new Socialist Party of François Mitterrand. It claims 7000 members (in January 1977), an optimistic claim that is taken seriously by no one. Among the other movements of the extreme Left are the Trotskyist Ligue Communiste Révolutionnaire led by Alain Krivine, a well-bred and well-spoken intellectual who perturbs rival revolutionaries by his ideas and his tie-wearing (he is nicknamed *Krivine-la-Cravatte*), and Lutte Ouvrière (headed by the attractive Arlette Laguiller, whose proletarian credentials are impeccable), and the Maoist Organisation Communiste des Travailleurs. These movements are elctorally weak (in the presidential elections of May 1974 Krivine won 0·37 and Laguiller 2·36 per cent of the votes), internally divided (the initiated can discern at least four rival currents in the Ligue Communiste Révolutionnaire) and hold one another in mutual lack of esteem.

The parties of the extreme Left are encumbered by a surfeit of ideas and embarrassed by the lack of a coherent or popular strategy, and they frequently resemble an army with very few troops and led by resentful and rebellious lance-corporals. But they are not without influence. They have an audience in certain academic circles, are active in certain factories, and support four newspapers (all of which are carefully dissected by the police) which have unearthed some of the seamier aspects of the régime. If they no longer enjoy the mobilizing capacity of the heady days of May 1968, they have successfully organized campaigns over Vietnam, over the soldiers who were accused of 'subversive' activities (they were complaining of their living conditions) in November–December 1975, over abortion, over prison reform, over the plight of immigrant workers and the eviction of tenants by property speculators – all subjects which bored or embarrassed the 'establishment' Left. They have also been very active in the environmental protest movement and especially in the growing opposition to nuclear power stations. If they dislike one another, they dislike even more the 'reformist' and 'revisionist' (two of the milder adjectives frequently employed) Left, which seems only too ready to work within the existing system.

The opposition centre Left

Within this category may be placed the Left-wing opposition Gaullists and the Left-wing Radicals. The Left-wing Gaullists are themselves divided into several groups, the main three being the Fédération des Républicains de Progrès and the Initiative Républicaine et Socialiste, headed respectively by Jean Charbonnel and Léo Hamon (both ex-ministers of the Fifth Republic), and the Union des Gaullistes de Progrès. Many of the leaders of the opposition Left-wing Gaullists previously belonged to the progressive wing of the Gaullist party; they were opposed to the conservatism of Pompidou and even more so to the pro-Europeanism and pro-Americanism of Giscard d'Estaing whom they dislike for his anti-de Gaulle declarations of the 1960s. Electorally they are weak, and politically they have very little weight, but their support is welcomed by the rest of the Left, since recent elections have been decided by such narrow margins.

Of greater importance are the Left-wing Radicals who belong to the Mouvement des Radicaux de Gauche (MRG). The MRG was created in 1972 as a break-away group from the Radical Party headed by Jean-Jacques Servan-Schreiber. In July of that year it signed the Joint Programme which had just been negotiated between the Socialists and the Communists, and it also entered into a first-ballot electoral agreement with the Socialist Party with which it continues to be closely associated. The party has no autonomous group in the National Assembly and lacks a charismatic leader (its present leader, Robert Fabre, is a provincial chemist who looks and acts like a provincial chemist). It is a loosely structured party which is dominated by a few provincial *notables*. But with its 18 Senators,

10 Deputies, 200 Departmental Councillors, over 3000 town councillors and 25000 members it is a useful addition to the Left, especially since its moderate policies and image reassure those electors
who are suspicious of the Socialists and afraid of the Communists.

The Left-wing Radicals are the rightful heirs to those Radicals
who founded the one, indivisible and secular Third Republic and
who provided the Fourth Republic with so many of its leaders.
Economically conservative, financially orthodox and socially progressive, they traditionally backed the Left at election times (in
the name of 'Republican discipline') and the Right between elections.
The more cynical observer might unkindly point out that most of the
party's Deputies owe their parliamentary seats (which are concentrated in the south-west) to the good will of the other parties of the
Left.

The Socialists

One of the most important political changes of the Fifth Republic
has been the renewal and transformation of the French Socialist
Party (Parti Socialiste, or PS). For the first ten years of the Fifth
Republic, the then Socialist Party – the S F I O – seemed incapable of
arresting its apparently inexorable decline. Its leadership was ageing
and politically insensitive, its image was tarnished (it was too closely
linked with the crises, the compromises and chaos of the Fourth
Republic), its membership was in decline (from the 1946 peak of
335000 to a generously estimated 70000 in 1969), its press had virtually disappeared, and its electorate was sharply decreasing (in 1946
it received 23·4 per cent of the votes and by November 1962 only
12·6 per cent of the votes). In the 1967 and 1968 legislative elections,
the decline of the party as a member of the Federation of the Left
was not stopped, and in the June 1969 presidential elections its
candidate, Gaston Defferre, won a humiliating 5 per cent of the votes.
Furthermore, the party has been deprived of office during the Fifth
Republic, and during the Fourth Republic office had compensated
for its decline and sclerosis.

After the disastrous legislative elections of June 1968 and the
débâcle of the presidential elections of June 1969, the French Socialist
Party, the party of Jaurès and Blum and the main party of Government from 1936 to 1938, 1944 to 1951 and from 1956 to 1958, was
reduced to a marginal and badly divided political force. But the
trauma of 1968 and 1969 proved salutary, and since 1969 the fortunes

of the party have so dramatically changed that within five years it had become the biggest electoral party in France. A new Socialist Party has been born, first under the leadership of Alain Savary and then under that of François Mitterrand. At successive congresses (Issy-les-Moulineaux in July 1969, Épinay in June 1971 and Paris in October 1974), a new and enlarged party has been forged. At present it is possible to detect six main elements within the party:

Members of the now defunct SFIO led by Mauroy (Mayor of Lille) and Defferre (Mayor of Marseilles);

Members of the CERES, a Left-wing ginger group which had previously belonged to the SFIO and which forms a powerful independent force within the present party;

Members of a group of political clubs – the Convention des Institutions Républicaines (CIR) – closely associated with François Mitterrand;

Members of the Left-wing clubs associated with Alain Savary or Jean Poperen;

Ex-PSU members who have entered in several waves and whose leader is Michel Rocard;

The previously unattached – a motley collection composed of those who are completely new to party politics (and many of whom were 'politicized' during the events of May 1968), some disabused ex-Gaullists, some idealistic Left-wing Catholics and the inevitable cohort of unprincipled opportunists and ambitious political adventurers.

The new Socialist Party has transformed its situation in several respects.

It has a leader of unquestioned ability and great popularity
Since June 1971, when he took over the leadership from Alain Savary, Mitterrand has established himself as the undisputed master of his party and of the Left-wing Opposition in general. Indeed, a great part of the Socialists' success is due to Mitterrand's brilliant leadership which was asserted during the presidential campaign of May 1974, when he came within an ace of winning, and which has been reaffirmed by his standing in the polls. Helped by his 'court' (composed of close friends), he dominates his party to such an extent that he has earned for himself the nickname of 'the Prince' and 'the Pope'. Mitterrand is an indefatigable organizer, a shrewd and tough negotiator and an ambitious politician. As a mass orator he is quite

outstanding, lacing his lyricism and brooding romanticism with literary allusion and acerbic wit, gentle irony and bitter sarcasm. Mitterrand is also the teacher, the poet, the author and the prophet. He is a man who exudes a sense of his own inner self-assurance, who seems secure in his achievement of having reconstructed the party of Jaurès and Blum, and who is aware that he has already achieved an honourable place in the history of his country. There are touches of de Gaulle in Mitterrand – the isolation, the aloofness, the haughtiness, the ingratitude towards his friends, the disdain for his enemies, the pretension to be 'above politics' whilst carefully and even cynically indulging in them, the skilful manipulation of language, the vision, and the quiet taste for publicized martyrdom. Like de Gaulle, he evokes respect and admiration but little affection.

The party has enlarged and completely renewed its elite
A new, young, more educated and more enterprising generation of Socialists now controls many of the directive organs of the party. Already under Savary's leadership (1969–71), 70 per cent of the secretaries of the local federations had been replaced and the average age of the holders of those key posts fell by twenty years. A study of the 687 delegates at the Nantes party congress in June 1977 showed that more than half (54 per cent) were under forty years old, that only a quarter (26 per cent) had belonged to the Socialist Party before 1969, and that more than half (51 per cent) had university degrees or the equivalent. The renewal of the party elite could also be seen in the National Assembly, where half the Socialist Deputies elected in 1973 were total newcomers to Parliament, and also in the departmental and local councils: in the town elections of March 1977, for example, the Socialist mayors elected in such important towns as Nantes, Rennes, Angoulême, Poitiers, Dreux, Chambéry and Castres were all under forty years old.

The party has increased its membership
By 1969, the membership of the Socialist Party had fallen to a mere 70000, and in certain parts of France (notably in Alsace, Lorraine and Brittany) organized party activity had virtually ceased. The recruitment drive has been considered disappointing by many party leaders, but with 170000 members (January 1978) it has more than doubled in eight years, and most of the present members are much more dynamic than those of the SFIO. It is clear that previously moribund local federations have been totally rejuvenated.

The PS has increased its electoral appeal

In the March 1973 legislative elections, the Socialists for the first time during the Fifth Republic not only arrested their electoral decline but actually reversed it. It formed a first-ballot alliance – the Union de la Gauche Socialiste et Démocrate (UGSD), with the Left-wing Radicals, which it dominated and which won 20·6 per cent of the votes, bettering the performance of the Federation of the Left (FGDS) – its previous electoral alliance – in 1967 (18·9 per cent of the votes) and in 1968 (16·5 per cent of the votes). In many respects, the 1973 electoral achievement of the party was its best since the Liberation, since not only did it increase its share of the poll but it also put down roots in Catholic areas such as Alsace, Lorraine, Brittany and Savoy where it had previously been very weak or even non-existent. The increased integration of the Catholics into French political life, the waning of passions in the Church–State dispute, the pronounced Left-wing sentiments of many younger members of the clergy, the political neutrality of most, and the sympathy of some, of the Church hierarchy, the increasingly important role played by young Catholic trades unionists within the party, all combined to attract Catholics to a party which had traditionally been one of the bulwarks of anti-clericalism. The party also improved its position in the growing urban areas of France and amongst working-class voters. In the 1978 elections the party increased its share of the poll by 4 per cent, consolidating and improving the gains of 1973.

The excellent performance of its leader in the May 1974 presidential elections, its progress in successive by-elections, its success in local elections in 1973, 1976 and 1977 and the general election of 1978 all demonstrate the electoral strength of the party. Its showing in the departmental elections is indicative of its growing success (in 1970 the party won 14·8 per cent of the votes, in 1973 21·9 per cent and in 1976 26·5 per cent).

The Socialist Party has undergone an 'ideological renaissance'

Since 1969 the party has indulged in an orgy of doctrinal debate: study groups on every conceivable subject have pullulated like weeds in a wet spring. Under the impact of its more radical, more Left-wing and more intellectually aggressive elements, and unbridled by the tiresome responsibilities of office, the party programme has become more radical, more aggressive, more Left-wing and more irresponsible. At the National Convention of the party at Suresnes in March

1972 it adopted a new programme – *Changer la vie* – a title which reveals both its ambition and its naïveté. Marxism, or rather Marxist terminology, has been rediscovered and often gives intra-party debates an esoteric and antediluvian flavour. Elements of Marxism have been amalgamated with the newer concepts of *autogestion* (workers' control), decentralization and citizen participation. Moreover, the party had to make concessions to the Communist Party when it signed the Joint Programme of Government in June 1972, and the result is that the party now appears committed to a vague and not always intellectually consistent set of doctrines. It is thought that the sobering reality of power will temper the wilder ideological excesses of the party, but disenchantment is bound to be widespread and profound amongst the party faithful who, unlike most of the members of the old SFIO or of the British Labour Party and the German Social Democratic Party, have learnt to distinguish between policies and rhetoric.

The party, from a position of relative strength, has renewed and reinforced its alliances with other parties of the Left
During the 1960s the Socialists were bitterly divided over their choice of allies. One group, comprising mainly SFIO notables (and including the mayors of several important towns), advocated the kind of 'Third Force' type alliance which had operated during periods of the Fourth Republic: this involved a wide-ranging alliance with most of the parties of the centre to the total exclusion of both the Gaullists and the Communists. A second faction of the party, led by Gaston Defferre, favoured a federation of centre parties which could count on the support, however reluctant, of the Communists at the second ballot of elections. Defferre attempted to create such a federation in 1964–5 to further his candidacy for the presidential elections by trying to forge a *Grande Fédération* composed of the Socialists, the Catholic MRP and a number of Left-wing clubs. But the venture failed and Defferre withdrew from the presidential race. A third element of the party emerged after the electoral catastrophes of 1968 and 1969: the new party leader, Alain Savary, backed by a majority of the party, preached the need for a firm and speedy alliance with the Communists. The fourth faction within the party was led by Mitterrand who argued that its first priority should be to strengthen the non-Communist Left, which, from a position of strength, would negotiate a formal electoral agreement with the Communists on the basis of a compromise programme. Essential to

Mitterrand's thinking was the need to *rééquilibrer la gauche* – to redress the balance of Left-wing forces in favour of the non-Communist Left. Mitterrand's strategy prevailed between 1965 and 1968 when he formed the Fédération de la Gauche Démocrate et Socialiste (the FGDS, not to be confused with the UGSD formed in 1973) comprising the SFIO, the Radicals and various Left-wing clubs and which had negotiated a second-ballot agreement with the Communists. The Federation collapsed in late 1968 under the strains imposed by the 'events' of May of that year, and contacts between Socialists and Communists were broken off. Mitterrand's strategy has prevailed again since 1971, especially after he had strengthened his own party, its machine and organization and his position within it. The Socialist Party has concluded a second-ballot agreement with the Communists, and negotiated a Joint Programme of Government with them which was signed on 27 June 1972 and which was supposed to be updated in the summer of 1977. However, negotiations between the two parties broke down on 23 September 1977, and relations between them since then have remained rather strained. The party has also cemented a first-ballot electoral alliance with the Left-wing Radicals: this coalition – the Union de la Gauche Socialiste et Démocrate (UGSD) – has now fought several elections together.

The Socialist Party is undoubtedly in a very strong position: it has a leader of international stature; it has a growing and enthusiastic membership; it enjoys encouraging electoral support; it is powerfully entrenched at the local level; it has concluded electoral alliances. It has also strengthened its links with the university world through bodies such as the Comité pour un Syndicat des Étudiants de France and Démocratie et Université, with certain sympathizers in the army through the Conventions pour l'Armée Nouvelle, with the trade unions (through the many leaders of the Force Ouvrière and the CFDT who are party members), and with the young (through bodies such as the Fédération Léo-Lagrange which in November 1976 claimed 37000 members). It has put down roots in the factories: in 1971 there were only 71 Socialist *sections d'entreprises* and by January 1977 there were 958 representing 20000 members. The party now organizes fêtes, processions, debates and discussions, and now has its own book club (the Club Socialiste du Livre created in 1976), its own record club (Club Socialiste du Disque), its own cine-club in Paris, and even its own anthem – the *Hymne au Socialisme* composed by Mikis Theodorakis for the 1977

Nantes Congress. More importantly, the party has moved into new and better-equipped headquarters at the Place Palais-Bourbon (which is next door to Parliament), enjoys greater financial security than the old SFIO and enjoys the support of a new daily newspaper – *Le Matin de Paris*.

The first main problem facing the PS is that of internal party unity. When François Mitterrand declared that 'if the PS is more than a mere gathering it is not yet a party' he was underlining the lack of tight organization, discipline and policy coherence within the party. The party is composed of a large number of feuding clans: Leninists rub shoulders with revisionists, self-styled revolutionaries with convinced reformists, Jacobins with decentralizers, idealists with opportunists, the dogmatic with the pragmatic. Ex-Communists, ex-members of the PSU, ex-SFIO activists, ex-Trotskyists and the previously uncommitted fight many of the battles of the past within the framework of the party, and these battles take place at every level of the party. Moreover, ideological animosities are frequently compounded by personal enmities. Mitterrand has his own personal 'court' composed of personal friends such as Georges Dayan and Roland Dumas and close political collaborators such as Mermaz and Claude Estier, and he has also firm allies such as Mauroy and Defferre. But he also has his political opponents, such as the leaders of the Left-wing CERES group of the party (which represents about a quarter of the party members), who view Mitterrand as an autocrat and, even worse, as a Social Democrat.

The present Socialist Party is a brittle alliance which is too young to have formed a basic party loyalty. It is divided over a large range of subjects which include the European Common Market, State aid to Church schools, the Middle East conflict, the French nuclear deterrent, the nature of the alliance with the Communists, the extent of future nationalization and the role of the market in Socialist France. It is held together by a brilliant leader, by its relative electoral success and by the prospects of office. The real test of its viability will come when it loses the first, is deprived of the second and is denied the third.

The second main problem facing the party is its relations with the Communist Party – a problem analysed later in this chapter.

The Communists

A number of facts strike the political observer about the French Communist Party (PCF) under the Fifth Republic: the first is that the party has become increasingly integrated into French political life; secondly, the party has liberalized its doctrines and its image if not its methods; thirdly, it has stagnated electorally, and fourthly, it has improved its organizational base; finally, it is facing a number of apparently intractable problems.

The integration of the PCF into French political life

The political isolation of the PCF in the very early years of the Fifth Republic was complete: its position recalled those earlier periods when the party was in a ghetto – the very early years following the Congress of Tours of December 1920 when the party was founded, the period of the 'phoney war' from September 1939 to May 1940 after the signing of the Molotov–Ribbentrop pact, and the height of the Cold War from 1947 to 1953. The isolation of the party at the beginning of the Fifth Republic was due to a number of factors: the bitter and recent memories of the Cold War; the party's slavishly pro-Moscow line which led it to support the Russian intervention in Hungary in 1956; its equally unpopular opposition to the Anglo-French fiasco in Egypt (opposed by the British Labour Party but inspired by French Socialist Premier Guy Mollet); its ambiguous position over the Algerian War (which was intensified after 1956 by Premier Mollet); its opposition to the popular return of de Gaulle in May 1958 and to the new Constitution which was approved by four-fifths of the French electorate in the September 1958 referendum.

Since the early 1960s the party has made a systematic attempt to break its political isolation which had such electorally disastrous consequences. Its electoral alliances with the Socialists and Left-wing Radicals were finally strengthened by the Joint Programme of Government which it signed with the Socialists in June 1972. Increasingly, the PCF, which in the past used to pride itself as unlike all the other parties, is perceived as a party like the others – especially by Left-wing sympathizers. This emerges from an IFOP poll taken in April and May 1977 (Table 10 overleaf).

Other polls suggest that opposition to the appointment of Communist ministers has slowly declined, and that the activity of the party is judged by the electorate as more positive than in the past. In its attempt to assimilate itself into French political life it has been helped by the changing international situation (the thaw in the Cold War and the policy of détente as well as Gaullist policy of *rapprochement* with the USSR all combined to make the party's pro-Moscow stances less 'treasonable' and less objectionable), by the changing

Table 10   *IFOP poll April–May 1977. Replies to the question, 'Do you think that the PCF has become a party similar to other French parties?'*

	Voters of presidential coalition	Left-wing voters (per cent)	Total
It will never become such a party.	60	27	35
It has already become such a party.	26	62	43
No reply.	14	11	22

tactics of the Socialists (who after apparently irreconcilable opposition sought some form of alliance) and by the party's own efforts in liberalizing its policies and images. But there are limits to the PCF's integration into the French body politic: the poll quoted above also makes it clear that there is still widespread opposition to the idea of Communists acquiring the key ministries of the Interior, of Foreign Affairs and of Defence. And opposition to the appointment of a Communist Prime Minister or the election of a Communist President of the Republic is very marked – even amongst Socialist voters, who are the allies of the party.

The liberalization of the party's doctrines and image
The liberalization of the PCF has been based on two interconnected strategies, summed up by the ugly yet useful terms *Italianization* and *deRussification*. The Italianization of the party has involved the acceptance of 'a democratic, parliamentary and governmental vocation' and the modification of many of its cherished dogmas: it has rejected the notion of the *parti unique* – the single revolutionary vanguard party – in favour of multi-partism; it has accepted the primacy of the ballot box as the sole source of democratic legitimacy; it has adopted the principle of alternate government (a Left-wing Government beaten at the polls must withdraw from office); it now resolutely defends the freedom of association of the press, of opposition groups and parties, freedoms which were previously dismissed as 'bourgeois', formal and meaningless; at the XXII Party Congress of February 1976 it officially sacrificed the doctrine of the dictatorship of the proletariat as 'outmoded'. The leader of the PCF, Georges Marchais, has constantly reaffirmed his party's attachment to democratic ends and means. Finally, greater discussion within the

party has been encouraged, and the party has been less neurotically secretive in its relations with the outer world (it has even allowed television cameras into its bullet-proof headquarters at the Place Colonel Fabien).

The deRussification of the PCF was a slow and painful process for the most pro-Stalinist Communist Party in Western Europe. Its reaction to Kruschev's denunciation of Stalin in 1956 was one of stunned disbelief, and it was not until 1966 that it was prepared to take an open stand against the USSR when *L'Humanité*, the party's newspaper, published an attack on the Daniel and Siniavski trial. Since then there have been many occasions when the PCF has ostentatiously taken its distance from the Soviet Union: in August 1968, Waldeck-Rochet, then the leader of the party, condemned the Soviet Union's invasion of Czechoslovakia; in December 1976, the PCF criticized the Soviet repression following the workers' insurrection in the Baltic ports; in early 1971 it publicly appealed for justice for Soviet Jews; in October 1975 it intervened successfully in favour of Leonid Plyusch, the dissident Soviet mathematician; in the following month it made a pointed attack on labour camps in the USSR: in October 1976, Pierre Juquin, one of the party's leading liberals, attended a public meeting which had been organized to demand the release of political prisoners in Latin America, in Czechoslovakia and in the USSR – Pinochet's Chile and Brezhnev's Soviet Union ('the motherland of socialism') were thus bracketed together. The party constantly reminds the Soviets – and the French electorate – that its policy is determined in Paris and not in Moscow, and that it is resolved to take 'the French road to socialism'. The deRussification of the PCF was greatly facilitated by the evolution of the international situation: the thawing of the Cold War following the death of Stalin; the process of deStalinization in the USSR; the break-up of Communist international solidarity especially following the Sino-Soviet split; the development of the doctrine of polycentrism inspired by the Italian Communist leadership.

Both the liberalization of the party and its policy of assertive independence *vis-à-vis* of Moscow were encouraged by the accession of Waldeck-Rochet – 'the Pope John of the PCF' – to the party leadership in 1964 after the death of Maurice Thorez, whose thirty-four years of autocratic and illiberal rule more readily recalled that of Pius XII. Both were also encouraged by the gradual promotion to key party posts of a new generation of Communists – *les nouveaux communistes* – who were less marked than their elders by the passionate and angry battles and memories of the past, and who were anxious to play an active role in the government of the country.

Liberalization of doctrines has not always been matched by liberalization of methods. Decision-making is still based on the Stalinist practice of democratic centralism, with the base sometimes merely informed of changes of policy: the party's dramatic switches, in 1977, over the French nuclear deterrent (which overnight became acceptable), over direct elections to the European Parliament (previously denounced by Marchais as 'crime against France' but adopted by the party barely a year later), and their relations with the PS are but three recent examples. Furthermore, the brutality and ruthlessness of the party's campaign against its Socialist ally after September 1977 quickly awakened disquieting memories of its Stalinist past.

The electoral stagnation of the PCF

Since the days of the Liberation, the size of the Communist Party electorate has first declined and has then stagnated. In November 1946 the party polled 28·6 per cent of the votes, in June 1951 26·4 per cent, in January 1956 25·6 per cent, and November 1958 only 18·9 per cent. In the November 1958 elections – the first of the Fifth Republic, the party won only 3 870 000 votes (compared with 5 503 000 less than two years previously), and its representation in the National Assembly was decimated, falling from 146 in 1956 to only 10 in 1958. Since 1958, the party has regained some ground, but it has never achieved the level enjoyed under the Fourth Republic: in November 1962 it polled 21·8 per cent of the votes, in March 1967 22·5 per cent, in June 1968 20·2 per cent, in March 1973 21·3 per cent. As can be seen, its best performance under the Fifth Republic is worse than its worst under the Fourth. Moreover, the evidence of successive by-elections, the local elections and the opinion polls which suggested that the party was unlikely to improve its position in the March 1978 elections proved correct: it won only 20·8 per cent of the poll. The PCF, once the biggest party of France, is now no longer even the biggest party of the Left, for it has been supplanted in that position by the Socialist Party of François Mitterrand.

The reconstruction of the party organization

The PCF has never enjoyed the mass membership of the British Labour Party, the German Social Democratic Party or the Italian Communist Party, and even at its peak, at the time of the Liberation, membership never reached a million. During the Fourth Republic the party lost two-thirds of its membership, which by 1958 had dwindled to about a quarter of a million. Membership oscillated between 225000 and 275000 throughout the 1960s, but since then the party leadership has made a successful effort to increase it: figures released by the party at the beginning of 1978 indicated that the party has passed the 600000 mark, which means, more realistically, however, a figure of about 450000.

The party has also in the 1970s increased the number of party cells, but although the 1972 total of 23178 (8072 factory cells, 9649 local cells and 5457 rural cells) represents a real jump since 1961, when there were 16072 (3819 factory cells, 7590 local cells and 4663 rural cells), it still constitutes only two-thirds of the total (of 36283) of December 1946. Nevertheless, whatever its weaknesses compared with the time of the Liberation, the PCF, with its 860 full-time agents (and another 14000 paid by Communist municipalities, the Communist-dominated CGT and other Communist bodies) and with its army of devoted activists, is the best-organized and most disciplined party in France. It is also the wealthiest party in the country. It owns an estimated 135 blocks of flats, a great deal of land, 25 printing shops and 50 bookshops, and controls over 300 firms: the self-proclaimed party of the poor is the richest party in France.

The problems of the PCF

The PCF faces a number of problems apart from its electoral stagnation and the widespread suspicion about its motives and intentions: it has continuously troubled relations with its Socialist allies whom it suspects of hegemonic designs; it is sensitive to the danger of being outflanked on the Left as in May 1968; its rapports with the CGT are much less smooth than are generally supposed, since the latter is frequently more syndicalist than Communist; it has always been plagued by the soul-searching of its own intellectuals; its membership may be growing in numbers but it is neither as subservient nor as militant as the leaders would wish; the party press is in a parlous state (in 1946 there were seventeen Communist newspapers, thirty years later only four, which are read by only the party faithful); many of its satellite organizations have disappeared, whilst others such as the Union des Femmes Françaises and the Mouvement de la Jeunesse Communiste are decreasingly effective.

There are even more fundamental problems confronting the PCF. First, it bases much of its electoral strategy on the working class. Indeed, its proudest claim is to be *the* party of the industrial working class, even though only half the voters of the party are working class and only about a third of the working class votes for the party. Furthermore, as elsewhere in Western Europe, the industrial working class is not only a minority but is not a growing minority. Secondly, the party has the difficult task of balancing the demands of its highly disparate electorate, and all too frequently it resembles less the vanguard of the proletariat than the broker of the conflicting demands of its discontented (and sometimes reactionary) constituent elements. Thirdly, the party has yet successfully to tackle the vexed problem of internal party democracy: in spite of increasing intra-party debate, the Leninist principle – or rather the Stalinist practice – of democratic centralism still holds good. Decisions are frequently *diktats*, imposed from above on a bewildered membership. Fourthly, in spite of reiterated declarations that the party is taking 'the French path to socialism' and in spite of increasing criticism of the USSR, the PCF refused to sever its umbilical link with the 'motherland of socialism'. The party now argues that socialism and democracy are inseparable, but whilst admonishing the Soviet Union and the East European régimes for lack of democracy it refuses to castigate them as being unsocialist. The illogicality was pointed out by Pierre Daix (who was expelled from the party for his audacity – one should never be right too early in the PCF) and is constantly highlighted by Jean Elleinstein, the Communist historian and *enfant terrible* of the party.

Finally, the party is faced with the seemingly irresolvable dilemma which arises out of its pursuit of revolutionary ends by reformist means. Ronald Tiersky, in his excellent study of the PCF, defines the four basic roles of the party as those of:

A revolutionary vanguard party – the self-styled exclusive repository and propagator of Marxist truth.

A counter-community, or what Annie Kriegel calls a 'microcosmic anti-society': the party provides an environment for its followers which is distinctive from, and even alien to the rest of French society, and which secretes its own organizations, rites, norms and languages.

A tribune or organ of the protest and frustrations of the underprivileged.

A governmental party with a managerial vocation.

According to Tiersky, the four basic roles develop simultaneously, 'partially in harmony and partially in contradiction', one or another being emphasized, depending on the prevailing circumstances. Now it is clear that in fulfilling these four roles, the party helps to stabilize the French political system: as a revolutionary vanguard party and the bearer of a chiliastic message it gives hope to the discontented of the advent of the new millennium; as a counter-community it provides a focus for the loyalty and potentially disruptive energy of its followers; as a tribune party it articulates grievances and diverts them into institutional channels, thus preventing them from finding expression in anti-system violence; as a government party with a managerial vocation its members have permeated innumerable commissions, committees and councils of both an appointed and elected nature, and often as a result they are more managerial than militant, becoming the 'objective collaborators' (one of their own favourite phrases) of the system. The cumulative effect is that the PCF, which has the avowed intention, however ultimate, of destroying the existing system, has become one of its principal props: far from undermining the system it underpins it and even, to some extent, legitimizes it. Thus, to use Annie Kriegel's expression, the party has become 'one of the agents of the pluralistic cohesiveness of established society'. The extreme Left, totally disabused by the timorousness of the PCF during the events of May 1968 and disillusioned by its subsequent moderation, vilify it for its lack of revolutionary zeal. The Right, however, denounces it for its revolutionary zeal, arguing that it is merely more skilfully disguised than in the past.

Table 11 *The electoral performance of the Left 1946–78 (percentage of votes cast)*

Election	PCF	Non-Communist Left	Total
November 1946	28·6	30·3	58·9
June 1951	26·4	24·3	50·7
January 1956	25·6	30·1	55·7
November 1958	18·9	24·0	42·9
November 1962	21·8	20·4	42·2
March 1967	22·5	21·1	43·6
June 1968	20·3	20·4	40·6
March 1973	21·3	25·0	46·3
March 1978	20·6	28·9	49·5

The Left under the Fifth Republic: the uneasy alliance

Since the beginning of the Fifth Republic the Left has not won a major national election. Its performance has been far from distinguished in legislative elections (Table 11) and in terms of representation in the National Assembly (Table 12).

Table 12 *Representation of the Opposition Left in the National Assembly 1958–78*

Election	PCF	Socialists and Radicals*	Other Left	Total Left Deputies	Total Deputies
November 1958	10	77	–	87	552
November 1962	41	104	2	147	482
March 1967	73	118	4	195	467
June 1968	34	57	–	91	483
March 1973	73	101	1	175	490
March 1978	86	114	1	201	491

* In 1973 Left-wing Radicals only.

In the presidential elections the fortunes of the Left have varied. In December 1965, François Mitterrand, the only candidate of the Left, won 31·7 per cent of the votes at the first ballot and a respectable 44·8 per cent at the second against de Gaulle. In the June 1969 elections which saw the victory of Georges Pompidou, there were no fewer than four Left-wing candidates (Defferre the Socialist, Duclos the Communist, Rocard the leader of the PSU and the Trotskyist Krivine), who together mustered only 30·9 per cent of the votes. Because the best placed Left-wing candidate, Duclos, ran third, the Left was eliminated from the election and was unrepresented at the second ballot. Five years later, in May 1974, the Left came within an ace of winning the Presidency when François Mitterrand, again the candidate of the Socialists and the Communists, won 43·2 per cent of the votes at the first ballot and 49·2 per cent at the second.

The Left has been deprived of national office throughout the Fifth Republic. It is true that it seemed poised for victory in March 1978, but as Jacques Chirac once unkindly remarked, 'the Left wins the opinion polls but never the elections'. It is also true that the coalition which presently embraces the Socialists and the Communists has been welded together a little more firmly in the past few years, both ideologically (because of the radicalization of the Socialists and the ....zation of the Communists) and also over specific policies where there is a closer identity of views. It has also fought several election campaigns together and it has drawn up a Joint Programme of Government which binds both parties of the period of a legislature. But the coalition remains very fragile, and the Joint Programme (the interpretation of which divides the signatories) was elaborated in part because neither partner basically trusted the other. Even its survival is in question. Each party accepts the alliance as a means of strengthening itself and furthering its own ends, and each party is determined to retain its separate identity. Tension between the partners is inherent in the alliance, for each views it not only as a means of beating the Right but also as an instrument for establishing its own hegemony. Tension heightens when one partner seems to be profiting more than the other: when, for instance, the Socialists fared very well and the Communists rather badly in the October 1974 by-elections, relations between the two were soured for more than a year. Furthermore, each party suspects the motives and intentions of the other: many Communists chastise the Socialists for being essentially electoralist and reformist, whilst many Socialists fear the fundamentally revolutionary, undemocratic and anti-parliamentary intentions of the PCF (fears which seemed to be confirmed by the PCF's support for the Stalinist Cunhal in Portugal in 1975). The PCF also dislikes the electoral growth of the PS, whilst the PS is suspicious of the organizational strength of the PCF.

Between the two partners there also remain wide differences over policies: over the French nuclear deterrent which, after a remarkable *volte face* in May 1977, the Communists now defend as indispensable (it had previously been pernicious); over the extent of nationalization in the event of a Left-wing victory at the polls, and over the means of compensating those whose property has been expropriated; over the Middle East conflict (since many Socialist leaders are pro-Israel); over the nature of workers' control, which the PCF suspects as a means of furthering and legitimizing class collaboration. Policy differences are exacerbated by ideological disagreements related to issues such as intra-party democracy, the role of the party (the PCF still views itself as the sole repository of scientific Marxism), the Communist Party's claim to be *the* party of the working class, the nature of the transitional phase to socialism, and the PCF's relations with Moscow. As the breakdown in the negotiations between the parties in September 1977 clearly revealed, there is even fundamental disagreement over the nature, the interpretation and the function of the Joint Programme of Government: for the

Communist Party leadership it is but a starting point and a mechanism for triggering off the activity of the masses as well as a means of 'irrevocably' transforming the French economy. For some Socialists, notably Michel Rocard, it is merely a compromise between two distinctive Left-wing cultures and traditions; for other Socialists, mainly those associated with the CERES group of the party, it is an *instrument de dépassement* – a part of a dialectical process which helps to transform both parties in a way which will facilitate ultimate unity.

For the moment, the Left-wing alliance must be considered as a tactical response to the challenges of the régime: the most powerful cement of Left-wing unity of action is Right-wing unity of action. Both parties are condemned to live together, but they remain distinct entities in terms of their electoral audience, their membership, their policies, their basic ideology, and even in their language, folklore and loyalties. Their relationship is inherently ambiguous: the self-interest of each dictates both complicity and competition with the other. The real test of the alliance will come when it is confronted with the unpopular choices of office. The suspicion lurks that over twenty years of opposition have blunted the sense of reality in the minds of many Left-wing leaders: absolute lack of power can corrupt as absolutely as absolute power. An ambitious and costly programme (based on the achievement of an unattainable growth rate) is envisaged when the country is still in the grips of the economic crisis which has afflicted the western world since 1973. And the Left will get little encouragement from the business world: the very idea of the Left winning an election worsens the investment crisis and panics 'patriotic' Frenchmen (for patriotism, according to the Right, is a preserve of the Right) into sending their money to Switzerland and the United States. Certainly, the historical augurs are not encouraging. The Popular Front experiment from 1934 to 1938 ended in ignominy and the period of Left-wing governmental collaboration from 1944 to 1947 was brought to an end in acrimony. All too often – in 1924, in 1936, in 1946 and 1956 – Left-wing coalitions elected at the polls collapsed long before the following elections to leave the Republic once more in the reassuring hands of the Right.

The powerless Left?

It has frequently been asserted that the Left has been 'out of power' since the beginning of the Fifth Republic. But such an assertion is too simplistic, for it confuses 'office' with 'power'. And even if the official organs of legislative and executive authority are seen as the unique repositories of power, the assertion would still rest on a highly restrictive interpretation of power, which is a ubiquitous commodity and a nebulous concept. It could be argued that in certain policy areas President de Gaulle (in foreign affairs) held, and Giscard d'Estaing (in social matters) holds, 'Left-wing' views. Certain ministers could also be described, with some justification, as Left-wing: Gaullist ex-ministers such as Buron and Pisani were to join the Socialist Party after 1971, while others such as Charbonnel, Hamon and Capitant were to enter into alliance with the Left after 1974. Prime Minister Chaban-Delmas fell foul of the very conservative private staff of President Pompidou because, as Chaban-Delmas was later to recount in his memoirs, he was considered to be doing the work of the Socialists. It is also clear that Left-wingers have been very influential in certain private staffs – those of Chaban-Delmas between 1969 and 1972 and of President Giscard d'Estaing since 1974 are good examples – and in certain parts of the administration: it is certainly powerfully entrenched in the lower echelons of the civil service where decisions are often made and unmade.

The power of the Left may be discerned in other ways. First, the parties of the Left have been deprived of national office but they are solidly ensconced at local level. Certain areas such as the great industrial ghettos of the Paris red-belt or parts of the Midi-rouge where the Socialists and Communists win more than 90 per cent of the votes are veritable rotten boroughs of the Left. The Left presently dominates the councils of eight of the twenty-two regions and it also enjoys a majority in the councils of forty-one of the ninety-six French *départements*, whilst the communal elections of March 1977 re-

Table 13 *Socialist and Communist mayors elected in main towns in March 1977*

Size of town	Number of towns	Socialists	Communists	Total Socialists and Communists
6000–9000	403	108	81	189
9000–30 000	605	193	156	349
More than 30 000	221	83	72	155
Total	1229	384	309	693

affirmed the supremacy of the two major parties of the Left, especially in the big towns. To the above figures shown in Table 13 must be added other towns which elected mayors belonging to other Left-wing parties. The performance of the Left in the biggest towns (those with more than 30000 inhabitants) was especially impressive: at present it controls four-fifths of those towns. Certain Left-wing leaders are the undisputed masters of their towns or *départements*: Mauroy at Lille, Defferre at Marseilles, Mitterrand in his *département* of the Nièvre.

The second main area of Left-wing power is in the numerous organizations which are either satellites or merely sympathetic: youth clubs, women's organizations, secular sports clubs and intellectual groups. The Left also has a complex and troubled but privileged relationship with the major trades unions, most of whose members are Left-wing party activists. Thirdly, the Left exercises an intellectual hegemony which amounts, according to the critics, to a 'pervasive terrorism' in certain circles which are not organically linked with it: the dominant ethos of the economic planning agencies, the educational establishment, influential sections of the press, the environmental groups, the consumers' associations, the social security system and many Catholic lay organizations is progressive, egalitarian and Leftish. *Nos idées sont au pouvoir* has been a traditional cry of the Left, which has derived some compensation for being denied the psychic gratification associated with national office.

Finally, the power of the Left may be seen in the constant electoral pressure it exerts on the Right. At each election the presidential coalition has been prodded or frightened into advocating reforms which have been part of the Left-wing programme. It is perhaps worth concluding that France, which has had only very rare and very short-lived bouts of Left-wing government, has none the less embraced many (if not all) of the basic economic and social principles of social democracy.

8 The State and the pressure groups

The first Prime Minister of the Fifth Republic, Michel Debré, proclaimed his intention in August 1959 of destroying 'the feudal forces' which were dismembering the French State: by 'feudal forces' he meant the powerful pressure groups. During the Fourth Republic, in his *Ces princes qui nous gouvernment*, he wrote that it was vital to make war upon those vested interests which 'divide the State and leech upon it with scarcely a thought for the nation or the citizens'. President de Gaulle also refused to see the State as a mere 'juxtaposition of particular interests, capable only of feeble compromises' and claimed that it was 'an instrument of decision, action, ambition, expressing and serving only the national interest'. Yet his view of the groups was less jaundiced than that of the Prime Minister, for numerous incidents showed that he was not against the groups as such: they could and should be consulted. Indeed, his April 1969 referendum, which sought to bring them into an enlarged and more powerful upper chamber, provoked widespread criticisms of neocorporatism. But President de Gaulle, whilst accepting their role in policy-making, refused to tolerate their direct interference in politics. It was a fine yet vital distinction. Hence he accepted the right of student leaders to discuss their working conditions but contemptuously dismissed their protests about the size of the educational budget and denied their right to criticize his Algerian policy. In March 1960, in a reply to the President of the National Assembly about the farmers' main pressure group, he noted that 'however representative this group may be in regard to the particular interests it defends, it is nevertheless, from the legal point of view, bereft of authority and political responsibility'. Whilst Debré hinted at an authoritarian and hostile approach to the 'intermediate bodies' in the name of State purity, General de Gaulle appeared to accept that they had a legitimate but subordinate place in policy-making. Whatever the differences, the views of both men involved an onslaught on the *régimes des intérêts* (another fashionable and misleading description of the Fourth Republic), and a radical change in the relationship between the State and the groups. It is the nature of that relationship which serves as the framework of the following discussion.

The four models

In the literature on pressure groups during the Fifth Republic – and it is unfortunately somewhat sparse – it is possible to discern four basic schools of thought on the relations between the groups and the State: for the sake of convenience they may be called the domination–crisis school, the endemic conflict school, the concerted politics school and the pluralist school. Each has its supporters who root their analysis in the nature of French political society. But whilst each has some justification, all are inadequate and somewhat simplistic in their explanations.

The domination–crisis school

This school is largely associated with Michel Crozier and Stanley Hoffmann, who reformulated in more systematic fashion the views and prejudices of a long line of observers. Those views are anchored in an analysis of French attitudes towards authority and change, and may be briefly summarized as follows:

The French fear face-to-face relations, and they very readily have recourse to impersonal, highly formalized, distant and hierarchized rules imposed from above to govern social intercourse; only such authority is likely to prevent arbitrariness. Hence a powerful and centralized bureaucracy exists.

French political culture is characterized by both 'limited authoritarianism' and 'potential insurrection against authority', and the French oscillate between a normal servility towards authority and sporadic rebellions against it. Closely associated with this idea is the fashionable view expressed by Michel Poniatowski (who echoed Tocqueville) that 'France is a profoundly conservative country which dreams of revolution but rejects reform'.

In a highly individualistic, atomized and anomic society, associational life is weak, for a Frenchman fears the loss of his liberty and individuality which results from belonging to groups. Those groups that do exist are highly fragmented, badly divided, thoroughly egotistical and generally anomic, all refusing the principle of fruitful interdependence. There is an absence of genuine bartering, of

dialogue, of compromising between the groups. Each group fero-
ciously defends its rights against other groups, and resists any
attempts by the State to impose change which might be prejudicial
to its acquired interests.

Since the groups defend the *status quo*, change within society must
be imposed by the bureaucracy: there is thus a gulf between a
modernizing administration and their highly conservative *administrés*.

The State is viewed with mistrust by the ill-organized groups, since
it threatens to impinge upon entrenched rights. Authority must,
therefore, be resisted. This 'perpetual resistance' to authority found
its early philosophical justification in the writings of *Alain* – the
pseudonym of Emile Charlier – who told his countrymen to build
themselves 'barricades' against the encroachment of the State: the
first rule in the handbook of government, he contended, was 'heroic
idleness'. The result of this unremitting and obscurantist resistance is
stalemate – *la société bloquée*.

The State authorities view the groups as 'delinquent communities'
(Jesse Pitts), as 'subservient clients' (Jack Hayward), which may be
treated with authoritariansim (because of their normal servility) and
with contempt (because of their obscurantism). Yet their traditional
rights must be respected, because of their predeliction for revolt.

In this political culture dominated by fear and suspicion and by a
'perpetual resistance to the ruling elites', change can be brought
about to break the stalemate not by peaceful means but only by
sporadic upheavals, by violent social spasms. But these 'functionally
innovative crises' which introduce reforms are then followed by long
periods in which the traditional rules of the game reassert themselves.
In the domination–conflict model, the State dominates the groups
and imposes its directives upon them in authoritarian fashion. But,
fearful of insurrection, it is unable to impose radical reformist
policies which can only be effected in a crisis situation.

There is some justification for the points outlined above: groups
in France are very fragmented and badly divided; the bureaucracy
does play an important role in the life of the nation; parts of that
bureaucracy have proved themselves modernizing as the economic
reconstruction of the country bears witness; Governments and the
administration have certainly acted with extraordinary authoritarianism on occasions (the way in which Prime Minister Barre formulated
and implemented his 1976 anti-inflation plan was but another
example of the mailed fist in the mailed glove); the obscurantist and

unremitting resistance of pressure groups may be seen in the activities, described below, of the small shopkeepers and certain farming groups; the absence of dialogue and compromise is evident in the relations between the employers' organizations and certain trades unions; May 1968 may be considered as yet another 'functionally innovative crisis' which has been followed by stifling and routine-ridden conservatism, since the important rights wrested by the trades unions have been whittled away, and the impetus towards important educational reform has been skilfully broken by the traditional academic establishment. Yet some of the points raise legitimate objections: certain parts of the administration may be modernizing in outlook but others have been obdurate defenders of the *status quo*, especially if its disturbance entails a possible diminution in their own power; the State may be authoritarian on occasions but it has also proved itself permanently sensitive to the demands of certain groups; the bloody-minded conservatism of some groups has been matched by the forward-looking dynamism of others such as the Young Farmers Association; constant compromise is evident in the behaviour of many groups, but it is by nature less spectacular and less obvious than its absence; if May 1968 and, more arguably, May 1958 constitute 'functionally innovative crises' it is also true that the Fifth Republic and its predecessor have shaken up large sectors of French society in a persistent and pragmatic way, unswayed by the pressures of immediate crisis. The social and political reforms introduced by President Giscard d'Estaing which have profoundly affected both the individual and the family were not introduced in a revolutionary spasm but under the normal and healthy impact of electoral fear. The domination–crisis model of State–group relations provides a useful series of insights but not a convincing total explanation. Like most models, it raises more questions than it answers, and it is too neat and too selective in its choice of facts to convey the full complexity of the situation.

The endemic and open conflict school

This school is linked with, but is distinct from, the previous school of thought. It shares certain assumptions about the authoritarian nature of the State, the fragmented nature of the groups and the impact of revolutionary crisis as a creative and reforming force. But it differs from the domination–crisis school in an important respect: its claims rest less on a view of the innate characteristics of French society than on an argument about the functioning of the political institutions of the Fifth Republic. It is maintained that with the decline of Parliament, the natural safety-valve of the Third and Fourth Republics, and the growth of a disciplined pro-governmental party coalition, the political leverage of the groups has been severely limited. Decreasing influence has led to increasing frustration. And frustration has led to mounting pressure of an extra-institutional and often violent nature: Jean Meynaud, writing in 1962, pessimistically observed that,

in spite of the end of the Algerian war and the political liquidation of the OAS [the secret army organization fighting for *Algérie française*] and the Poujadists, the political régime of the Fifth Republic will continue to live in the midst of protest movements, sometimes of a brutal nature. . . . This is not so much the result of the increasing difficulties of neo-capitalism; rather it is the quasi-automatic consequence of the functioning of the new institutions.

Extra-institutional pressure has become endemic and has taken the form of open conflict, and this pressure has been instrumental in wresting concessions from Governments. According to this school, the groups in their relations with the State are less quiescent clients than belligerent defenders of their interests.

Extra-institutional pressure has taken four basic forms throughout the Fifth Republic: strikes, demonstrations, illegal obstruction and violent confrontation. Strikes are more numerous in France than in Great Britain, but because of lack of militancy or lack of trades unions, or both, they rarely last as long. French workers normally resort to one-day stoppages or 'lightning' strikes (which may last only two hours), which are symbolic rather than effective. This is equally true of 'action days' (*journées d'action*), when all the unions call for a one-day general strike: there were nine such days between March 1975 and January 1978. French strikes rarely receive unanimous support: for instance, the national strike of 7 October 1976 against the Government's anti-inflation plan and which was considered by union leaders to be one of the most successful of the Fifth Republic involved four-fifths of the country's teachers and miners, but only two-fifths of the postmen and a third of the railwaymen, and in the private sector only a third of the workers joined the strike. French strikes also rarely last, those of the workers at the Crédit Lyonnais (beginning of 1974), the Post Office (autumn 1974), at Renault (spring 1975), Usinor (June 1975), Fos petrochemical complex (autumn 1975), the Caisse d'Épargne (winter 1976–7), the newspaper *Parisien Libéré* (1975–7) being exceptions to the rule. And with the exception of the *Parisien Libéré* strike, all were failures. It is not only the working class which has gone on strike. Middle-class university students and grammar school pupils, doctors, lawyers and architects have all employed this eminently proletarian weapon (often because they are appalled at the prospect of being proletarianized . . .). The militancy of the French students is no new factor in French history; the events of Algeria, May 1968, and the protests against certain unpopular Bills such as the Debré project of 1973 (which had the impertinence to treat middle-class students like all other Frenchmen by tightening up the law on national service deferment) and the proposed education reforms of Fontanet in 1975 and of Haby in 1975 surprised observers only by the numbers involved.

Illegal obstruction has taken various forms. Lorry drivers have blocked motorways and the more moderate farmers have tipped their artichokes, tomatoes, peaches and apples on to the streets – tactics designed to disrupt traffic and to slow down even French drivers. The ecologically minded also have blocked the sites of proposed motorways, closed down ports to protest against oil pollution and, in Brittany, have invaded proposed atomic energy stations. A favourite target of direct action groups is the local prefecture or sub-prefecture, the physical representation of State authority in the provinces. Mass demonstrations and processions have always been a traditional French means of expressing support or protest, and the Fifth Republic has had its fair share. In 1975, not a particularly troubled year, there were 612 demonstrations in Paris, of which 312 necessitated the mobilization of the police. The events in Algeria triggered off massive demonstrations in favour of peace, some of which degenerated into terrible bloodbaths. During May 1968 Paris, Bordeaux, Nantes, Strasbourg and other big university towns experienced massive processions, mixtures of the rally and the circus, both moving and cathartic.

Violence has been a frequent feature of the Fifth Republic, and has been resorted to by many groups. Extremists in the ranks of the normally mild-mannered environmental groups have been tempted into violent means: in May 1975 they blew up part of a nuclear power station at Fessenheim in Alsace; in July 1976 the offices of the main building of the atomic energy authority was blown up in Tours; in November of the same year a uranium mine was blown up in the Haute-Vienne by a COPEAU (the graphically named

Commando d'Opposition par l'Explosif à l'Autodestruction de l'Univers); in August 1977, there was a bloody confrontation between the police and environmentalists at the site of the proposed nuclear power station at Creys-Malville in the Rhône valley. Not unnaturally, the most violent groups have been those whose very existence appeared menaced. These marginal groups include small shop-keepers, the wine-growers of the south and certain national minorities. When cultural or national vulnerability is combined with economic or political deprivation, however relative, the danger of violence increases, as the activities of the marginal farmers of Brittany, Corsica and Languedoc amply demonstrate. Many poor peasants have developed a siege mentality, which is scarcely surprising, for nearly half the farm population has been forced from the land since 1954 and many of those who remain are heavily in debt (loans from the Crédit Agricole multiplied by eight between 1960 and 1974); most earn less than the minimum industrial wage. The peasants' response has been a series of violent outbursts in 1961, 1963, 1967, 1970, 1971 and every year since 1974.

Many of the threatened groups of the Fifth Republic have both their moderate spokesmen who try to negotiate peacefully with the authorities and also their *enragés* who are frequently grouped in para-military organizations. The small shopkeepers are represented by the CID–UNATI (which in November 1976 claimed 150000 members), which organizes discussion with the Government as well as running clandestine 'self-defence groups', created in 1976 and direct heirs to the *brigades anti-fisc* (a programme in a name!) founded in 1973. These self-defence groups or commandos comprise ten to fifteen members, are organized on a local basis, and their task is 'to oppose by any means the "abuses" of the tax inspectors' (which simply means the collection of taxes). The 'any means' have included armed attacks on tax offices, the theft of tax files and the threatening and manhandling of tax collectors. Many of the wine-growers of the south are represented in the official FNSEA, the biggest farmers' union, and the local Agricultural Chambers. But in the early 1960s, they also formed unofficial departmental action committees, veritable commando groups which have caused considerable damage. In 1975, for example, they overturned 112 lorries (and set light to another four) which were carrying cheap imported Italian wine, pillaged the wine cellars of a prominent Toulouse wine merchant, ripped up railway lines and blocked the port of Sète (where Italian wine arrived). On 4 March 1976, during a *journée d'action* in the *département* of the Aude, the local action committee clashed violently with the police, injured an unsympathetic journalist, pillaged or burnt down six tax offices, attacked a branch of the Crédit Agricole, interrupted rail traffic, damaged toll-booths on the A9 motorway, blew up a televion mast and blocked several roads.

In both Brittany and Corsica, moderate autonomous groups are flanked by more revolutionary and more unruly para-military factions. In Brittany the FLB–ARB (Front de Libération Bretonne–Armée Républicaine Bretonne) and the Résistance Nationale Bretonne (founded in September 1977) specialize in the destruction of television masts, although their other less laudable and more spectacular operations have included the blowing up of an aircraft at Quimper airport in August 1974. Between June 1976 and August 1977, the FLB–ARB carried out no fewer than fifty armed attacks on State property. In Corsica, there are four legal autonomotist movements and as many illegal ones. The principal legal body is the Association des Patriotes Corses (APC) which replaced the now banned Action pour la Renaissance de la Corse (ARC). The APC is essentially moderate (by Corsican standards) and demands not independence but a greater degree of autonomy for the island. The four clandestine movements, the two most active of which are the Front de Libération Nationale Corse (FLNC) and the Armée Révolutionnaire Corse, all demand the independence of the island from France. They have been responsible for some very spectacular actions which have included the destruction of wine cellars belonging to the *pieds noirs* (the French who left North Africa and who are accused of taking over the best land) and the blowing up of a Caravelle at Bastia airport in March 1974 and a Boeing 707 in September 1976 at Ajaccio airport. In 1975, there were 226 officially recorded *attentats* against life or property on the island, and in the first eight months of 1976 there were 176 such actions.

Grumbling resentment punctuated by occasional violence can suddenly erupt into bloody confrontation. There have been several recent incidents which highlight the importance of violence as an ingredient of French political life: the events of March 1976 at Montredon in the Languedoc when 3000 peasants gave battle to contingents from the police ended with the deaths of one policeman and one peasant, and those at Aléria, in Corsica, in 1975 and at the site of the proposed nuclear power station at Creys-Malville in August 1977 also ended in tragic deaths.

The history of the Fifth Republic appears to prove that extra-institutional methods frequently pay. There are numerous examples of a previously insensitive Government meeting demands in the face of conflict, muted or violent. The strikes of the miners in 1963 and of the wholesale vegetable and fruit merchants of 1973 both forced an apparently resolute Government to make major concessions. The small shopkeepers were rewarded for their turbulence with the Royer Act of December 1973 which gives them an important say in deciding whether supermarkets may be opened in the *département*: it was rather like placing the decision of the opening of new pubs in the hands of the Plymouth Brethren. Concessions have also been made to the wine-growers of the south: in 1976 a worried French government violated the rules of the Common Market and placed a temporary ban on Italian wine imports (it was at the same time crowing about the anti-European attitudes of the British . . .), and in January 1977 it announced a costly programme for the restructuring of the wine-growing areas of the Midi. The bloody events in Corsica extracted from the Government in February 1977 a massive long-term aid programme.

The endemic and open conflict model, whilst usefully underlining an important aspect of State–group relations, suffers on a number of accounts. First, it fails to note that extra-institutional means have frequently been totally ineffective in forcing concessions: the violence of the OAS in 1961 and 1962 was exploited by the Government and merely accelerated Algerian independence. Certain groups, through extra-institutional means, have been able to slow down policies, but they have rarely been able permanently to defy the weight of public opinion or the pressures of the market: the determination of the well-backed wheat-growers and of the bakers' lobbies has been unable to prevent the French from eating less bread and more meat and fruit; the antics of Gérard Nicoud, the militant leader of the small shopkeepers, has not slowed down the rush to the supermarkets; the rage of the southern wine-growers has not altered the French desire for better wine. Facts have a habit of taking their revenge.

The second defect of the model is that many of its assumptions about the Fifth Republic are no less valid for previous régimes. Extra-institutional activity by the groups – even violent – is a congenital characteristic of French political society and not an acquired inadequacy of its latest political offspring. Even in the last two generations, 1934, 1936, 1944, 1947 and 1953 stand out as conflict-ridden and violent years. And such bucolic pursuits as the tarring and feathering of tax-collectors who had the effrontery to demand tax payment stopped, not started, with the Fifth Republic. This is not to deny that the Fifth Republic has been spared or has prevented bloody violence – the campaign of the OAS in 1961 and 1962 and the events of May 1968 are eloquent affirmations to the contrary – it is merely to place the problem in a wider historical perspective.

The third major defect of the endemic and open conflict model is that, like the previous model, it seriously underestimates the degree of genuine, peaceful and fruitful dialogue between the groups and the State. Finally, the model often misinterpets the real nature of conflict and violent confrontation, for they are not always motivated by mindless, purposeless and uncontrollable frustration. Violence is often orchestrated in careful and ritualistic fashion, and has always been an intrinsic element in the French bartering process. The deliberate dramatization of a negotiation may enable a group not only to extract concessions from the sponsor ministry but it may also be exploited by both the group and the ministry in bringing pressure to bear on the Government as a whole. Occasionally such dramatization may help the Government to persuade tax-payers that concessions are vital or, in the case of the farmers and wine-growers, to convince her Common Market partners that without concessions revolution would be imminent.

The concerted politics school

If the two previous models of State–group relations lay stress upon the conflictual nature of those relations and emphasize the generally authoritarian and insensitive nature of the organs of the State, the concerted politics model describes the relationship as one of partnership, constant, permanent and mutually beneficial. Concerted politics, writes Jack Hayward,

stresses the interdependence of the Government and the interest groups, and the interpenetration of 'public' and 'private' decision-making characteristic of a mixed economy in which an increasing measure of State intervention has to be reconciled with an increasing measure of interest group intervention in all spheres of social activity.

It is clear that the concerted politics model is both descriptive and prescriptive: it sees the State–group partnership as both desirable and inevitable.

Since the Second World War several attempts have been made to institutionalize the dialogue between the State and the groups: at present both are represented in the various organs of the Five Year Plan, in the Economic and Social Council (a body composed essentially of representatives of employers', workers' and farmers' organizations which serves as 'a barometer of social and economic group opinion' (Jack Hayward)), in the regional economic and social committees (which are described on pages 201–2), and in the consultative and advisory committees which have proliferated in recent years.

Underlying the attempt to direct State–group intercourse into institutional channels was the search for consensus and for 'rational' decision-making. But the search has proved illusory, for it is based on the myth that such a consensus exists, that it is possible, by the alchemy of concertation, to reach decisions acceptable to all interests. Concerted politics implicitly denies the primacy and inevitability of politics, and rejects the intrinsically conflictual nature of decision-making: one protagonist of concerted politics could even proclaim the need 'to depoliticize the major policy options of the nation'. In a country so ideologically divided this was a pious and foolish aspiration. The organs of concertation may have provided useful forums for airing grievances and have occasionally played a useful educative role: but they have been less the instruments of concertation than the institutionalized agents of muted conflict. This has now been recognized, even by the economic planners: the present Head of the French Plan, Jean Ripert, has discreetly abandoned the concept of concertation in favour of consultation.

The pluralist school

The pluralist school argues that a Government, whatever it may proclaim, seeks less to implement the general interest than continually to bring about adjustments between the particular interests which are in constant and inevitable conflict. The State provides an institutional framework for the struggle; far from dominating the groups, it seeks by a policy of accommodation and incrementalism, to facilitate dialogue between them. It further argues that France has undergone a revolution in the last generation, and that the cultural stereotypes propagated by Michel Crozier are less and less convincing. Associational life may have been weak in the past (but even that proposition is highly questionable) but it certainly is not so today, France, it is contended, positively pullulates with pressure groups, ranging from the major economic groups to the ARAP, an association dedicated to the protection of foxes and other vermin. It was calculated that in 1976 there were nearly 200000 associations in France dealing with social questions such as consumer protection, housing, the aged and the mentally handicapped. And in July 1977 the Environment Minister estimated that there were more than 6000 environmental groups comprising 300000 members in the country, and that they were increasing at the rate of a hundred new groups a month.

In the pluralist model, power is not concentrated but diffused: there is a proliferation of decision centres, sometimes informal, often anti-hierarchical in structure, frequently transient, generally ever-shifting. The Government is essentially a broker which, in its search for social consensus, is obliged to modify its policies and to bring about concessions in the light of evolving circumstances. Decision-making is rarely 'heroic', and only rarely results from the imposition of rationally calculated policies, but is rather the negotiation of marginal adjustments to the *status quo*. It necessarily precludes major shifts in policy which would be offensive to certain groups who could jeopardize the harmony of social institutions. In short, Governments buy peace in the search for consensus. The pluralist case receives empirical underpinning by the endless list of 'concessions' or 'incremental adjustments' brought about in non-crisis situations by the normal, legitimate and peaceful bartering process: the Education Minister's unsuccessful attempts to cut school holidays in 1959 and 1969 as the result of resistance from the teachers' unions (who were, of course, motivated by a touching concern for the children); Edgar Faure's decision not to introduce selection at entrance to university in 1968; the withdrawal of the 1973 law on architecture which was adopted by the Senate but never reached the National Assembly; the presidential decision, in September 1976, to scrap the plan to charge motorists in eastern Paris who use the A4 motorway; the burying of the Deniau recommendations for the restructuring of French agriculture in 1976; the decision to prevent the price-cutting activities of a hypermarket chain in 1976 following protests from petrol station managers (yet another breach of the principle of competition which the régime proclaims as sacrosanct).

The list could be extended without difficulty. Yet even a complete list of measures directly influenced by the groups would give only a partial picture of their real and discreet power. First, it is almost impossible accurately to define the *self-imposed parameters of governmental action* – the area in which a Government *feels* free or able to act. The political and psychological limitations imposed upon governmental activity are often more easily discerned than defined, but they are none the less real. Any government knows that there are political no-go areas; limits that cannot be transgressed, conventions that cannot be violated, or rights that cannot be trampled upon, and those limits, conventions and rights are established and protected, often unconsciously, by the groups, Secondly, the extent of group influence even before the formal introduction of proposals in confidential and informal discussions in ministerial corridors cannot be accurately assessed: the introduction of the anti-trusts Bill in 1976 was preceded, according to the Government, by eighteen months of 'intensive negotiations', but it was never made clear with whom or what concessions were made. Finally, the power of certain groups may be manifested in their steady and successful resistance to legislation even after it has been passed. The 'treasures of imagination' released in the academic community during the heady days of May 1968 (*l'imagination au pouvoir* was a description as well as an exhortation) has been skilfully used to undermine some of the more important reforms of Edgar Faure's Higher Education Act: the 'mandarins', imaginative and otherwise, are back in firm control of their university departments.

The pluralist model suffers on a number of counts: it assumes that interests are generally organized when they are often not; it underestimates the extent of extra-institutional activity and even violence; it posits the free interplay of groups, when relations are in fact distorted by the presence of certain very powerful groups enjoying monopolistic positions; it underplays the extent to which the State can direct the activity by groups; it ignores the fact that there is frequently no interplay at all between groups and between the groups and the State even in the same policy area.

The untidy reality

The Fifth Republic has been described as crisis-ridden (because it too readily ignores the groups), as neo-corporatist (because it has attempted to insert them and subvert them in a proliferation of functionally organized institutions) and as 'an interest-dominated régime' (in a solemn protest of the chairmen of the parliamentary committees in July 1971, it was claimed that a régime dominated by the parties – the Fourth Republic – was being little by little replaced by a régime dominated by pressure groups). The reality is, of course, infinitely more complex. There is too ready a tendency in discussing State–group relations to think in terms of the confrontation of monolithic blocks, when, in reality, both are highly fragmented and highly divided. It has already been shown that both governmental and administrative institutions are riddled with functional, ideological and personal divisions. And the same is true of many of the major interest groups in France. In truth, the term 'pressure groups' hides an infinite variety of situations, for they differ in size, structure aims and power.

All the major economic and social interests of France are characterized by extreme fragmentation. The industrial workers who belong to trades unions – and they are a small minority – are distributed in five main peak organizations. The CGT (Confédération Générale du Travail) which has a close but complex relationship with the Communist Party (its General Secretary, Georges Séguy, is a prominent member of the party's *bureau politique*) is the most powerful, the biggest and the best organized of the workers' unions. Like the PCF it is gradually taking the reformist path. The second biggest union is the CFDT (Confédération Française Démocratique du Travail), the heir to a long Catholic social tradition, though since 1964 it has been officially secular. Since 1970 it has been committed to socialism and to workers' control (*autogestion*). The third workers' peak organization is the CFTC (Confédération Française des Travailleurs Chrétiens) formed in 1964 as a breakaway minority group from the CFDT, since it disagreed with the latter's policy of secularization. Fourthly, there is the CGT–FO (Force Ouvrière) which is slightly smaller than the CFDT, is unrepentantly reformist and officially apolitical (even though many of its leaders are active Socialists). The present General Secretary of the Force Ouvrière, André Bergeron, believes in negotiation with government and is reluctant to use the strike weapon. Finally, there is the CFT (Confédération Française du Travail), headed by Auguste Blanc, which totally rejects the use of the strike, denies the concept of class war and sturdily defends the existing capitalist State. Its size is debatable (it claims 100000 members, but a quarter of that figure would be more accurate) and its political docility is legendary. Between the various workers' unions there is a long legacy of bitter conflict: the Force Ouvrière, because of its readiness to negotiate with the employers, is viewed by its rivals as a tool of the Right; the CGT is feared for its connections with the Communist Party and accused of sclerosis and authoritarianism; the CFDT is accused of irresponsibility and 'puerile *gauchisme*'. The CFT elicits the ill-disgused contempt and dislike of all other unions. There have been sporadic displays of workers' unity of action, but they are never followed by any long-term united strategy.

The fragmentation of the industrial working class is matched by that of other socio-economic groups. The business community is divided between big business which dominates the Conseil National du Patronat Français (CNPF) and the owners of the smaller and medium-sized firms whose main spokesman is the Confédération Générale des Petites et Moyennes Entreprises (CGPME) led by Léon Gingembre. The professional middle classes are no less divided than the workers and businessmen, and all attempts to forge a minimum of united action have failed. Bodies such as the Comité National de Liaison d'Action des Classes Moyennes created in 1947, the Syndicat National des Classes Moyennes, founded in December 1975, or the Groupes Initiative et Responsabilité, formed in March 1977, are very weak because their potential constituents are themselves so badly divided. The doctors are a good example: most belong to the Confédération des Syndicats Médicaux Français (which is itself divided between an apolitical majority and a Socialist minority), although a few wealthy consultants who refused to enter the social security system are members of the Fédération des Médecins de France, and a small number of Left-wing general practitioners have joined the Syndicat de la Médecine Générale. Even their professional organization, the Ordre National des Médecins, a highly conservative and self-perpetuating Paris-dominated elite, is being called into question by a militant Left-wing minority.

The managerial and executive classes are equally divided: if most belong to the CGC (the Confédération Générale des Cadres) which was founded in 1944 and is presently headed by Yves Charpentié, militant and more Left-wing minorities belong to either the Union des Cadres et Techniciens, affiliated to the CGT, or the Union Confédérale des Ingénieurs et Cadres, which belongs to the CFDT.

The biggest farmers' union is the powerful FNSEA (the Fédération Nationale des Syndicats d'Exploitants Agricoles) to which half the farmers of France belong: it comprises 30000 local farming organizations with 600000 members and runs its own influential network of banks, schools and co-operatives. There are basically three constitutent elements: thirty-six produce organizations (cereals, meat, milk, wine, tobacco, etc.) of a specialized nature; ninety-three

departmental chambers of agriculture, which are 'horizontal' organizations; affiliated bodies such as the CNJA (Centre National des
Jeunes Agriculteurs). The FNSEA, which was founded in 1946
and is presently led by Michel Debatisse, is flanked (and often outflanked) by several hostile rival organizations: the FFA (the
Fédération Française de l'Agriculture, a Right-wing farmers' organization which resulted from a schism within the FNSEA in
December 1969) and three Left-wing farmers' unions – the MODEF
(Mouvement pour la Co-ordination et la Défense de l'Exploitation
Familiale) founded in 1959, which claims 200000 members, largely
amongst the small farmers of southern France and many of whose
leaders are Communist Party members or sympathizers), Paysans-
Travailleurs, a Left-wing organization which specializes in com-
mando-type operations and which gains most of its support in the
west, and the MONATAR (Mouvement National des Travailleurs
Agricoles et Ruraux), founded in February 1975 and close to the
Socialist Party.

The first consequence of the fragmentation of most groups is to
prevent them from aggregating group demands: they reflect and also
perpetuate the lack of social cohesion and instability. Secondly,
fragmentation weakens the groups in their relations with the
Government. A determined and clever minister may exploit divisions
so as more easily to impose his policy: for instance, important reforms
in medical training and teaching and in hospital structures were
introduced when the Health Minister succeeded in breaking up a
previously united doctors' front. Finally, fragmentation leads to
increased verbal militancy, since certain groups are competing for
the same clientele. There is a wide gulf between the expectations they
raise and the goods they deliver, and the result is disillusion and a
further weakening of the groups. The vicious circle closes.

The *intérêts* are not only fragmented. They also differ considerably
in their power and influence. But that power and influence is not
immutable: it is ever-changing, shifting according to new circumstances. Before returning to the question of State–group relations it
is worth considering the factors which contribute to a group's power.

Access to decision-makers
This can be considered as both a consequence and a cause of a
group's power. During the Fifth Republic the groups tend to focus
much more attention than under the previous régime on the Executive with its increased political power and on the administration

with its wide regulatory powers: favourite targets are the private staffs of the ministers and the highly compartmentalized and vertically organized divisions of the central administration. Links with Parliament and the parties are retained, however: the well financed Union Nationale de la Propriété Foncière has many connections with the parties of the Right, and it certainly brought considerable pressure to bear on them during the debates on the Land Tax Act of autumn 1975. The Aranda scandal which broke in 1972–3 also revealed a network of contacts between certain groups, the private offices of certain ministers and Gaullist Deputies. The farmers, the small shopkeepers and ex-servicemen's organization all have their parliamentary supporters: the farming lobby is well organized at parliamentary level by the Amicale Parlementaire Agricole et Rurale which embraces members of all parties.

Its strategic importance in the social and economic life of the nation
This is an obvious point: as elsewhere, doctors and dockers have greater influence than defenceless university teachers.

Its electoral importance
Many groups, such as old-age pensioners, have only one weapon – the vote – at their disposal, but it is a potent one, and in the feverish electoral atmosphere of the Fifth Republic such groups must be heard and heeded: since the collapse of the Fourth Republic, France has experienced three presidential elections, six general elections and six referenda (all of which were viewed as votes of confidence in the Government of the day), as well as several politically important local elections. The closer the election results (and some have been desperately close) the more sensitive the Government is likely to be: even the stern and apparently unbending de Gaulle allowed major tax concessions to the shopkeepers, self-employed craftsmen, farmers and small businessmen (the bulwark of his electoral support) during the 1965 presidential campaign. Social and economic changes which appear adversely to affect the influence of a group may be offset by electoral considerations. Thus, the farmers have dramatically declined in numbers during the Fifth Republic but their votes have been increasingly important in keeping the ruling Right-wing coalition in power. In 1962, Pisani, a determined Minister of Agriculture, could push through, with some concessions, an important agricultural Bill, but by the mid 1970s the situation had altered: successive plans for the restructuring of French agriculture have been osten-

tatiously scrapped. This need to reassure groups which, although diminishing in numbers, are vital to the survival of the *majorité* helps to explain the passage of the Royer Act of December 1973 which gave shopkeepers an important say in whether supermarkets could be built in their *département*.

The backing of public opinion

Although not essential, public support may be useful. The widespread popular support enjoyed by the miners during their strike in 1963 led to a slump in the Government's standing (President de Gaulle's popularity ratings in the opinion polls reached their lowest point during his ten years of office) and contributed to the Government's humiliating climb-down. All groups tend to marshal public support by presenting their sectional interests in terms of a wider national interest. In a study of the reform of French secondary education Donegani and Sadoun show that all the interests involved in the process tried to legitimize their corporate egoism by reference to ends such as 'democracy', 'pedagogical efficiency' or the economic exigencies of society. Businessmen who were in favour of raising the school leaving age (because a better educated school force was more likely to adapt rapidly to changing techniques) presented their arguments in the name of increasing equality of opportunity (an end which mysteriously disappears in their arguments about income distribution). Virtue was once again mobilized in support of utility. The Government and the administration are no less reticent in their recourse to higher abstract principles to buttress essentially selfish ends. That conveniently nebulous concept of 'the national interest' is frequently wielded against 'the particularist and egotistical interests', especially when civil servants are quite nakedly defending a departmental prejudice.

The power of countervailing forces

These forces almost always exist: indeed, without them there would be no conflicts and no politics. Employers conflict with employees, farmers with industrialists, environmentalists with the protagonists of growth, the small shopkeepers of the CID–UNATI with the much more discreet but no less effective Fédération Nationale des Entreprises à Commerces Multiples, which looks after the interests of the supermarkets, the Catholic Association des Parents d'Élèves de l'Enseignement libre (APEL), the vigilant defender of Catholic private schools, against the Centre National d'Action Laïque and the

Ligue Française de l'Enseignement, which are sturdy guardians of the secular State.

The degree of representativity enjoyed by a group
Thus, the FNSEA, the farmers' main peak organization which enjoys the support of half the French farmers is in a weaker position than its British counterpart, the National Farmers' Union, to which nine out of ten British farmers belong. It is also weaker than the FEN (Fédération de l'Education National) which, with a membership of 540000, embraces over three-quarters of all teaching and school administrative staff. The FEN's biggest component element, the SNI (Syndicat National des Instituteurs), draws a great deal of strength from its ability to speak for 90 per cent of all primary school teachers. But the FNSEA is in a far stronger position than the French trades union movement which is weakened not only by its ideological fragmentation and its internal political dissensions but also by its total lack of representativity: it has been calculated that only 24 per cent of the French work force belongs to a trade union (compared with 62 per cent in Denmark, 46 per cent in Britain and 39 per cent in Germany), and that in certain industries trades union activity is non-existent. The biggest union, the CGT, claims 2350000 members (it has dropped from 6000000 in 1946), the CFDT 820000, the CFTC 225000, the Force Ouvrière 900000, and the CGC 250000. But dividing those figures by half would give a more accurate picture.

Certain groups enjoy monopolistic positions: the powerful professional orders, for instance, the infamously antediluvian and reactionary Ordre des Médecins and the Ordre des Architectes are under increasing pressure from a discontented base, but they continue to insist on membership before allowing the practice of the profession; doctors who have refused to pay their annual subscription have been taken to court. Similarly, no one works on the production side of the Paris press if he is not a member of the Ouvriers Parisiens du Livre, which is affiliated to the CGT. When the *Parisien Libéré*, a Right-wing newspaper, decided to break the monopoly and transferred its printing presses to outside Paris, the workers responded by occupying the existing building and by occasionally stopping the publication of other Paris newspapers (seven times in 1975, six times in 1976 and twice in 1977).

Its internal cohesion

The workers' peak organizations are divided not only between themselves but within each other. All are organized on a functional and a
geographical basis, and all contain militant minorities politically
opposed to the leadership. The CFDT is particularly badly divided:
there are debates of peculiar theological intensity between the
supporters of the Socialist Party, those of more Left-wing PSU and
those of Ligue Communiste and Lutte Ouvrière (both Trotskyist
organizations). There are disputes between the national leadership
and many of the local organizations, who demand disciplined action
but crave autonomy, and there is a permanent battle between those
who see the union as a political force espousing and propagating a
global view of society and those who claim the union is an economic
movement dedicated exclusively to the material well-being of its
members. Like the CGT and the FO, the CFDT tries, generally
unsuccessfully, to resolve the conflicts between its distinctive and
conflicting ideological traditions: reformism, Marxism and anarcho-
syndicalism.

Most businessmen are grouped in the peak organization CNPF
(Conseil National du Patronat Français), but it is badly divided,
since it embraces highly disparate groups. It tends to be dominated
by the very big industries such as the Chambre Syndicale de la
Sidérurgie (headed by the influential steel magnate Jacques Ferry),
although since October 1969 it has been the accredited spokesman
for the entire business community. It is openly in favour of the existing economic order and its leader, François Ceyrac, gave his un-
qualified support to the Government in the 1973 and 1978 general
elections and to Giscard d'Estaing in the 1974 presidential elections.
Amongst its affiliated members is the PME (Confédération générale
des Petites et Moyennes Entreprises) which was founded in 1936 to
protect the interests of the small businessmen and which champions
the small man against big business, against multinational companies,
money-grubbing Governments and the technocrats of Paris. Its
leader, Léon Gingembre, is a flamboyant figure with a gift for colour-
ful threats. It has been affiliated to the CNPF since 1954. At the other
extreme is the CJP (Centre des Jeunes Patrons), which has strong
Catholic sympathies and which has become the spokesman of the
young, more dynamic and more progressive business elements.

The main peak organization of the farmers – the FNSEA – has
been described as 'a battleground of feudal warlords', and it has

certainly had problems in keeping together the wealthy farmers of the north and the marginal farmers of the centre and the south, the various specialist produce groups, the reactionary elements and the more enlightened young farmers belonging to the affiliated CNJA.

Its financial resources
Money is vital to employ an efficient full-time staff and organize adequate research facilities. Business, banking and insurance groups score heavily in this respect. Part of the weakness of the French trades unions may be attributed to their weak financial position (there are twice as many full-time trades union officials in Denmark even though the work force is ten times smaller: in 1975 the CGT employed only 171 full-time officials). Their inadequate finances also means that the CGT has no strike fund at all whilst those of the FO and CFDT are very small. Expertise and specialized knowledge are useful bartering counters, for politicians and officials need both: the success of the highly expert and specialized farmers' groups and the pharmaceutical lobby rests on the permanent dialogue that they enjoy with the Government and specialized sponsor divisions in the ministries.

Its ability to mobilize its members and its general level of combativity
The CNPF, the employers' peak organization, claims to represent 800 000 firms, but its control over those firms is largely fictional. At the other extreme, the *comité d'action vinicole* of the Aude, led by André Cazes, can quickly mobilize a thousand men and count on the unflinching support of all the wine-growers of the area. Other effective groups in this respect include the primary schoolteachers union (the SNI), and the Communist-dominated dockers union and typographical union, which are affiliated to the CGT and which enjoy the privilege of a closed shop.

The social and political circumstances
There is nothing immutable about the relations between Governments and groups. A change in the social and political climate may radically affect the standing of certain groups. The decline in anti-clerical sentiments partially undermined the strength of the secular school lobby, and the mounting desire for peace in Algeria from 1959 to 1962 weakened the previously influential North Africa lobby. The growing influence of the environment groups in the 1970s reflects a widespread urge to put an end to the process of making

France resemble an industrial suburb of Tokyo. Political change or crisis may also affect the influence of certain groups. The change of régime in 1958 led to the decline of the influence of groups such as the ex-servicemen's association and the notorious alcohol lobby (which during the Third and Fourth Republics had successfully defended the inalienable right of every Frenchman to drink himself to an early death), whose main leverage had been in Parliament and amongst the undisciplined, but strategically placed Deputies of the Right and Centre. The events of May 1968 convinced the Government that major concessions even to the working class were infinitely preferable to the prevailing chaos: the result was the 'Grenelle agreements' which gave the unions 'a charter of rights' and their members unprecedented wage increases.

Policy changes decided by the Government
A change of governmental policy may suddenly alter the position of certain groups. After the failure of the electricians' strike in 1969, which caused such damage and such bitterness, the Chaban-Delmas Government (inspired by Jacques Delors, the social councillor of the Prime Minister's private office) decided to introduce *une politique contractuelle* – a policy of negotiating contracts to put industrial relations on a more coherent and peaceful footing, based on negotiated and binding agreements for a specified period. To sugar the pill, the *politique contractuelle* was underpinned by a promise to guarantee an automatic 2 per cent annual increase in the standard of living. This introduction of collective bargaining inevitably involved close links with the unions, and if the CGT refused such close collaboration in principle (in later practice it was as supple as a medieval Pope) and if the CFDT was characteristically ambivalent in its attitudes, other unions were less reluctant to play the Government's game. Similarly, the influence of the PME (the small- and middle-sized business organization) was enhanced in 1976 when the Government decided to switch its industrial strategy from one based on the creation of massive industrial complexes by encouraging mergers and take-overs (the Japanese recipe for growth) to one resting on the strength of smaller businesses (the German model).

The attitude of individual ministers
Jacques Fommerand has shown how a politically sensitive minister such as Edgar Faure, aware of the need to legitimize his controversial reform of higher education in 1968, multiplied his contacts with

various university groups. The reformist Edgard Pisani as Minister of Agriculture assiduously courted the modernizing young farmers of the CNJA in order to push through his restructuring of French agriculture in the early 1960s.

The State and the pressure groups: some concluding remarks

The basic *leitmotiv* which runs through the preceding analysis is that it is misleading to speak of State–group relations and more accurate to think in terms of relations between a particular decision-maker and a specific group. There is, in truth, an infinite and bewildering variety of situations. The influential Rueff-Armand report made clear that some groups had been totally 'domesticated' and were essentially agents of the administration. Others, such as the FNSEA (the farmers' union), totally colonize and dominate their sponsor ministry or division within the ministry: some organs of State have been transformed into 'institutionalized pressure groups' (Henry Ehrmann). This so-called clientele relationship is most likely to be found in highly specialized and vertically organized divisions of the central bureaucracies. The practice is not necessarily corrupt: France is not a 'banana republic'. Money rarely exchanges hands and its defenders claim that such practices greatly facilitated industrial concentration – one of the Fifth Republic's early and obsessive priorities. Between complete domination and total subservience there is a large variety of other situations. The appropriate organs of State may adopt other attitudes:

Entering into collusion with certain groups

This appears the case in the building industry, where certain powerfully entrenched groups which form privileged clubs benefit from a disproportionate share of State contracts, even though free competition is proclaimed as a cardinal virtue of the régime. In some cases, collusion is even institutionalized: in the Association Professionnelle des Banques representatives of the State banks which dominate the market co-exist with those of the private banks and credit houses, and have on occasions come to collective decisions. Such collusion, as Ezra Suleiman rightly argues, is unfair (because it affects the privileged few) and is dangerous because it blurs the vital distinction between public and private interest and may lead to 'the imperceptible dilution of the public interest'.

Genuinely collaborating to form a symbiotic relationship, both sides
retaining their autonomy, independence and even aggressiveness.

Ezra Suleiman underlines three reasons for the administration's
willingness to collaborate with the groups: it facilitates the formulation and implementation of policies; it provides a Government with
information; it enables a Government to explain its decisions and to
foresee opposition. Perhaps the best example of this sort of relationship is that which exists between certain divisions of the Education
Ministry and the SNI, the primary schoolteachers union. Founded
in 1920, the SNI has managed to create a powerful organization at
national, departmental and local level which embraces nine out of
every ten primary school teachers. It clearly articulates the aspirations and disgruntlement of the base, and a strike call will always
mobilize at least 70 per cent of the members: in the May 1977
general strike 82·5 per cent of the primary school teachers went on
strike. The SNI is in permanent negotiation with its sponsor ministry
and has managed to wrest concessions concerning the size of classes,
sabbatical leave, the length of school holidays and the reduction in
working hours. It has frequently been accused of practising 'corridor
politics' and of unholy connivance with officialdom.

*Discriminating, for political reasons, in favour of some groups and
against others*
The CFT is frequently given as much weight and as many subsidies
as the CGT, which is twenty times bigger. But the CFT, unlike the
CGT, is against strikes, a sturdy defender of the existing economic
order and abhors class war. The subsidies given to students' unions
bear little relationship to their strength but rather to their political
docility. A group may initially be treated with hostility, but if it is persistent and is seen to be mobilizing public support an attempt may be
made to absorb it into an institutional framework with the aim of
more readily controlling it. This was clearly the case with the
CELIB, a Breton nationalist group which made itself an active
nuisance in the 1960s.

Viewing the groups as bodies simply to be resisted
Until recently, for example, Governments of the Fifth Republic
viewed the small and middle businessmen's organization, the PME,
as John Stuart Mill considered the House of Lords – 'an irritating
type of minor nuisance'. Its demands were invariably considered

unreasonable and reactionary and it was generally pacified by fiscal advantages of an obscure and complicated nature. Consultation was largely perfunctory.

Refusing all collaboration with certain groups
The unruly students' union UNEF was frozen out of all contacts with government departments from 1960 to 1963 by short-sighted and vindictive Governments. Annoyed by the students' noisy opposition to the war in Algeria, the Government stopped all sub-sidies, refused to meet its delegations and even helped to establish and then subsidize a rival union – the Fédération Nationale des Étudiants de France (FNEF). Throughout the Fifth Republic the Ministry of Agriculture has met representatives of the FNSEA – the farmers' main peak organization – every week, but it has always refused to recognize agricultural unions such as MODEF, Paysans-travailleurs and the Mouvement des Travailleurs Agricoles which are of Communist or Socialist persuasion.

Adopting an attitude of apprehensive and embarrassed toleration or appeasement
The tax evasion of certain groups such as small businessmen, shop-keepers, hotel-owners and farmers is denounced every year by the Minister of Finance but tolerated by successive Governments who have a wary eye on the electoral consequences of over-zealous tax-collecting. In the wine-growing areas of the south where there was a growing tide of violence in 1975 and 1976 the Government was unprepared to act against the action committees for fear of inflaming passions even further. It took the Government more than two years to put an end to the flagrant illegality of the typographers of the *Parisien Libéré* who were occupying the newspaper's Paris offices, and it finally did so by financing the climb-down of the newspaper's owners.

Finally, it should be noted that there are groups which eschew all con-tact with the organs of State and which exploit the latter's tolerance, laxity or ignorance. The massive property speculation in Paris and on the Côte d'Azur was accomplished by both rule-bending and, in some cases, rule-breaking. Other groups profit from the inefficiency of the State machine in the control of their activities: widespread price-fixing, recognized in the official reports of the Economic and Financial studies service of the Finance Ministry, goes largely unchecked. And the strengthening (in 1976) of the Commission de la Concurrence, the body which is supposed to look into abusive monopolies, was testimony to the inadequacy of the previous control.

In conclusion, the relationship between the different organs of official decision-making and the various groups ranges from domination to subservience, from collusion and complicity to baleful and begrudged recognition and even outright hostility. And there are cases where, out of choice or incapacity, no relationship exists at all. In short, the relationship between the State and the groups during the Fifth Republic is like the rest of government – infinitely complex and intrinsically untidy. Certainly, there is little evidence to suggest that Debré's desire to destroy the 'feudal forces' which he claimed (erroneously) to be dismembering the French State under the Fourth Republic has in any sense been fulfilled.

9 Provincial pressures in a Jacobin state

Economically, intellectually and culturally France is dominated by its capital. The Paris region, which covers only 2 per cent of the national territory, houses 20 per cent of the nation's population, 35 per cent of its business headquarters, 60 per cent of its research scientists, and almost all its actors and its few decent musicians. It is also frequently contended that Paris completely dominates the political life of the country, crushing the provinces under the weight of its *diktats* and whims. Traditionally, the capital was depicted as the malevolent centre of revolution which, in 1789, 1814–15, 1830, 1848 and 1871, disturbed the contented and peace-loving provincials. It was also portrayed as the diabolic purveyor of those modish doctrines and those timeless temptations which were designed to undermine the austere virtues of provincial life, and as a harlot whose mindless frivolity had brought the country at least once (in 1870) to the brink of humiliating disaster: the church of the Sacré-Cœur in Paris was the provincials' act of repentance (though some claim vengeance) for the impiety of the capital. Paris was, in short, a politically turbulent Babylon.

But the Jacobins who fashioned the First Republic and who bequeathed later régimes with most of their institutions and many of their attitudes did not see the capital in such a light. They saw it as an island of culture, a city of enlightenment, a torchbearer of progress assailed by oafish – and reactionary – rural clods, the ignorant troops of the Church and the château. Like the monarchs of the *ancien régime*, they imposed centralization as their means of strengthening the régime against internal opponents, but also against external enemies. Napoleon perfected and future régimes consolidated the centralizing work of the Jacobins. Each was uneasily aware not only of its own fragility but also of the very precariousness of the French national fabric. France is a country of great geographical and cultural diversity and was created by bringing together (with the persuasion of the axe and the sword) peoples as distinct as the

Basques and the Bretons, the Béarnais and the Burgundians, the Alsatians and the Auvergnats, the Normans and the Provençals. Parts of France such as Nice and Savoy are recent acquisitions (they were annexed in 1860), and Alsace has twice this century (1918 and 1945) been taken back from the Germans. Autonomous sentiments have always been regarded with obsessive suspicion and crass insensitivity because it was felt that they could lead to the temptation of secession if allowed to flourish. Centralization was also the instinctive reaction of Governments to successive wars, invasion and occupation when national boundaries were violated: 1814–15, 1870–1, 1914–18 and 1940–5.

Centralizing tendencies have been accentuated during the twentieth century. For latter-day Jacobins such as Michel Debré, the first Prime Minister of the Fifth Republic, centralized State authority was essential to combat not only the potential dissidence in the provinces but also powerful 'professional feudalities', those major groups who threatened the interest of the State in their pursuit of selfish particularist interests. Finally, centralization was the inevitable result of the need to impose minimum standards in electorally sensitive areas such as education, housing and health.

As the result of historical, cultural, social and economic pressures, decision-making became increasingly concentrated in Paris, and strong, unified and centralized authority became the basis of the one and indivisible Republic. It is argued, especially in Opposition circles, that France has become excessively centralized: Paris, it is contended, decides everything and imposes a rigid uniformity upon the unhappy and unwilling provinces. The latest critic is Alain Peyrefitte who, in his *Le Mal Français*, presents several examples of the idiocies of the Parisian stranglehold.

No one disputes that France is a unitary State, in which most major decisions are taken in Paris. But it is important to know not only where decisions are *taken* but from where they *emanate* and where they are *shaped*, and it will be shown in this chapter that in answering those two questions the weight of the provinces fully emerges, and that relations between Paris and the provinces are immensely subtle and complex. Before examining the precise nature of the relationship between the centre and the periphery it is useful to look at the main local institutions and the major local decision-makers.

The institutions and the actors

Local government in France is organized at three levels: regional, departmental and communal. In metropolitan France there are 22 regions, 96 *départements* (divided into 320 *arrondissements* and 3530 *cantons*) and 36 383 communes. The regions are a creation of the Fifth Republic (they were envisaged by an *ordonnance* of January 1959, created in June 1960 and given their present shape in March 1964 and July 1972) whilst the *départements* were created in 1790. The communes date from 1789 but are based on the parishes of the *ancien régime*.

Decision-making takes place at all three levels, and the local decision-makers belong essentially to four categories of institution: the representative assemblies; the prefectoral administration; the provincial field services of the Paris ministries; and the professional associations and the local pressure groups.

The representative assemblies

At all three levels may be found representative assemblies: at the regional level there are two indirectly elected assemblies, the regional council and the economic and social committee, whose powers were defined by the 1972 Act; at the departmental level there is the departmental council, whose basic powers have remained largely unaltered since the 1884 Act; at the level of the commune is the town council, whose main powers date from the two Acts of 1871 and 1884.

The twenty-two regions are essentially organs 'for the concerted action of the constituent *départements*' (President Pompidou) with the task of contributing to regional development through studies, proposals or financial participation in State public investment projects, or even, to a limited extent, by carrying out their own projects. The executive officer of the region is the regional prefect who is assisted by two assemblies: the regional council and the economic and social committee. The regional council is composed of three groups: the Deputies and Senators of the region; representatives of the departmental councils; and representatives of the communal councils. Its task is to vote the budget of the region, and it may vote resolutions within its decision-making competence which are enforceable *per se* by the regional prefect. It also debates and is consulted about the regional options of the Five Year Plan and about the allocation of State grants for public investment of a local nature. The economic and social committee comprises representatives of the various professional associations and pressure groups within the region; its role is largely consultative.

In each of the ninety-six *départements* there is a departmental council (Conseil Général) composed of members who each represent a canton. The departmental councils range in size from seventeen (Lozère) to 109 (Paris). Unlike the members of regional councils, departmental councillors are elected by universal suffrage, with elections taking place every three years when half the members of the council are elected: a councillor's term of office is thus six years. The departmental council meets for a maximum of only six weeks a year, although it has a small permanent standing committee called the departmental commission. Its executive head is the departmental prefect who prepares its agenda, its timetable and its budget. It meets twice a year to discuss and vote the departmental budget which it does, often after ritualistic grumbling and symbolic resistance. The departmental council is a servicing agency for the State (for matters such as roads, schools and certain welfare services), and it also enjoys a limited initiative and discretion in areas not specifically precluded by the law.

There is a local council (conseil municipal) in each commune which is elected by universal suffrage every six years by an electoral system which varies according to the size of the commune. The size of the local councils ranges from nine to 109 (Paris). The local council is the deliberative organ of the commune and has two main tasks. The first is to implement the duties assigned to it by the State: it is a servicing agency incurring obligatory expenses. Its second task is to exercise its competence in areas which are not specifically forbidden by law. It is obliged to present a balanced budget. In most cases the local council merely gives its official blessing to decisions made by the mayor it has elected. Indeed, it is no great exaggeration to claim that the main task of the 475000 local councillors of France is to elect the 36000 mayors.

Unlike his British counterpart, the French mayor is an important and influential personality. Almost all mayors remain in office for at least six years, and the great majority are re-elected after their first term of office. The mayor has two main official roles. First, he is the *representative of the State in the commune*; as such he promulgates and ensures the implementation of laws, regulations, circulars and instructions emanating from Paris. He is also the official registrar of births, deaths and marriages, and he is responsible for drawing up the electoral list and for compiling official statistics (such as the census figures) for the State. Secondly, he is the *executive officer of the local council*; in that capacity he represents the commune in judicial proceedings, is the head of all communal staff, implements the decisions of the council, supervises its accounting and manages its revenues. He is officially responsible for the order, safety, security and sanitation of the commune. In practice, the mayor is the gentle autocrat of the commune, its principal arbitration officer, its father confessor and the guardian of its interests. Endowed with undeniable prestige, *Monsieur le maire* readily feigns a plausible political agnosticism, and in his quest for communal consensus constantly invokes the 'general interest' of the commune. He is judged largely by his ability to keep peace in the commune, ensuring that the norms that govern communal behaviour are not transgressed, and also by his capacity to intervene for his citizens with the prefectoral authorities.

The prefectoral authorities

The prefectoral corps is composed of regional prefects, departmental prefects and sub-prefects (one in each *arrondissement*).

The regional prefect is a recent creation, dating only from 1959. His headquarters is in the principal town of the main *département* of the region, and in spite of his heavy responsibilities he also remains the prefect of that *département*. His powers were defined in measures taken in June 1960, March 1964 and July 1972. His basic task is to impart stricter unity and greater cohesion to administrative activity, particularly in the area of economic planning. To that end, he must, in practice, co-ordinate and direct the work of the departmental prefects in regional development planning. He is helped by a regional mission (*mission régionale*), a kind of brains trust of young civil servants which advises him and executes his decisions, and a regional administrative conference (known as the CAR) which brings together every two or three months the departmental prefects of the region, members of the mission, the regional representative of the Ministry of Finance and appropriate members of the field services of the Paris ministries. He is also aided by the two regional assemblies described above. In principle, the regional prefect has to guide and direct local investment policies in a co-ordinated and rational regional manner. In practice, he has become the main agent for articulating departmental grievances and for transmitting to Paris an economic package which bears all the marks of traditional incrementalism. The position and authority of the regional prefects were much contested in the early years and it is only recently that they have fully established their place in the local decision-making structure.

In each of the ninety-six *départements* of France there is a prefect who is helped by a small number of sub-prefects (one in each *arrondissement*). The prefect is an essentially Napoleonic creation (but he can trace his ancestry to the intendant of the *ancien régime*) and his official roles have not changed since then.

He is the representative of the State in the département. He is the personification of State authority, the living embodiment of the One and Indivisible Republic. He has an unofficial uniform, an official residence in the main town of the *département* – the *Hôtel de la préfecture*, normally the best *hôtel* in the *département* and certainly the most sumptuous – an official car and sometimes princely living expenses. He receives all visiting dignitaries and presides all important ceremonies.

He is the representative of the Government in the département, with the task of supervising and co-ordinating the work of the field services of the Paris ministries (with the exception of Justice, Education and Labour, which escape his official jurisdiction) and he ensures that laws and governmental directives are implemented. His powers as the 'departmental overlord' were considerably augmented by reforms announced in March 1964.

The prefect is the main agent of the Ministry of the Interior in the département, and, as such, exercises an administrative tutorship (*tutelle*) of the local authorities. He may dissolve illegal meetings of councils or suspend meetings which, in his opinion, act outside the scope of their competence. He has an ultimate (although increasingly remote) control over communal budgets. As the agent of the Ministry of the Interior he directly supervises all the field services of the Ministry responsible for the maintenance of law and order. He has the right to ban a film, a demonstration or a procession if he feels it is likely to be prejudicial to public order. Finally, the prefect is still considered to be the main electoral agent of the Minister of the Interior, although there is no doubt that this aspect of his work has steadily declined. He still gives advice, information and warnings to pro-governmental candidates but he rarely intervenes overtly in election campaigns. He realizes the inefficacy of such intervention, accepts that after the election he will have to live with politicians from all the parties, and is aware that if the Opposition wins the elections his chances of survival are negligible.

The prefect is the executive officer of the departmental council: he prepares the timetable, the agenda and the budget of the *département*, and implements the measures decided by the council.

The local field services

Each ministry has its representatives in the provinces. The Ministry of Defence is represented by a general in each *département* (and is responsible for the local *gendarmerie* amongst other things), the Ministry of Education by a rector, the Ministry of Justice by a procurator. But the four most powerful officials in any *département* are the treasurer and paymaster general (TPG, who is the main agent of the Ministry of Finance), the director of infrastructure (Directeur de l'Équipement or DDE), the Director of Labour (DDT) and the Director of Agriculture (DDA). Each of these officials heads an army of lesser State officials, and his task is to implement decisions coming from Paris and also to supervise the work of the local authorities. Some of these men, especially those belonging to highly prestigious technical corps which have their own national networks of influence, are very powerful figures.

The professional associations and the local pressure groups

The three most influential local professional associations are the Chambres de Commerce et d'Industrie, the Chambres d'Agriculture and the Chambres des Métiers, which are composed of representatives of the main economic groups and which are present in all the *départements* and all the main towns. Most of the major national pressure groups have local branches, although some pressure groups, notably in the cultural field, are exclusively local in character. Information on the power of these groups is scant, but there is some evidence to suggest that they are occasionally very influential. Studies of Bordeaux and Abbeville have shown that the chambers of commerce enjoy close and fruitful relations with the mayors. Other studies have revealed that the building of the great petrochemical complex at Fos in the south of France was organized largely in co-operation with the local chamber of commerce, and that the Chamber of Commerce of Rennes inspired and facilitated the building of the giant Citroën car plant in the town. It is also clear that in many rural *départements* the agricultural groups enjoy easy access to, and influence with local officials. Many prefectoral decisions are made on the advice of committees on which these interest groups are represented.

The bases of French centralization

It is possible after that brief description of the principal institutions and local decision-makers to return to the main problem of centre–periphery relations, and to examine the main reasons for the intrinsic weakness of the local authorities in their relations with Paris. It is argued that the weakness of the local authorities derives from four main sources:

The statutory weakness of the local authorities and the obsessive control exercised by Paris and its provincial agents, the prefects and the technical field services.

The archaic nature of the present structures renders local government especially ineffective.

The unrepresentative nature of local elites deprives them of legitimacy in their dealings with State officials.

The financial dependence of the local authorities on Paris is almost complete.

The statutory weakness of the local authorities and the obsessive control exercised by Paris and its provincial agents

The texts which define the powers and competence of local authorities are very restrictive. This is especially true at regional and departmental level, where the prefects prepare the timetable, the agenda and the budgets of the assemblies which do not have their own administrations to enable them to control or propose counter-measures to prefectoral plans. At present, if a local authority wishes to beg or borrow, add a new tax, build a new school or even name a street after someone Paris can, and often does, intervene. By its laws, decrees, circulars, recommendations, instructions and warnings it exercises a constant control of local decision-makers. And that control is further reinforced by that of the financial inspectorate and the Court of Accounts (which examine the accounts of the local authorities) and the administrative tribunals and the Council of State (which judge any complaints against the local authorities). Paris control is thus of a technical, financial and judicial nature, and it is all the more effective since its agents are omnipresent in the provinces: it must be emphasized that many of the tasks carried out by local government staff in Britain are executed by State-paid officials in France.

Heading the vast army of State civil servants are the prefects, described by the more charitable as 'colonial governors', 'miniature emperors', and 'provincial potentates'. Indeed, two leading Socialists, Defferre (the Mayor of Marseilles) and Mauroy (the Mayor of Lille) have referred to the Fifth Republic as the *'régime des préfets'*, and they are only two of many provincial *notables* who have been critical of the powers of the prefects, whose supervision of the regional and departmental assemblies is apparently so overwhelming. Certainly, the texts endow the prefects with considerable powers over the local assemblies. To the general supervision of the prefect must be added the financial control of the Treasurer and Paymaster General and his agents, and the technical control of other field services. Moreover, many local authorities even encourage the technical control of their plans by inviting the field services to draw them up: they do so because they lack qualified staff, because they recognize the need to send well-presented plans to Paris in order to get permission to implement them, and because they wish to exploit the wide network of relations enjoyed by many of the local technical services. The legal, financial and technical assessments of local projects by State officials in the provinces soon spill over into judgements about their very desirability, and are frequently used as mechanisms for blocking those projects.

The archaic nature of the present structures renders local government especially ineffective

Local government structures date from a period when France was almost entirely rural and when social and economic expectations were non-existent. The population explosion and the rapid industrialization and urbanization of the country, growing demands for better social services and minimum standards throughout the country have combined to render totally inadequate the old uniform structures. That inadequacy has been demonstrated by the emergence of absurd anomalies: for example, the 1977 Peyrefitte report on violence and crime in France revealed that the town of Vitry in the Paris region, which has a population of over 100000 and an alarming crime rate, has no police station merely because it is not the main town of a canton (which was a criterion defined in 1871). The inadequacy of the traditional system was amply shown in the 1950s and 1960s by the economic planners who found that the *départements* were far too small to be viable planning units. But the most glaring inadequacy concerns the vast majority of small communes which are clearly incapable of meeting the demands placed upon them.

France, with 36 383 communes, has more units of local government than the rest of her Common Market partners together. All but 2 per cent of those communes have fewer than 10 000 inhabitants, whilst 32 746 have fewer than 2000 inhabitants; 11 206 (or nearly 30 per cent of the total) have fewer than 200 inhabitants. There are even about 100 communes with no population at all! This vast mosaic of small communes no longer reflects the demographic, occupational and economic reality of the country. The very small communes do not have the financial resources to build or to maintain the basic social facilities now widely demanded: the squeamish British visitor to rural France will note that deserted public swimming pools are in much greater evidence than the much more expensive rubbish disposal centres. The rapidly growing towns, on the other hand, soon ran into the problems of rational urban planning, for they lacked the space to expand.

Several attempts have been made to ensure collaboration or co-operation between the communes, but the painstaking efforts of the reformers have met with conspicuous lack of success. Those attempts have taken basically six forms:

Single-purpose syndicates (*syndicats à vocation unique*) which involve a voluntary grouping of communes for only one specific and defined purpose. There are presently just over 10 000 such syndicates.

Multiple-purpose syndicates (*syndicats à vocation multiple*). Since the January 1959 *ordonnance* communes have been allowed to co-operate on a voluntary basis to carry out any number of tasks which they themselves specify. By mid 1977 there were 1738 multiple-purpose syndicates grouping 16 940 communes.

Districts are the heirs to the urban districts (also created by the January 1959 *ordonnance*) and are designed to induce co-operation between communes in the same conurbation. The present 148 districts are *obliged* to carry out certain services such as housing and fire-fighting, and they also have competence over any other areas defined by the constituent communes. The districts have greater financial control than the multi-purpose syndicates over the constituent communes.

Urban communities (communautés urbaines). The law of December 1966 created the four urban communities of Strasbourg, Lyons, Lille and Bordeaux which involved the grouping of 199 communes. Since then five new urban communities have been voluntarily formed in the conurbations of Cherbourg, Le Mans, Dunkirk, Le Creusot and Brest. The creation of an urban community involves the obligatory transfer from the constituent communes to the community of services such as housing, fire-fighting, the construction and equipment of primary and secondary schools, water, rubbish disposal and cemeteries, public transport, town planning and public works. The council of the urban community is composed of representatives of the councils of the constituent communes.

New towns. In December 1972 the Government created nine new towns in the rapidly developing Paris region. This involved the disappearance of sixty-four communes.

The merging (fusion) *of communes* has been encouraged by a series of measures taken during the Fifth Republic. But in spite of prefectoral pressure, ministerial exhortation and financial inducements the number of mergers remains obstinately small: between 1959 and 1970 only 746 communes agreed to merge into 350. The July 1971 Act was designed to speed up the process, but local resistance proved too effective: in the year following the 1971 Act only 300 communes had agreed to some form of merger, and by the beginning of 1975 only 779 mergers had taken place involving the disappearance of 1130 (or less than 3 per cent of the total) communes.

It seems likely that France will live with her vast mosaic of communes for many years hence. The latest recommendations on local government reform, contained in the Guichard report of October 1976, envisage the creation of 750 urban communities and 3600 communal communities (in rural areas) which would have jurisdiction over the main tasks of planning, transport, housing, education and health. The existing 36000 communes would remain and their mayors would carry out minor administrative tasks. Guichard recommends that the *first* stage of the changes be completed by 1985 – an indication of the foolhardy alacrity with which local government is reformed in the Paris-dominated Republic! And even that distant date seems wildly optimistic, for already the serried ranks of rural mayors have made clear their opposition to a reform which would relegate them to the role of second-class officials.

The profoundly unrepresentative nature of the local elites deprives them of legitimacy in their dealings with State officials

The unrepresentative nature of the local elites is both geographical and social. The size of local constituencies varies widely. In the *département* of the Hautes-Alpes, for example, the canton of Embrun had in March 1976 7191 inhabitants whilst that of Barcilonnette had only 318, yet both had one representative in the departmental council. In all the departmental councils rural cantons are given undue weight: until 1973, in the *département* of the Haute Garonne, Toulouse, the main town with a population of 450000, had four councillors, whilst the rest of the *département*, with a population of only 250000, shared thirty-five councillors.

The socially unrepresentative nature of local councils is notorious (Table 14). Only 2 per cent of the departmental councillors elected in 1974 and only 693 of the 37708 mayors elected in 1971 were women, who comprise over half the population. The manual working class is also vastly under-represented: only 1·72 per cent of departmental councillors and only 2·9 per cent of mayors issue from that class, which represents nearly a third of the French population. At present,

Table 14   *Occupations of locally elected elites*

Occupation	Département Councillors elected in 1974 (*per cent*)	Mayors on 31 December 1976 (*per cent*)	Population
Upper management and liberal professions	35·13	11·1	12·8
Industrialists, shop-keepers and small businessmen	15·30	15·4	5·0
White collar and middle management	20·95	10·5	19·7
Workers	1·72	2·9	32·3
Farmers and farm-workers	13·59	45·4	7·9
Retired or not working	13·11	14·7	22·3

amongst departmental councillors there are five times more doctors than workers.

Mayors and departmental councillors tend also to be elected from amongst the ageing and the aged: four-fifths of both groups are over fifty years old. The not totally inaccurate portrait of the average mayor or departmental councillor projects him as an ageing male representative of a traditional social elite from a rural area. He is seen as cautious and conservative, totally unsympathetic to the moods and needs of *la nouvelle France* and technically ill-equipped to meet its challenges.

The financial dependence of the local authorities on Paris is almost complete

For the critics, what little autonomy is left to the local authorities is rendered illusory by financial restrictions. Almost all French communes are heavily in debt: it has been calculated that about three-quarters of new loans are contracted to pay back old debts. Local authorities complain that Governments create public services but then leave the whole or part of their financing to the local authorities – which they then accuse of profligacy: for British observers it all has a familiar ring. Nor has the financial crisis of local government been solved by the rapid rise in local taxes: between 1959 and 1973 they rose by an annual average of 12 per cent, in 1974 by 20 per cent and in 1975 by 30 per cent.

The subject of local government finance has always been politically explosive, and Governments have always moved with the utmost circumspection in tampering with the basic structures. The independent resources of the regions were limited by law to 35 francs per inhabitant, which produces in the smaller (and poorer) regions only derisory sums. In the communes the situation is no better. In spite of no fewer than ten governmental or parliamentary reports between 1920 and 1970 the shape of local government finance remained unchanged, and it is only in the last five years that limited reforms have been introduced.

The independent resources of the communes, which amounted to 35 000 million francs in 1975, are totally inadequate, and increasingly the communes have had to turn to the State for loans (12 000 million francs in 1975) and subsidies (45 000 million francs in 1975). The system of loans and subsidies resembles a statistical maze: a senatorial report in 1973 enumerated no fewer than 150 kinds of State subsidy available to the communes. State aid to the communes may be summarized as follows:

State grants for capital investment projects or programmes, often available through specialist public agencies such as the Caisse d'aide à l'équipement des collectivités locales (CAECL).

Long-term loans, four-fifths of which are filtered through bodies such as the Caisse des Dépôts et Consignations and the Crédit Foncier.

Transfers of items of expenditure. The State may reduce the expenditure of the local authorities by transferring to the general State budget items previously on local budgets. One of the recent complaints of local authorities is that the reverse is now happening.

At present the State provides, through loans or subsidies, about 70 per cent of the finance for local capital investment projects and for about 60 per cent of their current operating costs. To obtain a loan a local authority must submit its project to officials of the Ministry of Finance and the TPG, their representative in the provinces, who may modify, slow down or even reject it.

In conclusion, it is argued that local authorities have their autonomy severely circumscribed by the texts which govern the competence of local assemblies, by the intrinsic weakness and archaism of their structures, by the general supervision of the prefects. And that even when they are allowed autonomy, Paris restricts their freedom by a constant flurry of circulars and recommendations and by its manipulation of its financial powers: indeed, by insisting that certain technical norms or financial stipulations be met before the grant of a subsidy or a loan the State controls either directly or indirectly an estimated four-fifths of all local investment projects. The picture appears, therefore, a sombre one, with the innocent and virginal provinces assailed and violated by a brutal and insensitive capital. In truth, however, the situation is much less melodramatic and infinitely more complex.

Local influences in the One and Indivisible Republic

One cannot understand the political and governmental system of the Fifth Republic without taking into account the influence of local forces. The rigours of centralization are tempered by various factors which ensure that local decision-makers are not the inactive spectators of their own collective fate. Those factors may be summarized as follows:

Centre–periphery relations are based less on domination than on an intrinsic mutual dependence.

Provincial elites are able to exploit differences of opinion and outlook in Paris.

State officials are often sensitive to local requirements.

The position of locally elected notables is much more powerful than the texts suggest.

The power of the prefects is exaggerated and its nature misunderstood.

There has been an increase in the number, the size and the autonomy of big towns.

Let us examine each point in turn.

Centre–periphery relations are based on an intrinsic mutual dependence

Relations between Paris and the provinces are all too frequently presented as antagonistic when, in reality, there is frequently a large measure of agreement between them. Often they are pursuing common objectives which are defined, in large measure, by electoral pressures to which both are equally sensitive. In the 1950s and 1960s both were involved in encouraging industrialization and both were trying to contain an explosion of socio-economic expectations. Both are now frantically concerned with improving the 'quality of life' under pressure from the increasingly popular environmentalists. But interdependence is rooted not only in the pursuit of common objectives; it is also embedded in mutual self-interest. Whilst many decisions made in Paris automatically affect the provinces it is frequently forgotten that local decisions may have national repercussions. For instance, the policies of the big towns towards immigrant workers have not only local but also national and even international consequences. It is also clear that if the local authorities need the financial assistance of the State, the State frequently calls upon the financial help of the provinces: thus, for example, in July 1977, Paris decided to go ahead with its plans to improve the Canal du Midi only when the three regions involved promised to pay two-fifths of the cost. Whilst it is true that the budget of the local authorities represent only 15 per cent of the total budget of the State, compared with 50 per cent in Sweden, Denmark and Great Britain and 80 per cent in the German Federal Republic, it must be emphasized that local authorities in those countries are paying for many more services imposed upon them by the State: the actual degree of financial autonomy based on *real disposable income* is much less than implied by the above figures. It should also be recalled that about a third of the State budget in France is spent by the local authorities, which are directly involved in about two-thirds of the State's capital improvements expenditure.

In the 1950s and 1960s an effort was made to integrate the local system into a framework of national economic imperatives. The problems of economic growth, regional imbalances and urban planning led rationally minded State technocrats and bureaucrats into an assault on the 'irrational' incrementalism of the existing system. The prefects and the technical field services were to be the transmission belts of Paris orders to the localities. The planners soon acknowledged that local consultation and co-operation were vital to legitimize decisions and also to acquire vital information. They also discovered that tawdry electoral considerations had also to be taken into account: the DATAR carried out its work of industrial decentralization with one eye on economic imperatives and the other on the polling booths. Moreover, it soon became apparent that local officials, far from being the agents of enlightened national economic rationalism, readily remained the spokesmen for local interests and the instruments of self-interested incrementalism.

Provincial elites are able to exploit differences in Paris

Paris in its relations with the provinces is far from being a homogeneous entity. It is not 'Paris' or the 'State' which has relations with the periphery: both are convenient shorthand terms (even if the French do want to invest them with some quasi-mystical quality) embracing a vast variety of political, administrative, public and semi-public agents. Jacques Antoine, in his book *Le Pouvoir et l'opinion*, reveals that the administrative group established to study concrete proposals for regionalization in the 1969 referendum had great difficulty in pinpointing all the various Paris bodies concerned with local affairs. The group reporting on local finance for the Sixth Five Year Plan (1971–5) noted that an application for a loan or subsidy normally involved no fewer than sixty procedures in nine ministries, whilst the Bouvard senatorial report of 1976 indicated that before the March 1964 reforms a local application for a loan to build a secondary school required the intervention of at least seven Paris administrations.

Between the various Paris decision-makers involved in local affairs conflict is endemic and sometimes bitter. All is not always sweetness and light between, for example, the Ministries of the Interior and Finance, between the Ministry of Infrastructure and the DATAR, between the Ministry of Finance and the Caisse des Dépôts. These disputes and dissensions can – and frequently are – exploited by astute and unscrupulous local *notables*. Finally, as Sidney Tarrow has rightly insisted, the effectiveness of the Paris bureaucracy has declined as its size and scope for intervention have increased. As already noted in other spheres (see page 102) the administration is overwhelmed by the weight of its tasks and responsibilities.

State officials are often sensitive to local requirements

Some Paris-based bureaucrats hold local office. Unlike their British counterparts, top civil servants in France are allowed to stand for local office, and they do so frequently on highly partisan lists or under well-defined political labels. It has been argued that such men are merely 'technocrats in search of a spurious legitimacy', but the truth is much simpler: many Paris officials have firm family roots in the provinces and wish to retain and even to strengthen them by serving their local community. The result is that no departmental council is complete without at least one top civil servant based in Paris, and that amongst the French mayors may be found members of the Paris administrations, of the private staffs of ministers (the *cabinets*) and of the *grands corps*. For a commune it is immensely useful to have a top civil servant as mayor, for he can speak on equal terms with the prefect, bring pressure to bear upon him through Paris or even bypass him completely. Such officials seek patronage for their own communes or cantons and generally sensitize the administration to local needs and problems.

At the local level, too, State officials are far from impervious to local influences. The field services are given a certain discretion in interpreting directives from Paris, and often display great inventiveness in ignoring, modifying or even violating them: indeed, one of the main problems for Paris bureaucrats is to make their provincial subordinates obey them. Local field services are frequently manned by officials who remain a long time in the same area and who are gradually sucked into the whirlpool of local pressures.

The position of the locally elected notables *is much more powerful than the texts suggest*

This observation, according to André Tudesq, was true as early as the July Monarchy (1830–48). The position of the local *notables* is reinforced by their justifiable claim that, unlike the prefects and most other officials, their roots are firmly planted in the locality: Marchand noted that in 1958 and in 1964 fewer than 3 per cent of the departmental councillors lived outside the *département*, and that almost nine-tenths lived in the cantons they represented. Secondly, most elected *notables* hold office for a considerable length of time. Howard Machin has pointed out that during de Gaulle's Presidency (1959–69) thirty-five of the eighty-seven departmental councils outside the Paris region voted no change in their chairmanship whilst another forty saw only one change. A study of the *département* of the Ardennes in 1973 showed that since 1945 only one departmental councillor had not been re-elected after his first six years of office, and that six of the thirty-one members of the departmental council had represented their canton, without interruption, since the end of the Second World War, a period of twenty-eight years. There are even more astonishing cases of elective longevity: the indestructible Antoine Pinay has been departmental councillor of Saint Chamond since 1925 – a period of fifty-two years.

Stability of office is also the case in the communes. A study of the mayors of the rural *département* of the Calvados in Normandy in December 1976 revealed that more than a third had headed their commune for at least a quarter of a century. Some of the main towns of France have elected the same mayor since the war: Chaban-Delmas in Bordeaux, Defferre in Marseilles and Pflimlin in Strasbourg are amongst the better known examples. Local office is often handed on amongst the family heirlooms. When Médecin, the Mayor of Nice since 1928, died in 1965 he was immediately replaced by his son who is still Mayor of the town. Jeanne Becquart in her study of four northern *départements* showed that half the mayors were the sons of mayors or town councillors. Some rural areas are dominated by the same family for generations: the Basque canton of Saint-Étienne-de-Baïgorry has been represented in the departmental council by a member of the Harispe family since the 1830s. The position of the elected *notable* is undoubtedly strengthened by his claim that he knows the people and their problems of the area far better than the appointed emissaries of Paris, many of them mere birds of passage who are anxious to pass on to more prestigious and lucrative posts.

The third factor which strengthens many of the local *notables* in their relations with State officials is the phenomenon of *cumul des mandats* – the accumulation of offices. These offices may be purely local: most departmental councillors are also mayors and chairmen of a number of local associations. But frequently the offices are national in character. Most national political figures feel the need for local roots and stand for local office, and this is seen as eminently desirable by the electors, who view their Senators and Deputies as the spokesmen for local grievances and as intermediaries for extracting favours from Paris. The phenomenon of *cumul des mandats* is widespread: amongst the candidates in the March 1971 local elections were 36 of the 41 Ministers and Junior Ministers, 379 of the 487 Deputies and 191 of the 283 Senators, and in the departmental elections of March 1976 18 Ministers, 251 Deputies and 174 Senators were elected (others were not up for re-election that year). Amongst the dominant political figures of the Fifth Republic who have held or hold local office are Presidents Pompidou and Giscard d'Estaing, and Prime Ministers Debré, Messmer, Chaban-Delmas and Chirac. Some politicians collect posts like some men collect postage stamps: it is both an obsession and an investment. Ex-Premier Jacques Chirac, presently leader of the Gaullist party, for example, is the Mayor of Paris, Chairman of the departmental council of the Corrèze and deputy of that *département*, member of the regional council, and president of many local organizations. Edgar Faure, the President of the National Assembly and hence a Deputy, is Chairman of the regional council of Franche-Comté, Vice-President of the departmental council of the Doubs, local councillor in Pontarlier (he was Mayor until March 1977), and chairman or vice-chairman of a host of other national or local associations. Now it is clear that the relationship between a State official and a local *notable* is bound to be affected by the national notoriety of that *notable*. Put at its most extreme, no State official is likely to make life difficult for the mayor of a tiny commune if that mayor happens to be the minister in charge of his administration. Certainly there was never any doubt during Pompidou's Presidency that the most influential man in the *département* of the Morbihan was not the prefect but Marcellin, Mayor of Vannes, Chairman of the Departmental Council . . . and Minister of the Interior (the prefect's hierarchical head). These *grands notables*, local political bosses with extensive Paris contacts, expect and invariably receive deferential and preferential treatment from State officials. Even influential members of the Opposition (especially as they might be influential members of the Government in the near future) must be treated with courtesy, concern and consideration (however discreetly): for instance, only the most imprudent prefect would forget that François Mitterrand, Mayor of Château-Chinon and member of the local departmental council, is the political boss of the *département* of the Nièvre.

The interpenetration of local and national elites which is one of the most distinctive features of the French system completely distorts the formal relationship between certain *notables* and the State officials: official subservience underlined by the texts may become, in practice, domination.

The power of the prefects is exaggerated and its nature misunderstood

In theory, a prefect exercises vast regulatory and discretionary powers which enable him closely to supervise the activities of local authorities. In practice, however, his power is circumscribed by several important factors:

(i) Paradoxically, the extension of his formal *powers* has led to a diminution in his *power*, for he has been trapped in a tissue of roles and regulations which frequently hamper his freedom of manoeuvre by restricting his area of initiative and discretion – the real basis of his influence.

(ii) There has been a gradual weakening of the formal control he is able to exercise over the local authorities: during the Fifth Republic, for example, his control over local budgets has virtually disappeared.

(iii) An elaborate system of administrative law has evolved under the guardianship of the Council of State which sets judicial limits to prefectoral action.

(iv) Prefectoral control over the activities of the field services has always been tenuous, and there have been some legendary clashes between prefects determined to establish their authority and the heads of the field services resolved to rule alone. If there is necessarily a great deal of co-operation between the generalist prefect and the specialist field services there is also chronic tension and intermittent conflict. Generally, the prefect has neither the time, the technical expertise, the qualified staff nor the inclination to supervise the work of the field services. And the March 1964 reforms which were designed to strengthen prefectoral authority as the 'overlord' of the departmental administration have proved largely ineffective.

(v) The local prefect has little control over many pressure groups or big industrial concerns, which have their headquarters in the capital and which negotiate directly with the Paris bureaucracy.

(vi) His monopoly in the distribution of local patronage was quickly expropriated by the *notables*, particularly those who also sat in Parliament: the prefectoral monopoly became a parliamentary oligopoly. In the absence of a strong party system, Governments in Paris bought parliamentary favour by granting individual Deputies and Senators the right to distribute local manna to their constituents.

(vii) From the Restoration Monarchy (1815–30), and especially from the July Monarchy (1830–48), it became the practice of governments to consult Deputies and Senators over the appointment, promotion and dismissal of prefects in their constituencies – a fact that few prefects were allowed – or were likely – to forget. Members of Parliament (local figures holding several offices), who could make or break a prefect, supplanted the prefects during the Third and Fourth Republics as the most influential decision-makers in the *départements*, and in spite of the decline in the power of the French Parliament since 1958 its members remain very influential at local level.

(viii) A prefect's own career ambitions are frequently prejudicial to his success in controlling local government. In practice, promotion is related to mobility; only shortly after moving to a particular *département* a prefect is assailed by desires to be transferred to a more important, more lucrative and more prestigious prefecture. Prefectoral instability is a real source of weakness for the corps, and the problem is particularly acute in the small rural *départements*, far from Paris and inhabited by the uncultured and the unwashed. Since prefects already disappear with the inevitability of Puccini heroines (they are sacked or transferred on the slightest pretext), their own *wanderlust* merely aggravates an acute problem. In many *départements* prefects have little time to get acquainted with the people or the problems, and their authority is lessened in their relations with the local politicians and certain officials who have firmer local roots.

The prefect is thus in a much weaker position than is suggested by the texts or emphasized by his critics. He holds a precarious and vulnerable position, and his success depends on the goodwill and co-operation of men over whom, in principle, he exerts his 'tyranny'. The main role of the prefect, in practice, is as departmental troubleshooter. Helped by his sub-prefects, his police and the staff of the prefecture (many of them local men) and in daily contact with the *notables*, he is quickly confronted with the conflicts and tensions of the *département*. He can no longer impose solutions in authoritarian fashion: the *préfet à poigne* (the mail-fisted prefect of popular folk-lore who was defined as a man who would not hesitate, if ordered, to execute an opponent twice) no longer exists. The present prefect listens, persuades, cajoles gently and rarely bullies. He conciliates rather than coerces, and his main weapons are tact and common sense and not the vast panoply of formal powers at his disposal. A good prefect can enjoy great influence by careful use of his innate prestige, but a bad prefect can destroy his prestige by careless abuse of his influence. The prefect is a politician, an administrator, a priest, a policeman, a peacemaker, a safety valve and a scapegoat. He performs the most demanding, the most difficult and the most delicate job in the French administration.

His relationship with the local *notables*, far from being a dominant one, is one based on 'complementarity and interdependence' (Jean-Claude Thoenig). The links of mutual dependence which bind the prefect and the mayor, for example, are numerous and strong: their nature has been summarized by Mark Kesselman as follows:

Each needs to lean on the other to strengthen his own legitimacy. The prefect reinforces his position *vis-à-vis* of Paris by underlining his privileged *rapports* with the mayors, and the mayors reinforce their standing with their own electors by pointing to their strategic bargaining position with the local prefect.

Each needs the other to ensure local peace and harmony. Each is anxious to *éviter les histoires*, to avoid being embroiled in politically compromising and personally damaging conflicts.

Each needs the other as a scapegoat to explain *lack* of success.

Their active collaboration is frequently required to carry out specific projects.

They share similar defensive roles especially in their relations with the field services, the pressure groups and the Paris bureaucracies.

Both are ardent defenders of the present local system and both have effectively resisted any real reforms.

The relationship between the *notables* and the prefect is closely symbiotic, each buttressing the other against those outside elements which seem so keen to undermine both.

There has been an increase in the number, the size and the autonomy of big towns

In March 1977 there were 221 towns with more than 30000 inhabitants, compared with 193 in 1971 and 159 in 1965 . . . and 47 at the beginning of the Third Republic, when the Act which still largely defines the powers of local authorities was passed. At present there are 39 towns with populations of over 100000, and there are 8 big urban communities (see page 209). Less than 1 per cent of the 37000 communes in France contain more than 20 per cent of the population.

The relations between the big towns and the centre are, in practice, totally different from those which obtain between the vast majority of communes and the centre. First, there has always been a tradition of jealous autonomy in certain big towns such as Toulouse and Marseilles: their independence was facilitated by distance and often fed by political enmity. Secondly, the big towns have big and powerful bureaucracies led by a General Secretary who is frequently of very high calibre. Thirdly, they have their own technical services which rival those of the State. Fourthly, although they are, like all communes, financially dependent upon the State they nevertheless enjoy some degree of financial autonomy. Fifthly, they have greater scope of initiative in important areas such as town planning (by the judicious use of building permits and land expropriation), housing and public transport, the creation of industrial zones, social and cultural matters. Sixthly, in certain big towns, notably those held by the Communists (and 72 of the 221 towns of over 30000 inhabitants were won by the Communists in March 1977) the local authority is helped by a well organized party machine which provides technical expertise and advice. Finally, they frequently enjoy the dynamic leadership of a powerful, long-serving, full-time and paid mayor. Defferre in Marseilles, Chaban-Delmas in Bordeaux, Crépeau in La Rochelle, Dubedout in Grenoble, Pradel in Lyons until his death in 1976, Pflimlin in Strasbourg, Fréville in Rennes until his retirement in 1977, Médecin in Nice, Mauroy in Lille, Lecanuet in Rouen and Duromée in Le Havre are amongst the many important mayors who have determined the programmes and shaped the priorities of their towns, often giving them a particular image: Strasbourg and Grenoble have the reputation of being havens of culture (and by French provincial standards they are); La Rochelle is the 'ecological town' in which free bicycles are available to the inhabitants; Angoulême pioneered the idea of putting factories in pleasant rural surroundings; Lyons under Mayor Pradel covered itself with concrete. A recent study has pinpointed the key roles played by Fréville, Mayor of Rennes and 'an elected autocratic monarch', and by Médecin, Mayor of Nice, in shaping the destinies of their towns. The relative autonomy of the big towns has been attested to by several studies: it has even been claimed (by a regional TPG) that a patient and determined mayor can do virtually anything he wishes. Jérôme Milch has shown in his study of Montpellier and Nîmes (the former ruled by a Centrist mayor, the latter run by a Communist-dominated council) that they developed different policies in at least three distinct areas: the stifling uniformity which Paris is supposed to impose on local authorities was far from being the dominant characteristic of the two towns' policy outputs. It is also clear that Left-wing municipalities generally spend a greater proportion of their budgets (which are generally bigger) on public housing and public transport than Right-wing municipalities: many have also managed to renovate their town centres without expropriating the homes of the poor (who in Paris and Lyons have been forced to move to the inconvenient suburbs). These variations in the policies and styles of the big towns suggest a reasonable degree of independence in their relations with Paris.

Some concluding remarks

It has been claimed by the critics that the French centralized State is *inefficient, insensitive to local needs, stultifying* and *undemocratic*.

It is inefficient because it multiplies time-consuming procedures. Jean Lecanuet, Mayor of Rouen, once complained that it took him thirteen years before getting permission to rebuild one of the main squares of the town because an obstructionist Paris bureaucracy rejected successive plans (the final result suggests that Paris should have persisted). More seriously, because of the proverbial slowness of Paris it may take up to twenty years between a local decision to build a hospital and its completion, and Paris has been known to block the building of secondary schools for up to ten years. But decentralizing decision-making to the local field services does not necessarily speed up the process: the Bouvard senatorial report of 1976 concluded that the measures of administrative decentralization decreed in March 1964 led to 'growing complexity [of procedures] which increased delays and increased administrative costs'. It must also be conceded that many decisions on certain plans are, and have to be, *intrinsically* time-consuming, for they have not only major financial and technical implications but also wide-ranging social and political consequences. The decision of one town, for example, to build a new hospital may drain doctors from other towns which are already medically deprived.

The present system is also denounced as insensitive to local needs, since it applies uniform policies by its rules, regulations, directives, instructions, recommendations and warnings: areas with differing needs are treated to rigidly similar policies. The criticism merits three main observations. First, as already noted, different areas and towns have been able to pursue differing policies. Secondly, much of the uniformity that does exist springs from the electors, who demand minimum standards in a whole range of social services. Finally, lack of uniformity in certain areas such as defence and foreign affairs would be manifestly absurd and that is readily admitted. But in other areas, too, it would lead to absurd anomalies: for example, allowing practising Catholic regions to have separate legislation on abortion would merely lead to weekend coachloads of Basques and *Bretonnes* with unwanted pregnancies and sufficient means leaving for the more socially tolerant clinics of Paris. Furthermore, decentralizing economic decision-making might lead to greater regional disparities, with the poor getting poorer and the rich richer. Champions of decentralization frequently forget that 'malevolent' Paris has sometimes used its powers to ensure greater equity.

The third accusation levelled against the present system is that it is stultifying, since it kills local initiative and leads to a spirit of resignation and lassitude amongst local officials. The evidence for such an assertion is decidedly slim, and the dynamism, the resolution and the imagination of many mayors who have transformed their towns must raise doubts about the accusation.

Finally, the system is denounced as undemocratic, for decisions are made by non-elected Paris bureaucrats or their field services who ride rough-shod over the aspirations of locally elected officials. Again, a number of observations are called for. First, national exigencies and local requirements frequently coincide because both are shaped by similar electoral pressures. Secondly, for the numerous complex reasons outlined in this chapter the centre is often sensitive to local needs expressed by the *notables*. Thirdly, the present system with its mosaic of small communes ensures that at least 37 000 mayors and some of the 470 000 local councillors play some part – however marginal in some cases – in decision-making. In no other country in Europe is it easier for the ordinary citizen to locate an *identifiable* and *accessible* articulator and transmitter of a grievance than in France: the existence of 37000 mayors may be inefficient to the protagonists of economic rationalism, but it is a source of immense strength for local democracy. Fourthly, transferring decision-making to the local authorities may involve handing over increased powers to self-perpetuating political cliques. In France certain areas are impregnable bastions of the Right and others are rotten boroughs of the Left, where minority rights may be catered for less well than on the national level, since a small swing in any election may produce a change of Government.

Finally, however deplorable it may seem to the decentralizors, most of the local elites are generally content with the present system, as several official inquiries have demonstrated. It may be that some prefer the dictatorship of the distant and the impersonal centre to the closer and more oppressive tyranny of other local potentates. But the reason for the general contentment of the local elites springs from their appreciation of the practical possibilities of a system which is inflexible only in appearance.

If locally elected decision-makers have so few powers it is tempting to ask why local elections are fought with such passion and why the electors turn out in such large numbers to vote for such 'impotent' elites:

Table 15 *Abstention rates in national and local elections 1946-77*

General elections	Abstention (*per cent*)	Local elections	Abstention (*per cent*)
November 1946	21·9	October 1947	23·2
June 1951	19·8	April 1953	20·4
January 1956	17·3	March 1959	25·3
November 1958	22·9	March 1965	21·8
November 1962	31·3	March 1971	24·8
March 1967	19·1	March 1977	21·2
June 1968	20·0		
March 1973	19·1		

Given the 'tyrannical' nature of Paris control over the provinces, it is also curious that the reform of local government, willed by successive Governments, has been so 'piecemeal and gradualist'

(Jack Hayward): the reform of local finances announced in early 1959 was *commenced* only fifteen years later and is far from complete; the *first* stage of the 1976 Guichard Report recommendations will take, if accepted (and nothing is less certain), until 1985 to complete; the 1974 promises of President Giscard d'Estaing to introduce regional reforms have been discreetly shelved. The reluctance to touch the structures of local government must be attributed to the unwillingness to upset key parts of the administration (especially the prefects) and most of the local elites who, whatever their public protests, find the system generally so satisfactory that they resist all attempts to change it. Those elites are well represented in the French Parliament and are grouped in the influential Association des Maires de France, which has good contacts with the Ministry of the Interior.

The texts may suggest a hierarchy of decision-makers, with the local elites firmly entrenched at the bottom. In reality, however, behind a highly centralized formal system lurks a complex and highly personalized web of 'parallel powers' (Michel Crozier): Parisian bureaucrats and their provincial agents, prefects and locally elected officials are condemned to live together in a chaos of surreptitious bargaining, illicit agreements, hidden collusion, unspoken complicity, simulated tension and often genuine conflict. The present system of tempered or attenuated centralization is sustained by the customary combination of inertia, apathy and self-interest. There is also a touch of hypocrisy, with Paris and the provinces exploiting each other as the scapegoat responsible for its own deficiencies.

The exact nature of the relationship between Paris and a locality depends on a range of factors: the size of the commune and the quality of its technical and financial resources; the relations of the local *notables* with the field services, the prefect and the Paris bureaucrats; the dynamism and leadership of the mayors of the big towns; the general sensitivity of State officials to local needs; the prevailing economic situation; the electoral impact of particular issues. Simply to view decision-making in France as completely dominated by power-hungry Jacobins impervious to the demands of frustrated and impotent provincial *notables* is to misunderstand the complexity and subtlety of the relations which exist between a fragmented power structure in the capital and the splintered power structure in the provinces.

Conclusion: the Presidency and decision-making under the Fifth Republic

The political aims of the founders of the Fifth Republic were clearly stated: to destroy the weak and despised régime of the Fourth Republic which had been undermined by a defective Constitution, by unstable and short-lived Governments, by a Parliament which was omnipotent in theory but impotent in practice, by divided and undisciplined parties, by a ubiquitous and powerful administration, by a resentful and disobedient army and by overactive pressure groups. The new Republic was to be both strong and respected, underpinned by a Constitution which strengthened the powers of the Executive and which ensured presidential pre-eminence (if not predominance), and in which Parliament, the parties, the army, the administration and the pressure groups were relegated firmly to their proper – and subordinate – place. In some important respects, the founders have proved successful in the fulfilment of their basic aims: diplomatically, France is no longer the subject of international derision as she was before 1958; also in contrast with the situation before 1958, successive opinion polls indicate a high level of satisfaction with the régime; Governments now give the appearance of stability, and Prime Ministers enjoy longer periods of office; the powers of Parliament have been effectively curbed; small and undisciplined parties no longer dominate the political scene; the army – 'the State within the State' during the previous régime – has been reduced to silent obedience to the civil authorities.

Perhaps the most important, and certainly the most striking, change since 1958 has been the emergence of the Presidency as the major focus of political decision-making in France. The reasons for the growth of presidential power have been analysed at length in this book: the desire of successive Presidents to extend the scope of their powers; their careful use and abuse of the 1958 Constitution; the strengthening of their electoral legitimacy by the referendum of October 1962; the reinforcement of the presidential private office;

the transformation of ministers into presidential servants; the backing in Parliament of a sympathetic and disciplined party coalition; the weakness and divisions of the political opposition; the exploitation of propitious political circumstances. Personal, constitutional and political factors combined, therefore, to ensure presidential supremacy. That supremacy has been demonstrated on innumerable occasions. For instance, President de Gaulle's unilateral decision not to devalue the franc in the autumn of 1968 was matched by Giscard d'Estaing's personal decision to halt the extension of the Paris left-bank motorway in the summer of 1974. Moreover, the general guidelines of important policy areas bear the unmistakable personal imprint of successive Presidents: the foreign, European and defence policies of France were shaped by General de Gaulle; the country's industrial policy bears the Pompidou hall-mark; the liberalizing measures in the social field taken since 1974 owe much to the personal determination of President Giscard d'Estaing. In some respects, therefore, it is not totally misleading to describe the French political system as 'presidential'. Certainly, the Presidency is *perceived* as the major focus of decision-making by the general public, by the political and administrative elite and by the pressure groups. Yet the President of the Republic is not omnipotent. His powers are considerable, but they are not unlimited, for he is enmeshed in a complex web of personal, historical, constitutional and political restrictions.

The constraints on presidential power

The first type of restriction upon presidential power is constitutional and judicial in character. There are things that the President cannot do, since he is specifically prevented from doing so by the Constitution. For instance, he may not dissolve the National Assembly more than once a year. Moreover, the Constitutional Council, a creature of infinite docility during the early years of the Fifth Republic, has recently rejected certain controversial pieces of government legislation on the grounds of unconstitutionality. It should also be recalled that many of the constitutional provisions which limit presidential power and which have fallen into abeyance since 1959 may well be invoked if a politically hostile National Assembly is elected. The President is, in fact, in a peculiarly vulnerable position, for some of his power rests upon an ambiguous Constitution which may be quoted against him and upon several controversial conventions which may be rejected. He is also dependent upon the goodwill and co-operation of the Prime Minister, the Government and Parliament – a goodwill which may disappear after any election.

The second – and perhaps most obvious – restriction upon the President's power is the limited time at his disposal. As official Head of State, he is inevitably involved in time-consuming ceremony and travel, and, conscious of the need for support for his policies, he has to spend a great deal of time in political management. The time left for policy-making is fairly limited, and he has, therefore, to delegate some of his powers to his Prime Minister and other ministers, who, in turn, are obliged to devolve authority to an army of civil servants.

The President's own perception of his role provides the third major constraint upon his power. That perception is shaped not only by the personality and the tastes of the President but also by political calculation. There are a number of reasons why a President may voluntarily, if sometimes unconsciously, impose limitations upon his policy-making role. First, by becoming totally absorbed in the minutiae of legislation he may disqualify himself as the impartial arbiter and as the judge of its wider political implications. Second, too intimate an involvement in making policy, some of it bound to be politically controversial, may damage his image as the statesman above the political battle, the embodiment of the unity of the nation, the guide to its future action and the guardian of its basic interests. Opinion polls clearly reveal that the more politically active the President becomes the more his popularity declines. Third, the President of the Republic is elected for seven years – a very long time in politics – and an over-interventionist role may become physically crushing. Finally, the over-concentration of political power in the hands of the President may lead to public identification of the President with the régime itself – an identification assiduously fostered by de Gaulle himself in his dire warnings to the electors of *après moi le déluge*, but which was not without its dangers. When de Gaulle was absent or indecisive during the turbulent days of May 1968 there was a power vacuum, with certain members of the Government and the top civil service displaying the sense of purpose and direction of freshly decapitated chickens. A similar power vacuum, though less apparent, was no less real during the last year of Pompidou's period of office when the President was suffering from the appalling and enervating disease which was to kill him. The sense of drifting was equally evident during the summer of 1976 when inflation was increasing and the value of the franc was decreasing: ministerial procrastination was attributed to the absence of the President, hunting big game in Africa.

The fourth major restriction upon presidential power lies in the inefficacy of the administrative instruments at the disposal of the office. The machinery of government is overloaded, defective and inefficient. It has been given tasks that it is incapable or unwilling adequately to fulfil: its record has been lamentable in areas as vital as the forecasting of the population growth of the country (indispensable to any forward planning in health, education, housing), the balancing of the State budget (all the 'balanced' budgets between 1974 and 1977 ended in substantial deficit), the controlling of the money supply (an important factor in inflation), the prevention of the illegal flow of French capital to safer political havens abroad. In other important policy areas its control is tenuous or non-existent: for instance, it has no method of checking the 'irrational' behaviour of the Paris stock exchange or of effectively influencing the investment programmes of most big profit-making companies. Recent studies by Zysman and by McArthur and Scott have underlined some of the powerful constraints upon French Governments in industrial policy-making. Finally, Governments are confronted with problems which many consider insoluble: drug-taking, increasing violence and crime, racialism and loneliness, which are amongst the major social problems of the day.

The fifth major constraint on presidential power is political. As has been constantly emphasized in this book, the electorate (and especially his own supporters), his party and parliamentary backers and the pressure groups all impose limits upon his freedom of action.

There exists, therefore, a combination of personal, constitutional, administrative and political factors which severely constrain the President. The Presidency may be the major *focus* of political decision-making, but it is only one element (albeit an important one) in the vast and complex process of policy formulation and implementation.

The parameters of governmental decision-making

Decision-making in the Fifth Republic takes place within severely circumscribed limits drawn by history, by the outside world and, within France, by a jungle of private, semi-public and public interests.

It is a banality worth reiterating that the biggest decision-maker in any political system is the past. The Fifth Republic, in spite of claims to the contrary by its apologists, inherited a great deal from its predecessor. After May 1958 the upper part of the political super-structure may have been modified, but there was no upheaval in the social, economic and political substructure. Nor did basic cultural traits disappear with the waving of a Gaullist wand. The same social forces remained intact, the same economic interests continued to strive for superiority, the same administrative machine still func-tioned, and no one dismantled the vast and complex web of com-mittees, commissions and councils which had proliferated since the end of the Second World War. The Fourth Republic bequeathed much to its successor: *a booming economy and a rapidly changing occupational structure*; *a vague, yet pervasive ideology rooted in a not always consistent series of traditions* such as the primacy of universal suffrage, 'Republican legality', the independence of the judiciary, the legitimacy of governmental interventionism within the framework of a mixed economy, the respect for free speech and association; *its basic institutional framework*; *most of its political and administrative elite* (sixteen years after the fall of the Fourth Republic, in the May 1974 presidential elections the three leading contenders were Chaban-Delmas, Giscard d'Estaing and Mitterrand, who had been colleagues in the last Parliament of the Fourth Republic); *a jumble of political norms and conventions* (such as the desirability of *cumul des mandats* described in Chapter 9) that could be transgressed only with the utmost caution; *a wide-ranging series of domestic, diplomatic and defence commitments* (for example, to an extensive system of social welfare, to the North Atlantic Alliance, to the European Common Market); *a tangle of social and economic expectations* (full employ-ment and steadily rising living standards were taken for granted); *a welter of established rights and privileges* involving many powerfully placed groups; *a number of seemingly intractable problems* such as the Algerian war, which dominated and poisoned the politics of the early years of the Fifth Republic.

The future historian studying the Fourth and Fifth Republics might find more to compare than to contrast. He might also empha-size the increased vulnerability of France to outside pressures during the Fifth Republic. The growing demands for public participation in decision-making, for sexual liberation, the questioning of traditional morality and of organized religion were amongst the many social phenomena imported from other western industrialized countries. The uncharitable might also remind the chauvinistic French that their defence continues to depend essentially on the USA, and that the state of their economy is determined to some extent by decisions taken by the German and American governments, by the multi-national companies who have invested in France and by the members of OPEC. Paradoxically, often as the result of decisions taken by Governments of the Fifth Republic France's vulnerability to the outside world has become more acute: a determined and highly successful effort to make France a major exporting power in the world has made it more sensitive to the vagaries of international trade; many decisions, especially those affecting farmers, are now taken by organs of the Common Market in Brussels and not in Paris; foreign capital was welcomed but has penetrated French industry to such an extent that the Cotta Report of 1977 could warn the French Government that key sectors of the French economy (such as petroleum, ship-building, pharmaceuticals and electronics) were effectively controlled by foreigners; in certain border regions of France labour and capital increasingly move across the frontier with a facility that now alarms French government officials.

Decision-making under the Fifth Republic takes place, therefore, within limits defined by history and by the outside world. Within those limits, decisions emerge as the result of the interaction – or non-interaction (for mutual avoidance may be profitable) of a chaos of decision-makers who function at national, regional and local level. Power is diffused amongst a host of bodies – the Executive (which itself resembles a huge Byzantine court riddled with feuding factions), Parliament, the political parties (including those of the Left), the pressure groups, the banks, industrial firms and insurance companies – all of which are fragmented and divided. Even bodies such as the nationalized banks and industries and the administration, although nominally servants of the State, are badly divided, with each part secreting and protecting its own corporate interests. Relations between the decision-makers – when they exist – range from noisy confrontation to quiet collusion, from the parasitic to the symbiotic, from the permanent to the sporadic. Often the real point of decision-making is difficult to locate, for it is hidden from the public gaze. Analysing the political process in France – as in any complex industrial society – is rather like peering down a dimly-lit kaleidoscope held in a gently inebriated hand: after a while it is possible to distinguish some of the more significant pieces, but the pattern is ever-changing and is sensitive to the slightest shudder. Furthermore, there are pieces that remain in obstinate obscurity.

To ask the question, 'Where does power lie in the Fifth Republic?' is to invite the obvious rejoinder, 'Power to do what?' It was a President of the Republic who decided to withdraw France from NATO, who decided that Britain could enter the EEC and who decided to liberalize the divorce, abortion and contraception laws. But it was a small group of Communist-led workers, grouped in closed shops, who shut down the port of Le Havre for several weeks and who, on several occasions between 1975 and 1977, brought the Paris press to a complete standstill. The power of such strategically placed veto groups is often manifest and easy to assess, but how is it possible accurately to measure the effect of the spiritual power of the Church, the impact of the mass media, the electoral influence of the old-age pensioners? Governments are, therefore, inevitably enmeshed in a concatenation of competing and contradictory forces: they are hemmed in by historical, social, administrative, political and constitutional factors. And if they are not always the helpless spectators of the fate of their country (for they can make or encourage adjustments to the *status quo* by creating a climate which favours certain groups or policies) their freedom of action is often singularly limited.

It has been claimed by the apologists of the present régime that, because of greater governmental powers, stability and authority, decision-making is more 'efficient' and more 'rational' than during the Fourth Republic. Certainly, the Fifth Republic has *attempted* to improve the procedures of decision-making: constant reforms of the machinery of government at national, regional and local level; efforts to improve the administrative co-ordination and implementation of policies; the introduction of RCB (the French equivalent of PPBS); the improvement of statistical and forecasting techniques. The régime has also produced ambitious long-term programmes in order, for example, to restructure the steel industry, to create a national computer industry, to combat monopolies and restrictive practices, to provide the country with nuclear energy, to encourage industrial decentralization and to iron out regional disparities. Yet, compared with the Fourth Republic, the overall picture does not suggest any greater coherence in a system of decision-making which still bears as much the stigmas of fitful and supine incrementalism as the marks of thoughtful rationality. In truth, successive Governments of the Fifth Republic have been torn between the competing and often conflicting needs to satisfy *national grandeur* (hence Concorde), *rationality* (hence the nuclear energy programme), *electoral opportunism* (hence the totally 'irrational' handouts to the farmers and the steel industry, and the benevolent attention afforded industrial ducks which were not only lame but in some cases totally crippled), and *social consensus* (hence the financial help to Corsica). In the conduct of economic affairs they have lurched between an authoritarian *dirigisme* and a casual liberalism with, reassertions of State authority punctuated by acts destined to undermine it. The general lack of direction in French economic decision-making led one critic, Jacques Chirac, to describe the system as '*dirigisme* without direction'. In other areas, too, 'coherence' has been manifestly lacking, with Governments changing the policies of their predecessors with unnerving readiness and alacrity: the Haby Secondary Education Act of 1975 was the fifteenth such Act since 1958, whilst the Barre anti-inflation programme of 1976 was preceded by innumerable similar programmes. It is, of course, possible to point to major policy options which have been consistently and successfully pursued. President Pompidou's obsessive drive to modernize the French economy is frequently quoted in that respect. Yet it is legitimate to ask whether its success was due to deliberate policy, or whether it was the consequence of other factors: the end of the economically and financially ruinous colonial wars; the impetus of the Common Market; the zeal of the business community, which made huge profits; the weakness of the Opposition Left, which in France is always good for business; the preparedness of the French to work longer hours than any other Western European people in order to improve their standard of living. Certainly, the policy of vigorous growth has not survived the death of Pompidou: the Arabs, the environmentalists and the prospects of a Left-wing victory at the polls have combined to destroy it.

And the general record of the Fifth Republic? There are certainly some black spots: it has a judiciary which can be disquietingly susceptible to political pressure and a police which is frequently not; it has created a radio and television network which is politically disgracefully biassed; it has occasionally displayed a crass insensitivity to the aspirations of the provinces: it has tolerated property speculation of the most outrageous (and often illegal) sort; it has condoned tax evasion and avoidance by groups considered vital to its electoral survival, and it has done little to modify a tax system which is the least progressive in the Common Market; its leaders have sometimes shown a disconcerting disregard for the Constitution, and they have frequently been contemptuous of the rights of the Opposition; it has allowed too much public squalor in the midst of often indecent affluence. Yet the total balance sheet is far from dishonourable. The Fifth Republic has been a period of unprecedented change which has seen the transformation of the family, the Church, the occupational structure of the country, the means of communication and the mass media, moral values and sexual mores. During that period the régime has given the country peace (with the ending of the colonial wars), prosperity (purchasing power almost doubled between 1959 and 1975), a political system which is respected, and an international prestige which it singularly lacked during the Fourth Republic.

Appendices

Appendix 1: *Regions and* départements

Paris region

PARIS

VAL D'OISE

HAUTS-DE-SEINE

SEINE-SAINT DENIS

YVELINES

VAL-DE-MARNE

ESSONNE

SEINE-ET-MARNE

Charleville
Mézières
DENNES

NE
MEUSE
Metz
MOSELLE

s/ Marne
LORRAINE

ALSACE

PAGNE
Bar le Duc
Nancy

ENNE
MEURTHE-ET-
MOSELLE

BAS-
RHIN

Strasbourg

HAUTE
I-MARNE

VOSGES

oyes

Epinal

Chaumont
Colmar

HAUTE-
SAÔNE

HAUT-
RHIN

CÔTE-D'OR
Vesoul
Belfort

Dijon
DOUBS

TERRITOIRE
DE BELFORT

GOGNE
Besançon

FRANCHE-COMTÉ

JURA

NE-ET-LOIRE
Lons le
Saumier

Mâcon

Bourg
en Bresse

HAUTE-
SAVOIE

RHÔNE
AIN
Annecy

Lyon
Chambéry

ne
ISÈRE
SAVOIE

RHÔNE-ALPES

Grenoble

Privas
Valence
HAUTES-
ALPES

ÈCHE
DRÔME
Gap

D
VAUCLUSE
ALPES
DE HAUTE
Digne

nes
Avignon
PROVENCE

ALPES
MARITIMES

PROVENCE-CÔTE D'AZUR
Nice

BOUCHES-DU-
RHÔNE
Draguignan

ier
Marseille
VAR

- departmental préfecture
- regional préfecture
— departmental boundaries
— regional boundaries

CORSICA

HAUTE
CORSE

Ajaccio

CORSE-
DU-SUD

Appendix 2: *France 1967–77: some figures*

	1967	1977
Population (million)	49·8	53
Purchasing power: managers	240	300
(100 = 1950) workers	200	300
Savings (thousand million francs)	144	280
Number of families with: car (per cent)	53·7	65
television (per cent)	58	85·7
refrigerator (per cent)	68·5	90·8
washing machine (per cent)	47·5	73·2
Number of telephones (million)	3·34	9·9
Number of colour televisions (million)	0	4
Number of pocket calculators (million)	0	4·6
Annual sale of: records (million)	44	113
tapes (million)	0·67	7·3
Motorways (km)	975	4400
Supermarkets	900	3450
Hypermarkets	0	357
Number of students (thousand)	450	730

SOURCE: *Expansion*, September 1977, p. 121.

Appendix 3: *Chronological table of the main events from the Revolution to the collapse of the Fourth Republic*

1789	July	Fall of the Bastille.
	August	Abolition of all feudal rights.
1792	August	Fall of the Monarchy.
	September	Establishment of the First Republic.
1793	January	Execution of Louis XVI.
1799	November	Bonaparte becomes First Consul.
1804	May	Establishment of First Empire.
1814	April	First abdication of Napoleon I and restoration of Louis XVIII.
1815	June	Battle of Waterloo, second abdication of Napoleon and a second monarchical restoration.
1824	September	Charles X succeeds Louis XVIII.
1830	July	Revolution in Paris, abdication of Charles X, accession of Louis-Philippe.
1848	February	July Monarchy overthrown, Second Republic proclaimed.
	December	Election of Louis Napoleon to the Presidency of the Republic.
1851	December	*Coup d'état* by Louis Napoleon.
1852	December	Proclamation of the Second Empire, Napoleon III proclaimed Emperor.
1870	July	Outbreak of the Franco-Prussian War.
	September	Battle of Sedan, collapse of the Second Empire and proclamation of the Third Republic.
1871	January	Armistice.
	March–May	Revolutionary Commune in Paris.
1875	January–December	Constitutional laws voted in Parliament.

1877	May–June	Dissolution of the Republican-dominated Chamber of Deputies by President Mac-Mahon.
	October–December	Victory of the Republicans in the elections.
1879	January	Resignation of the President of the Republic, Republican victory in the Senatorial elections, foundation of the 'Republican Republic'.
1887	November–December	Wilson scandal, leading to resignation of President Grévy.
1887–1889		Republic threatened by General Boulanger and his supporters.
1892–1893		Panama scandal.
1894	June	President Carnot assassinated.
1897		Beginning of the Dreyfus affair, which dragged on for seven years.
1903–1905		Anti-clerical legislation culminating in the separation of Church and State.
1914	July	Assassination of Jaurès, Socialist leader.
	August	Outbreak of the First World War.
1918	November	Armistice.
1919	June	Versailles treaty signed.
1920	December	Tours Congress, foundation of the French Communist Party.
1923	January	French occupation of the Ruhr (until 1930).
1934	February	Violent Right-wing demonstrations in Paris.
1936	March	German re-militarization of the Rhineland.
	April–May	Victory of the Left-wing Popular Front in the elections.
	June	Popular Front Government under Léon Blum.
	October	Spanish Civil War began.
1937	June	Collapse of the Popular Front Government.
1938	September	Munich.

1939	March	Germany occupied Czechoslovakia.
	September	Outbreak of the Second World War.
1940	May–June	France invaded, Pétain became head of Government, de Gaulle to London, armistice. Half of France occupied.
1941	June	Germany invaded Russia.
1942	November	Allied invasion of North Africa, the whole of France occupied.
1944	June	Allies landed in Normandy.
	August	Paris liberated.
	September	General de Gaulle set up Government.
1945	May	End of the Second World War.
	October	French voted by referendum to end the Third Republic.
1946	January	General de Gaulle withdrew from the Government.
	May	France voted against first proposed Constitution.
	November	Constitution of the Fourth Republic accepted by referendum, and outbreak of the war in Indo-China.
1947	January	Election of Auriol as President of the Republic.
	April	Foundation of the first mass Gaullist movement – the RPF.
	May	Communists left the Government.
	June	Marshall speech on financial aid to Europe.
	November–December	Wave of political strikes.
1949	April	North Atlantic Treaty signed.
1951	April	Coal and steel agreement between France, Germany, Italy and the Benelux countries.
	June	General Election.
1952	March–December	Pinay Prime Minister.
1953	January	Official end of the RPF.
	August	Sultan of Morocco deposed.
	December	Coty elected President of the Republic.
1954	May–July	Dien-Bien-Phu, end of war in Indo-China negotiated by Premier Mendès-France.
	November	Outbreak of the Algerian war.

1956	January	General elections in France, Poujadists fared well.
	February	Demonstrations in Algiers against Premier Mollet.
	March	Independence of Tunisia and Morocco.
	October	Anglo-French intervention in Suez.
1957	March	Treaty of Rome establishing European Economic Community.
1958	May	Revolt by Algerian settlers in Algiers.
	June	General de Gaulle became head of Government.
	September	Referendum on the Constitution of the Fifth Republic.

Appendix 4: *Chronological table of main events under the Fifth Republic*

1958	September	Referendum on the Constitution of the Fifth Republic; 79·25 per cent voted in favour.
	October–November	Creation of the Gaullist UNR, general elections, big Gaullist gains.
	December	General de Gaulle elected President by 78·5 per cent of the votes of the electoral college.
1959	January	De Gaulle proclaimed President of the Republic, Michel Debré appointed Prime Minister.
1960	January	Uprising in Algeria.
	April	Creation of the PSU.
1961	January	Referendum ratifying de Gaulle's policy of self-determination in Algeria: 75·26 per cented vote in favour.
	April	Army coup in Algeria against French Government.
1962	March	Evian agreements on Algeria. Pompidou became Prime Minister.
	April	Referendum ratifying Evian peace settlement with Algeria: 90·7 per cent of voters in favour.
	August	Unsuccessful attempt on de Gaulle's life at Le Petit Clamart.
	October	Motion of censure passed against Pompidou Government, Parliament dissolved. Referendum for direct election of President of the Republic: 61·75 per cent in favour.
	October–November	General elections, big gains for Government.

1963	March–April	Miners strike, Government obliged to climb down.
1965	September	Creation of the FGDS (Fédération de la Gauche Démocrate et Socialiste) of Socialists, Radicals and Left-wing clubs.
	December	De Gaulle elected President of the Republic at the second ballot against Mitterrand.
1966	February	France withdrew from NATO.
1967	March	General elections: narrow victory for the Government.
	November	Creation of the Gaullist UDVe.
1968	May	The 'Events' – student revolt and general strike, National Assembly dissolved.
	June	Big victory of the Government in the general elections.
	July	Couve de Murville, replaced Pompidou as Prime Minister.
	November–December	Collapse of the FGDS, Mitterrand withdrew temporarily from political life.
1969	April	Referendum on the Senate and on regional reforms: de Gaulle resigned after 53·1 per cent voted against.
	June	Pompidou elected President of the Republic at the second ballot against Poher. Chaban-Delmas appointed Prime Minister.
	July	Creation of the CDP and of a new Socialist Party under the leadership of Alain Savary.
1970	November	Death of General de Gaulle.
1971	June	Creation of the new Socialist Party: Mitterrand became First Secretary.
1972	April	Referendum ratifying enlargement of the Common Market to include Great Britain, Ireland and Denmark: 67·7 per cent in favour.
	June	Joint Programme of Government signed between the Socialists and the Communists.
	July	Messmer replaced Chaban-Delmas as Prime Minister.

1973	March	General elections: victory for the Government, but with much reduced majority.
1974	April	Death of President Pompidou.
	May	Election of Giscard d'Estaing to the Presidency at the second ballot against Mitterrand.
	June	Jacques Chirac became Prime Minister.
	October	Many leaders of the PSU joined the Socialist Party.
1976	February	Congress of the Communist Party.
	March	Departmental elections: big gains for the Left.
	August	Chirac replaced as Prime Minister by Raymond Barre.
	December	Creation of the RPR headed by Chirac.
1977	March	Local elections: sweeping victory for the Left.
	May	Creation of the Republican Party (ex-Independent Republicans).
	September	Breakdown of negotiations between Communists and the Socialists.
1978	February	Creation of the Union pour la Démocratie Française (UDF), electoral alliance grouping non-Gaullist parties of presidential coalition.
	March	General elections: victory for the Government by comfortable majority.

Appendix 5: *Presidents and Prime Ministers of the Fifth Republic*

Presidents

Charles de Gaulle from 8 January 1959 to 28 April 1969
Georges Pompidou from 20 June 1969 to 2 April 1974
Valéry Giscard d'Estaing from 21 June 1974

Prime Ministers

Michel Debré from 8 January 1959
Georges Pompidou from 15 April 1962
Maurice Couve de Murville from 11 July 1968
Jacques Chaban-Delmas from 20 June 1969
Pierre Messmer from 7 July 1969
Jacques Chirac from 27 May 1974
Raymond Barre from 26 August 1976

Appendix 6: *Results of the referenda of the Fifth Republic*

Date	Subject	Abstentions	Percentage of votes cast in favour
28 September 1958	New Constitution	15·4	79·3
8 January 1961	Self-determination for Algeria	23·5	75·3
8 April 1962	Independence for Algeria	24·4	90·7
28 October 1962	Direct election of President	22·8	61·8
27 April 1969	Senate and regional reforms	19·4	46·8
23 April 1972	EEC enlargement	39·6	67·7

Appendix 7: *Results of the presidential elections of 1974*

First ballot 5 May	*Number*	*Percentage of electorate*	*Percentage of voters*
Electors	29 778 550		
Voters	25 285 835		
Abstentions	4 492 715	15·1	
Spoiled votes	228 264	0·8	
François Mitterrand (Socialist)	10 863 402	36·5	43·3
Valéry Giscard d'Estaing (Independent Republican)	8 253 856	27·7	32·9
Jacques Chaban-Delmas (Gaullist)	3 646 209	12·2	14·6
Jean Royer (Right-wing Independent)	808 885	2·7	3·2
Arlette Laguiller (Trotskyist Lutte Ouvrière)	591 339	1·9	2·3
René Dumont (Environmentalist)	336 016	1·1	1·3
Jean-Marie Le Pen (Extreme Right Front National)	189 304	0·6	0·7
Emile Muller (Right-wing Social Democrat)	175 142	0·6	0·7
Alain Krivine (Trotskyist Front Communiste Révolutionnaire)	92 701	0·3	0·4
Bertrand Renouvin (Royalist)	42 719	0·1	0·2
Jean-Claude Sebag (Fédéraliste Européen)	39 658	0·1	0·1
Guy Héraud (Parti Fédéraliste Européen)	18 340	0·05	0·07

Second ballot 19 May			
Electors	29 774 211		
Voters	26 168 442		
Abstentions	3 605 769	12·1	
Spoiled Votes	348 629	1·2	
Valéry Giscard d'Estaing	13 082 006	43·9	50·6
François Mitterrand	12 737 607	42·7	49·3

Appendix 8: *Votes for Giscard d'Estaing at the second ballot of the May 1974 presidential elections by* département

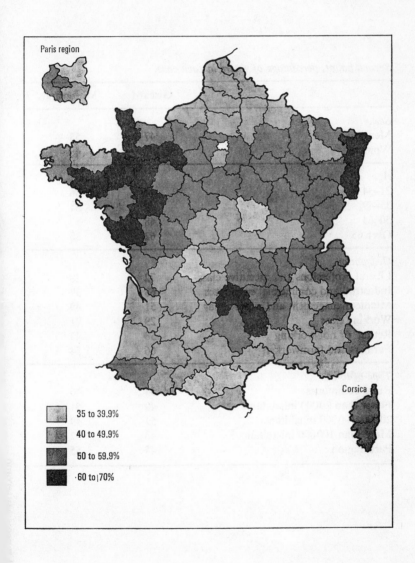

Paris region

Corsica

35 to 39.9%

40 to 49.9%

50 to 59.9%

·60 to¦70%

Appendix 9: *Voting behaviour in the May 1974 presidential election by socio-economic categories*

Second ballot, percentage of voters in each case.

	Giscard	Mitterrand
Sex		
Men	47	53
Women	52	48
Age		
21–34	44	56
35–49	49	51
50–64	48	52
Over 65	62	38
Occupation		
Liberal professions and executive class	72	28
Industrial and commercial employees	63	37
Middle-management and white collar	51	49
Working class	29	71
Retired or not working	58	42
Farmers and farmworkers	66	34
Type of town		
Rural communes	54	46
Fewer than 20000 inhabitants	49	51
20000–100000 inhabitants	51	49
More than 100000 inhabitants	48	52
Paris region	45	55

Appendix 10: *Results of the general elections of March 1978 (first ballot)*

Electors	35 179 654
Voters	29 125 025
Abstentions	6 054 629
Spoiled votes	583 963

Party	Votes	Percentage of votes cast
Extreme Left	952 661	3·33
Communists	5 870 340	20·56
Socialists	6 450 134	22·59
Left-wing Radicals	603 932	2·11
Gaullists (RPR)	6 451 454	22·60
UDF (pro-Govt Centrists + Republican Party)	6 122 180	21·45
Other pro-Government	684 985	2·39
Environmentalists	612 100	2·14
Others	793 276	2·77

Appendix 11: Voting behaviour in the March 1978 general elections (% of category)

	Percentage of population	Extreme Left	Communists	Socialists and Left-wing Radicals	Environ-mentalists	UDF	RPR	Rest
Sex								
Men	48	3	21	30	3	19	21	3
Women	52	2	20	26	4	21	22	5
Age								
18–24	⎱ 35	6	26	28	9	13	16	2
25–34	⎰	4	23	33	5	16	18	1
34–49	25	3	20	31	2	20	20	4
50–64	20	2	20	26	2	22	25	3
Over 65	20	2	17	22	0	28	28	3
Profession								
Farmers	8	2	13	23	2	27	31	2
Shop-keepers and self-employed	⎱ 14	2	12	24	3	26	29	4
Upper managers and liberal professions	⎰	4	11	24	7	24	24	6
Middle managers and white collar	19	4	20	31	6	18	19	2
Workers	32	3	34	32	2	14	14	1
Inactive and retired	27	2	19	24	1	24	26	4
How voters of 1974 voted in 1978								
Giscard d'Estaing	51	1	3	12	2	37	39	6
Mitterrand	49	4	40	46	2	3	3	2

Source: Louis Harris France in *L'Express*, 13 March 1978.

Appendix 12: *Political composition of the French Parliament on 1 April 1978*

National Assembly		*Senate*	
Gaullist party (RPR)	153	Gaullist party	30
Union pour la Démo-		Republican Party	57
cratie Française	137	Centrists	57
		'Peasants'	15
		Democratic Left	38
Pro-Government	**290**	**Pro-Government**	**197**
Socialists and		Socialists and	
Left-wing Radicals	114	Left-wing Radicals	52
Communists	86	Communists	20
Other Left	1		
Opposition Left	**201**	**Opposition Left**	**72**
		No group	10

Bibliographical guide to main books

General historical background

ANDERSON, R. D., *France 1870–1914: Politics and Society*, London 1977

BROGAN, DENIS, *The Development of Modern France 1870–1939*, 11th ed., London 1967

BURY, PATRICK, *France 1814–1940*, 4th ed., London 1969

CAHM, ERIC, *Politics and Society in Contemporary France (1789–1971,)* London 1972

COBBAN, ALFRED, *A History of Modern France*, 3 vols., London 1965

DUPEUX, GEORGES, *French Society 1789–1970*, London 1976

EARLE, EDWARD M. (ed.), *Modern France*, Princeton 1951

GOGUEL, FRANÇOIS, *La Politique des partis sous la IIIe République*, 3rd ed., Paris 1958

JACKSON, J. H., *A Short History of France*, 2nd ed., Cambridge 1974

RÉMOND, RENÉ, *La Vie politique en France depuis 1789*, 2 vols., Paris 1973–4

THOMSON, DAVID, *Democracy in France since 1870*, 5th ed., London 1969

WRIGHT, GORDON, *France in Modern Times*, Chicago 1962

ZELDIN, THEODORE, *France 1848–1945*, 2 vols., London 1973–77

The Fourth Republic

BARSALOU, JOSEPH, *La Mal-Aimée*, Paris 1964

ELGEY, GEORGETTE, *La République des Illusions 1945–1951*, Paris 1965

ELGEY, GEORGETTE, *La République des Contradictions*, Paris 1968

FAUVET, JACQUES, *The Cockpit of France*, London 1960

FAUVET, JACQUES, *La Quatrième République*, Paris 1959

FONTVIELLE-ALQUIER, FRANÇOIS, *Plaidoyer pour la IVe République*, Paris 1976

GOGUEL, FRANÇOIS, *France under the Fourth Republic*, Ithaca 1952

MACRAE, DUNCAN, *Parliament, Parties and Society in France 1946–1958*, New York 1967

PICKLES, DOROTHY, *France: The Fourth Republic*, London 1955

PRIOURET, ROGER, *La République des partis*, Paris 1947

WILLIAMS, PHILIP, *Crisis and Compromise: Politics in the Fourth Republic*, London 1964

WRIGHT, GORDON, *The Reshaping of French Democracy*, New York, 1948

General political and social background

ALEXANDRE, PHILIPPE, *Le Duel de Gaulle–Pompidou*, Paris 1970

ANDREWS, WILLIAM G., *French Politics and Algeria*, New York 1962

ARDAGH, JOHN, *The New France: A Society in Transition 1945–1977*, 3rd ed., Harmondsworth 1977

ARON, RAYMOND, *The Elusive Revolution: Anatomy of a Student Revolt*, London 1969

BEAUJOUR, MICHEL and EHRMAN, JACQUES, *La France contemporaine*, Paris 1965

BIRNBAUM, PIERRE, *Les Sommets de l'État*, Paris 1977

BIRNBAUM, PIERRE, et al., *La Classe dirigeante française*, Paris 1978

BREDIN, JEAN-DENIS, *La République de M. Pompidou*, Paris 1974

BROWN, BERNARD E., *Protest in Paris: Anatomy of a Revolt*, New Jersey 1974

CROZIER, MICHEL, *La Société bloquée*, Paris 1970

DEBBASCH, CHARLES, *La France de Pompidou*, Paris 1974

DUVERGER, MAURICE, *La Monarchie Républicaine*, Paris 1974

FABIUS, LAURENT, *La France inégale*, Paris 1975

FOURNIER, JACQUES, and QUESTIAUX, NICOLE, *Traité du Social*, Paris 1976

FRAZER, W. R., *Education and Society in Modern France*, London 1963

HARRISON, MARTIN, *French Politics*, Lexington (Mass.) 1969

HOFFMANN, STANLEY, *Decline or Renewal: France since the 1930's*, New York 1974

HOFFMAN, STANLEY, *In Search of France*, Cambridge (Mass.) 1963

HORNE, ALISTAIR, *A Savage War of Peace: Algeria 1954–1962*, London 1977

MARTINET, GILLES, *Le Système Pompidou*, Paris 1971

METRAUX, RHODA, and MEAD, MARGARET, *Themes in French Culture: A Preface to a Study of the French Community*, Stanford 1964

PEYREFITTE, ALAIN, *Le Mal français*, Paris 1976

REYNAUD, J. D., *et al.*, *Tendances et volontés de la société française*, Paris 1966

VIANSSON-PONTÉ, PIERRE, *Histoire de la République Gaullienne*, 2 vols., Paris 1970–1

WALLACE-HADRILL, D. M., and MCMANNERS, J. (eds.), *France: Government and Society*, London 1970

WYLIE, LAURENCE, *Village in the Vaucluse*, 2nd ed., New York 1964

WYLIE, LAURENCE, (ed.), *Chanzeaux: A Village in Anjou*, Cambridge (Mass.) 1966

General economic background

BAUCHET, PIERRE, *Economic Planning: the French Experience*, London 1964

CARRÉ, J. P., DUBOIS P., and MALINVAUD, E., *La Croissance française*, Paris 1972

CATHERINE, ROBERT and GOUSSET, P., *L'État et l'essor industriel*, 2nd ed., Paris 1972

CLOSON, F. L., and FILIPI, J. (eds.), *L'Économie et les finances*, Paris 1959

COFFEY, PETER, *The Social Economy of France*, London 1973

COHEN, STEPHEN, *Modern Capitalist Planning: the French Model*, Cambridge (Mass.) 1969

GUIBERT, BERNARD, *La Mutation industrielle de la France*, Paris 1976

HACKET, J. and A. M., *Economic Planning in France*, London 1963

HANSEN, NILES, *French Regional Planning*, Edinburgh 1968

HAYWARD, JACK, and WATSON, MICHAEL (eds.), *Planning Politics and Public Policy*, London 1975

KINDLEBERG, CHARLES, *Economic Growth in France and Britain*, Cambridge (Mass.) 1964

LIGGINS, DAVID, *National Economic Planning in France*, Lexington (Mass.) 1974

MCARTHUR, J. H., and SCOTT, BRUCE R., *Industrial Planning in France*, Boston 1969

PARODI, MAURICE, *L'Économie et la société française de 1945 à 1970*, Paris 1971

SHEAHAN, JOHN, *Promotion and Control of Industry in Post-war France*, Cambridge (Mass.) 1963

SHONFIELD, ANDREW, *Modern Capitalism*, London 1965

ULLMO, YVES, *La Planification en France*, Paris 1975

ZYSMAN, JOHN, *Political Strategies for Industrial Order: State, Market and Industry in France*, London 1977

Political institutions of the Fifth Republic – general

AMBLER, J. S., *The Government and Politics of France*, Boston 1971

AVRIL, PIERRE, *Politics in France*, London 1969

AVRIL, PIERRE, *Le Régime politique de la Ve République*, 2nd ed., Paris 1967

BERGER, SUZANNE, *The French Political System*, New York 1974

BLONDEL, JEAN, *The Government of France*, 2nd ed., London 1971

CHAPSAL, JACQUES, *La Vie politique en France depuis 1940*, 3rd ed., Paris 1972

DUVERGER, MAURICE, *La Cinquième République*, 5th ed., Paris 1974

EHRMANN, HENRY, *Politics in France*, 3rd ed., Boston 1976

GOGUEL, FRANÇOIS and GROSSER, ALFRED, *La Politique en France*, 5th ed., Paris 1975

HAMON, LÉO, *Une République présidentielle?*, 2 vols., Paris 1975–7

HAYWARD, JACK, *The One and Indivisible French Republic*, London 1973

LAPONCE, J. A., *The Government of the Fifth Republic: French Political Parties and the Constitution*, Berkeley 1961

LAVROFF, D. G., *Le Système politique français – la Ve République*, Paris 1975

MACRIDIS, ROY C., *French Politics in Transition*, Cambridge (Mass.) 1975

NOONAN, L. G., *France: The Politics of Continuity in Change*, London 1970

PICKLES, DOROTHY, *The Government and Politics of France*, 2 vols., London 1972–3

PIERCE, ROY, *French Politics and Political Institutions*, 2nd ed., New York 1973

PIQUEMAL, M., and DEMICHEL, F. and A., *Institutions et pouvoir en France*, 2nd ed., Paris 1975 (for a Marxist point of view)

WATERMAN, HARVEY, *Political Change in Contemporary France*, Columbus (Ohio) 1969

WILLIAMS, PHILIP and HARRISON, MARTIN, *Politics and Society in de Gaulle's Republic*, London 1971

Executive and legislative powers

ANDERSON, MALCOLM, *Government in France – an Introduction to the Executive Power*, London 1970

ANTONI, P. and J-D., *Les Ministres de la Ve République*, Paris 1976

AVRIL, PIERRE, *Les Français et leur Parlement*, Paris 1972

BAECQUE, F. DE, *Qui gouverne la France?*, Paris 1976

CAYROL, R., et al., *Le Député français*, Paris 1973

CHANDERNAGOR, A., *Un Parlement, pour quoi faire?*, Paris 1967

CLAISSE, ALAIN, *Le Premier Ministre de la Ve République*, Paris 1972

CORBEL, P., *Le Parlement français et la planification*, Paris 1969

COTTERET, JEAN-MARIE, *Le Pouvoir législatif en France*, Paris 1962

DEBRÉ, JEAN-LOUIS, *La Constitution de la Ve République*, Paris 1975

DEBRÉ, JEAN-LOUIS, *Les idées constitutionnelles du Général de Gaulle*, Paris 1974

DELVOLVÉ, P., LESGUILLIONS, H., *Le Contrôle parlementaire de la politique économique et budgétaire*, Paris 1964

DUPUIS, G., GEORGEL, J., and MOREAU, J., *Le Conseil Constitutionnel*, Paris 1976

GICQUEL, JEAN, *Essai sur la pratique politique de la Ve République*, Paris 1967

GUICHARD-AYOUB, E., et al., *Études sur le Parlement de la Ve République*, Paris 1965

LIDDERDALE, D. W. S., *The Parliament of France*, 2nd ed., London 1954

LORD, GUY, *The French Budgetary Process*, Berkeley 1973

MAOUT, JEAN-CHARLES, and MUZELLEC, R., *Le Parlement sous la Ve République*, Paris 1971

MASSOT, JEAN, *La Présidence de la République en France*, Paris 1977

PARODI, JEAN-LUC, *Le Rapport entre le législatif et l'exécutif sous la Ve République*, Paris 1972

Pour Connaître le Sénat, Paris (Documentation française) 1976

RIVOLI, JEAN, *Le Budget de l'État,* Paris 1975

VERRIER, PATRICE, *Les Services de la présidence de la République,* Paris 1971

WILLIAMS, PHILIP, *The French Parliament: Politics in the Fifth Republic,* London 1968

Parties and elections

General

BORELLA, FRANÇOIS, *Les Partis politiques dans la France d'aujourd' hui,* Paris 1973

BRAUD, PHILIPPE, *Le Comportement électoral en France,* Paris 1973

CAMPBELL, PETER, *French Electoral Systems and Elections since 1789,* 2nd ed., London 1966

CHARLOT, JEAN, *Quand la gauche peut gagner,* Paris 1973

CHARLOT, JEAN, *Les Français et de Gaulle,* Paris 1971

CHARNAY, P., *Le Suffrage politique en France,* Paris 1965

DEUTSCH, E., LINDON, D., and WEIL, P., *Les familles politiques,* Paris 1966

FOUGEYROLLAS, PIERRE, *La Conscience politique dans la France contemporaine,* Paris 1963

FREARS, JOHN, *Political Parties and Elections in the French Fifth Republic,* London 1977

GOGUEL, FRANÇOIS, *Modernisation économique et comportement politique,* Paris 1969

LANCELOT, ALAIN, *Les attitudes politiques,* 3rd ed., Paris 1969

LELEU, CLAUDE, *Géographie des élections françaises depuis 1936,* Paris 1971

MEYNAUD, J., and LANCELOT, A., *La Participation des Français à la Politique,* 3rd ed., Paris 1971

MICHELAT, GUY, and SIMON, MICHEL, *Classe, religion et comportement politique,* Paris 1977

RÉMOND, RENÉ, *et al., Forces religeuses et attitudes politiques dans la France contemporaine,* Paris 1965

WILLIAMS, PHILIP, GOLDEY, DAVID, *et al., French Politicians and Elections 1951–1969,* London 1970

Parties of the presidential coalition

ANDERSON, MALCOLM, *Conservative Politics in France,* London 1974

AVRIL, PIERRE, *UDR et Gaullistes*, Paris 1971

CHARLOT, JEAN, *Le Gaullisme*, Paris 1970

CHARLOT, JEAN, *The Gaullist Phenomenon*, London 1971

COLLIARD, J. C., *Les Républicains Indépendants*, Paris 1971

HARTLEY, A., *Gaullism; The Rise and Fall of a Political Movement*, London 1972

IRVING, R. E. M., *Christian Democracy in France*, London 1973

LECOMTE, BERNARD, and SAUVAGE, CHRISTIAN, *Les Giscardiens*, Paris 1978

NORDMANN, JEAN-THOMAS, *Histoire des Radicaux 1820–1973*, Paris 1974

RÉMOND, RENÉ, *The Right-wing in France from 1815 to de Gaulle*, 2nd ed., Chicago 1969

VIANSSON-PONTÉ, PIERRE, *Les Gaullistes*, Paris 1963

Parties of the Opposition Left

BARILLON, RAYMOND, *La Gauche française en mouvement*, Paris 1967

BIZOT, JEAN-FRANÇOIS, *Anatomie du parti socialiste*, Paris 1975

BLACKMER, DONALD L. M., and TARROW, SIDNEY G., *Communism in Italy and France*, Princeton 1975

BON, FRÉDÉRIC, *et al.*, *Le communisme en France*, Paris 1969

CAUTE, DAVID, *Communism and the French Intellectuals*, London 1964

CHEVÉMNEENT, JEAN-PIERRE, *Les Communistes, les Socialistes et les autres*, Paris 1976

DREYFUS, FRANÇOIS GEORGES, *Histoire des gauches en France*, Paris 1975

FAUVET, JACQUES, *Histoire du Parti Communiste*, 2nd ed., Paris 1977

GUIDONI, PIERRE, *Histoire du nouveau parti socialiste*, Paris 1973

HURTIG, CHRISTIANE, *De la SFIO au nouveau parti socialiste*, Paris 1970

KRIEGEL, ANNIE, *The French Communists*, London 1972

LAURENS, ANDRÉ and PFISTER, THIERRY, *Les Nouveaux Communistes*, Paris 1973

LICHTEIM, GEORGE, *Marxism in Modern France*, New York 1966

LIGOU, DANIEL, *Histoire du Socialisme en France 1871–1961*, Paris 1961

MINGALON, J.-L., and ANDREAU, *La Nouvelle Vague du Parti Communiste*, Paris 1975

NANIA, GUY, *Un parti de la gauche, le PSU*, Paris 1966

PFISTER, THIERRY, *Les Socialistes*, Paris 1977

PHILIP, ANDRÉ, *Les Socialistes*, Paris 1967

POPEREN, JEAN, *L'Unité de la Gauche 1965–1974*, Paris 1975

Programme commun de gouvernment, Paris 1972

ROCARD, MICHEL, et al., *Le PSU et l'avenir de la France*, Paris 1969

SIMMONS, HARVEY G., *French Socialists in Search of a Role 1956–1967*, London 1970

TIERSKY, RONALD, *French Communism 1920–1972*, London 1974

VERDIER, ROBERT, *PS – PC: une lutte pour l'entente*, Paris 1976

WILSON, FRANK, *The French Democratic Left 1963–1969*, Stanford 1971

WOHL, ROBERT, *French Communism in the Making 1914–1924*, Stanford 1966

Pressure groups

AMBLER, J. S., *Soldiers against the State; The French Army in Politics 1945–1962*, 2nd ed., New York 1968

BARJONET, ANDRÉ, *La CGT*, Paris 1968

BARJONET, ANDRÉ, *La CFDT*, Paris 1968

BAZEX, MICHEL, *L'Administration et les syndicats*, Paris 1973

BERGER, SUZANNE, *Peasants against Politics, Rural Organisations in Brittany 1911–1967*, Cambridge (Mass.) 1972

BERGOUNIOUX, ALAIN, *Force Ouvrière*, Paris 1975

BRIZAY, BERNARD, *Le Patronat*, Paris 1975

CAIRE, GUY, *Les Syndicats ouvriers*, Paris 1971

CAPDEVIELLE, JACQUES, and MURIAUX, RENÉ, *Les Syndicats ouvriers en France*, Paris 1973

CLARK, JAMES, *Teachers and Politics in France*, Syracuse (NY) 1967

EHRMANN, HENRY, *Organized Business in France*, Princeton 1957

FAURE, M., *Les Paysans dans la société française*, 2nd ed., Paris 1967

FIELDS, A. B., *Student Politics in France a study of the Union Nationale des Étudiants de France*, New York 1970

FRAZER, W. R., *Education and Society in Modern France*, London 1968

GIRARDET, RAOUL, *La Crise militaire française 1945–1962*, Paris 1964

KELLEY, GEORGE A., *Lost Soldiers; The French Army and Empire in Crisis 1947–1962*, Cambridge (Mass.) 1964

LA GORCE, P. M. DE, *La République et son armée*, Paris 1963

MENDRAS, H. and TAVERNIER, Y. (eds.), *Terre, paysans et politique*, Paris 1969–70

MEYNAUD, JEAN, *Les Groupes de pression*, Paris 1958

MEYNAUD, JEAN, *Nouvelles études sur les groupes de pression*, Paris 1962

REYNAUD, JEAN DANIEL, *Les Syndicats en France*, 2 vols., Paris 1975

TAVERNIER, YVES, *La FNSEA*, Paris 1965

TAVERNIER, YVES, *Le CNJA*, Paris 1966

VERNON, RAYMOND, *Big Business and the State*, Harvard 1973

WRIGHT, GORDON, *Rural Revolution in France*, Paris 1964

Administration

ARMSTRONG, JOHN A., *The European Administrative Elite*, Princeton 1973

BAECQUE, F. de., *L'Administration centrale de la France*, Paris 1973

BELORGEY, GÉRARD, *Le Gouvernement et l'administration de la France*, 2nd ed., Paris 1970.

BLANC, LAURENT, *La Fonction publique*, Paris 1971

BROWN, L. NEVILLE, and GARNER, J. F., *French Administrative Law*, London 1967

CATHERINE, ROBERT, *Le Fonctionnaire français*, 2nd ed., Paris 1973

CATHERINE, ROBERT, and THUILLIER, GUY, *Introduction à une philosophie de l'administration*, Paris 1969

CLOSON, F. L., and FILIPPI, J., *L'Économie et les finances*, Paris 1968

CROZIER, MICHEL, *The Bureaucratic Phenomenon*, Chicago 1964

CROZIER, MICHEL, *et al., Où va l'administration?*, Paris 1974

DARBEL, ALAIN, and SCHNAPPER, DOMINIQUE, *Morphologie de la haute administration française*, 2 vols., Paris 1969–72

DEBBASCH, CHARLES, *L'Administration au pouvoir*, Paris 1969

DEBBASCH, CHARLES, *Institutions administratives*, Paris 1966

DEROCHE, HENRI, *Les Mythes administratives*, Paris 1966

DOGAN, MATTEI (ed.), *The Mandarins of Western Europe; The Political Role of Top Civil Servants*, London 1975

ESCOUBE, P., *Les Grands corps de l'État*, 2nd ed., Paris 1977

FOURNERET, PIERRE, *L'Administration économique*, Paris 1972

FREEDEMAN, CHARLES E., *The Conseil d'État in Modern France* New York 1961

GOURNAY, BERNARD, *et al., Administration publique*, Paris 1967

GRÉGOIRE, ROGER, *The French Civil Service*, London 1954

KESLER, MARIE-CHRISTINE, *Le Conseil d'État*, Paris 1968

KOSCIUSKO-MORIZET, JOSEPH A., *La 'Mafia' polytechnicienne*, Paris 1973

LECA, DOMINIQUE, *Du Ministre des Finances*, Paris 1966

LETOURNEUR, M., BAUCHET, J., and MERIC, J., *Le Conseil d'État et les tribunaux administratifs*, Paris 1970

NEGRIN, J. P., *Le Conseil d'État et la vie politique en France depuis 1956*, Paris 1968

RIDLEY, F. F. (ed.), *Specialists and Generalists*, London 1968

RIDLEY, F. F. and BLONDEL, JEAN, *Public Administration in France*, 2nd ed., London 1969

SULEIMAN, EZRA, *Politics, Power and Bureaucracy in France*, London 1974

Superstructures des administrations centrales, Cahier de l'Institut Français des Sciences Administratives, Paris 1973

THOENIG, JEAN-CLAUDE, *L'Ère des technocrates*, Paris 1973

Local government

Administration des grandes villes, Cahier de l'Institut Français des Sciences Administratives, Paris 1977

BECQUART-LECLERQ, JEANNE, *Paradoxes du pouvoir local*, Paris 1976

BERNARD, PAUL, *Le Grand Tournant des communes de France*, Paris 1969

BOUCHET, C., *et al.*, *Institution communale et pouvoir politique*, Paris 1973

BOURJOL, MAURICE, *Région et administration régionale*, Paris 1970

CHAPMAN, BRIAN, *Introduction to French Local Government*, London 1953

CHAPMAN, BRIAN, *Prefects and Provincial France*, London 1955

DETTON, H., *L'Administration régionale et locale en France*, 2nd ed., Paris 1963

GRÉMION, PIERRE, *La Structuration du pouvoir au niveau départemental*, Paris 1969

GRÉMION, PIERRE, *Le Pouvoir périphérique*, Paris 1976

GRÉMION, PIERRE and WORMS, J. P., *Les Institutions régionales et la société locale*, Paris 1969

KESSELMAN, MARK, *The Ambiguous Consensus; A Study of Local Government in France*, New York 1967

LAGROYE, JACQUES, *Société et Politique; Jacques Chaban-Delmas à Bordeaux*, Paris 1973

LAVAU, GEORGES, *La Région et la reforme administrative*, Paris 1964

LONGEPIERRE, MICHEL, *Les Conseillers généraux dans le système administratif français*, Paris 1971

MABILEAU, ALBERT (ed.), *Les Facteurs locaux de la vie politique nationale*, Paris 1972

MACHIN, HOWARD, *The Prefect in French Public Administration*, London 1977

MARCHAND, MARIE-HÉLÈNE, *Les Conseillers généraux en France depuis 1945*, Paris 1970

SCHMITT, CHARLES, *Le Maire de la commune rurale*, Paris 1972

SOUCHON, MARIE-FRANCE, *Le Maire, élu local dans une société en changement*, Paris 1968

TARROW, SIDNEY, *Between Center and Periphery*, London 1977

Useful biographies, autobiographies and works by prominent politicians

ARON, ROBERT, *An Explanation of de Gaulle*, New York 1966

BASSI, MICHEL, *Valéry Giscard d'Estaing*, Paris 1968

BORZEIX, JEAN-MARIE, *Mitterrand lui-même*, Paris 1973

BUNEL, JEAN, and MEUNIER, PAUL, *Chaban-Delmas*, Paris 1972

BURON, ROBERT, *Le plus beau des métiers*, Paris 1963

CHABAN-DELMAS, JACQUES, *L'Ardeur*, Paris 1976

CHENOT, BERNARD, *Être Ministre*, Paris 1967

CLESSIS, CATHERINE, *et al.*, *Jacques Chirac ou la République des cadets*, Paris 1972

CROZIER, BRIAN, *De Gaulle*, 2 vols., London 1973

DEBRÉ, MICHEL, *Une certaine idée de la France*, Paris 1972

DEBRÉ, MICHEL, *Ces princes qui nous gouvernent*, Paris 1957

DEBRÉ, MICHEL, *Sur le Gaullisme*, Paris 1967

DEBRÉ, MICHEL, *Au service de la nation*, Paris 1963

DEBRÉ, MICHEL, *La mort de l'État Républicain*, Paris 1947

DUCLOS, JACQUES, *Mémoires*, 6 vols., Paris 1968–72

FOUCHET, CHRISTIAN, *Au Service du Général de Gaulle*, Paris 1971

GAULLE, CHARLES DE, *Discours et messages*, Paris 1970

GAULLE, CHARLES DE, *Memoirs of Hope*, 2 vols., London 1971

GIROUD, FRANÇOISE, *La Comédie du pouvoir*, Paris 1977

GISCARD D'ESTAING, VALÉRY, *La Démocratie française*, Paris 1976

GUICHARD, OLIVIER, *Un chemin tranquil*, Paris 1975

GUISBERT, OLIVIER, *François Mitterrand ou la tentation de l'histoire*, Paris 1977

LACOUTURE, JEAN, *De Gaulle*, London 1970

LA GORCE, PAUL-MARIE DE, *De Gaulle entre deux mondes*, Paris 1964

LAGROYE, JACQUES, *Chaban-Delmas à Bordeaux*, Paris 1973

LANCEL, FRANÇOIS, *Valéry Giscard d'Estaing*, Paris 1974

LANDE, DAVID, *François Mitterrand*, Paris 1974

MALRAUX, ANDRÉ, *Les Chênes qu'on abat*, Paris 1971

MARCHAIS, GEORGES, *Le Défi démocratique*, Paris 1973

MARCHAIS, GEORGES, *Parlons franchement*, Paris 1977

MENDÈS-FRANCE, PIERRE, *A Modern French Republic*, New York 1963

MITTERRAND, FRANÇOIS, *Ma part de vérité*, Paris 1969

MITTERRAND, FRANÇOIS, *La Paille et le grain*, Paris 1975

MITTERRAND, FRANÇOIS, *Le Coup d'État permanent*, Paris 1964

MITTERRAND, FRANÇOIS, *La rose au poing*, Paris 1975

MITTERRAND, FRANÇOIS, *Politique*, Paris 1977

MOLLET, GUY, *13 mai 1958–12 mai 1962*, Paris 1962

MOREAU, ALAIN, *Chirac ou la fringale du pouvoir*, Paris 1977

PAUTARD, ANDRÉ, *Valéry Giscard d'Estaing*, Paris 1974

PISANI, EDGARD, *Le Général indivis*, Paris 1974

POMPIDOU, GEORGES, *Le Nœud Gordien*, Paris 1974

PONIATOWSKI, MICHEL, *Cartes sur table*, Paris 1972

PONIATOWSKI, MICHEL, *Conduire le changement*, Paris 1975

POUJADE, ROBERT, *Le Ministère de l'impossible*, Paris 1975

ROUANET, P., *Pompidou*, Paris 1969

SERVAN-SCHREIBER, JEAN-JACQUES, *Le Manifeste Radical*, Paris 1970

SOUSTELLE, JACQUES, *Vingt-huit années de gaullisme*, Paris 1968

VALLON, LOUIS, *L'Anti-de Gaulle*, Paris 1968

WERTH, ALEXANDER, *De Gaulle*, London 1965

List of Abbreviations

APC   Association des Patriotes Corses

APEL   Association des Parents d'Élèves de l'Enseignement Libre

ARC   Action pour la Renaissance de la Corse

CAR   Conférence Administrative Régionale

CD   Centre Démocrate

CDP   Centre Démocratie et Progrès

CDS   Centre des Démocrates Sociaux

CERES   Centre d'Étude, de Recherche et d'Éducation Socialistes

CFDT   Confédération Française Démocratique du Travail

CFT   Confédération Française du Travail

CFTC   Confédération Française des Travailleurs Chrétiens

CGC   Confédération Générale des Cadres

CGPME   Confédération Générale des Petites et Moyennes Entreprises

CGT   Confédération Générale du Travail

CID–UNATI   Comité d'Information et de Défense–Union Nationale des Artisans et Travailleurs Indépendants

CIR   Convention des Institutions Républicaines

CNIP   Centre National des Indépendants et Paysans

CNJA   Centre National des Jeunes Agriculteurs

CNPF   Conseil National du Patronat Français

DATAR   Délégation Générale à l'Aménagement du Territoire

DGRST   Délégation Générale de la Recherche Scientifique et Technique

ENA   École Nationale d'Administration

FEN   Fédération de l'Éducation Nationale

FFA   Fédération Française de l'Agriculture

FGDS   Fédération de la Gauche Démocrate et Socialiste

FLB–ARB   Front de Libération Bretonne – Armée Républicaine Bretonne

FLNC   Front de Libération Nationale Corse

FNSEA   Fédération Nationale des Syndicats d'Exploitants Agricoles

FO   Force Ouvrière

INSEE   Institut National d'Études Statistiques et Economiques

MDSF   Mouvement Démocrate Socialiste de France

MODEF   Mouvement pour la Co-ordination et la Défense de l'Exploitation Familiale

MONATAR   Mouvement National des Travailleurs Agricoles et Ruraux

MRP   Mouvement Républicain Populaire

PCF   Parti Communiste Français

PPBS   Planning, programming, budgeting systems

PS   Parti Socialiste

PSU   Parti Socialiste Unifié

RCB   Rationalisation des Choix Budgétaires

RI   Républicains Indépendants

RPF   Rassemblement du Peuple Français

RPR   Rassemblement pour la République

SFIO   Section Française de l'Internationale Ouvrière

SNI   Syndicat National des Instituteurs

TPG   Trésorier Payeur Général

UDCA   Union de Défense des Commerçants et des Artisans

UDR   Union des Démocrates pour la République

UDT   Union Démocratique du Travail

UDV^e   Union des Démocrates pour la Ve République

UGSD   Union de la Gauche Socialiste et Démocrate

UNEF   Union Nationale des Étudiants de France

UNR   Union pour la Nouvelle République

Index